SACREDSPACE

SACREDSPACE
the prayer book 2006

from the web site www.sacredspace.ie

Jesuit Communication Centre, Ireland

ave maria press  Notre Dame, Indiana

Acknowledgment

The publisher would like to thank Gerry Bourke, SJ, and Alan McGuckian, SJ, for their kind assistance in making this book possible. Gerry Bourke, SJ, can be contacted at feedback@jesuit.ie

First published in Australia 2006 by
Michelle Anderson Publishing Pty Ltd

www.avemariapress.com

International Standard Book Number: 1-59471-062-7

Cover and text design by K. H. Coney

Printed and bound in the United States of America.

how to use this book

We invite you to make a sacred space in your day and spend ten minutes praying here and now, wherever you are, with the help of a prayer guide and scripture chosen specially for each day. Every place is a sacred space so you may wish to have this book in your desk at work or available to be picked up and read at any time of the day, whilst traveling or on your bedside table, a park bench ... Remember that God is everywhere, all around us, constantly reaching out to us, even in the most unlikely situations. When we know this, and with a bit of practice, we can pray anywhere.

The following pages will guide you through a session of prayer stages.

Something to think and pray about each day this week:

The Presence of God
Freedom
Consciousness
The Word (leads you to the daily scripture and provides help with the text)
Conversation
Conclusion

It is most important to come back to these pages each day of the week as they are an integral part of each day's prayer and lead to the scripture and inspiration points.

Although written in the first person the prayers are for "doing" rather than for reading out. Each stage is a kind of exercise or mediation aimed at helping you to get in touch with god and God's presence in your life.

We hope that you will join the many people around the world praying with us in our sacred space.

contents

Something to think and pray about each day this week:

A time of preparation

December prepares us for the coming (Advent means "coming") of God as a baby. Christians are not the only ones who prepare for Christmas. Some people have been preparing since January, not for the feast, but for selling, which is the main thing they associate with Christmas. Rather than be dismayed by their commercial focus, we might admire their far-sighted industry, ordering stocks, calculating what customers will go for. Do we look ahead as carefully to this extraordinary event?

Advent is a time to prepare not just our stocks for sale, but our minds for an encounter. You meet someone and they have been looking forward to seeing you. When I'd meet my friend Bill after an absence, he would approach me with curiosity. He had scanned my face with concern, seeing how I was on the outside, and when he asked "How are you?" he wanted a detailed answer—How was I on the inside? You meet another friend and her first words are: I have to be gone in twenty minutes. She does not look at you, she's just fitting you in.

Lord, in these four weeks may I prepare my mind with the thought of you, deepening my sense of what you brought to us in Bethlehem. I want it to be a real meeting, not just fitting you in or "getting over Christmas."

The Presence of God
I remind myself that, as I sit here now,
God is gazing on me with love and holding me in being.
I pause for a moment and think of this.

Freedom
I will ask God's help,
to be free from my own preoccupations,
to be open to God in this time of prayer,
to come to love and serve him more.

Consciousness
How do I find myself today?
Where am I with God? With others?
Do I have something to be grateful for? Then I give thanks.
Is there something I am sorry for? Then I ask forgiveness.

The Word
God speaks to each one of us individually. I need to listen to
what he is saying to me. (Please turn to your scripture on the
following pages. Inspiration points are there should you need
them. When you are ready, return here to continue.)

Conversation
Remembering that I am still in God's presence,
I imagine Jesus himself standing or sitting beside me,
and say whatever is on my mind, whatever is in my heart,
speaking as one friend to another.

Conclusion
Glory be to the Father, and to the Son, and to the Holy Spirit,
As it was in the beginning, is now and ever shall be,
World without end. Amen

Sunday 27th November, First Sunday of Advent
Isaiah 63:16b–17, 19, 64:1–2

You, O Lord, are our father; our Redeemer from of old is your name. Why, O Lord, do you make us stray from your ways and harden our heart, so that we do not fear you? Turn back for the sake of your servants, for the sake of the tribes that are your heritage. We have long been like those whom you do not rule, like those not called by your name. O that you would tear open the heavens and come down, so that the mountains would quake at your presence—as when fire kindles brushwood and the fire causes water to boil—to make your name known to your adversaries, so that the nations might tremble at your presence!

- There are a lot of mixed emotions expressed in this passage, and strong ones: repentance, regret, yearning, pleading. Do any of them express something of what I am feeling now?
- Most of all, this passage is asking God to make his presence known.
- God is present here now, and listening to me. What do I want to say?

Monday 28th November
Matthew 8:5–11

When Jesus entered Capernaum, a centurion came to him, appealing to him and saying, "Lord, my servant is lying at home paralyzed, in terrible distress." And he said to him, "I will come and cure him." The centurion answered, "Lord, I am not worthy to have you come under my roof; but only speak the word, and my servant will be healed. For I also am a man under authority, with soldiers under me; and I say to one, 'Go,' and he goes, and to another, 'Come,' and he comes, and to my slave, 'Do this,' and the slave does it." When Jesus heard him, he was amazed and said to those who followed him, "Truly I tell you, in no one in Israel have I found such faith. I tell you, many will come from east and west and will eat with Abraham and Isaac and Jacob in the kingdom of heaven."

- I view the scene in my imagination. A confident, self assured Roman, born to lead, turns to a simple Jewish rabbi with a problem that is beyond his power.
- What is going on here? How am I moved by what I see and hear?
- When I look at this scene, how am I moved to respond to Jesus?

Tuesday 29th November   Luke 10:21–24

At that same hour Jesus rejoiced in the Holy Spirit and said, "I thank you, Father, Lord of heaven and earth, because you have hidden these things from the wise and the intelligent and have revealed them to infants; yes, Father, for such was your gracious will. All things have been handed over to me by my Father; and no one knows who the Son is except the Father, or who the Father is except the Son and anyone to whom the Son chooses to reveal him." Then turning to the disciples, Jesus said to them privately, "Blessed are the eyes that see what you see! For I tell you that many prophets and kings desired to see what you see, but did not see it, and to hear what you hear, but did not hear it."

- There is more to our lives than our clever eyes can see. It's a mystery that a child, a trusting child, can grasp.
- Where am I with this? Do Jesus' words excite me, leave me feeling cold and excluded, or do they strike a chord of desire in me?
- Advent is a time for watching and hoping—waiting for an infant. Am I open to learning about the mystery from the infant?

Wednesday 30th November, St. Andrew   Matthew 4:18–22

As he walked by the Sea of Galilee, he saw two brothers, Simon, who is called Peter, and Andrew his brother, casting a net into the sea—for they were fishermen. And he said to them, "Follow me, and I will make you fish for people." Immediately they left their nets and followed him. As he went from there, he saw two other brothers, James son of Zebedee and his brother John, in the boat with their father Zebedee, mending their nets, and he called them. Immediately they left the boat and their father, and followed him.

- In this passage, Peter, Andrew, James, and John respond to Jesus' invitation, walking away from their past without hesitation. It is so simple.
- Jesus comes into your workplace or your home; he invites you to follow him out. How do you react?
- Do you hesitate? Perhaps you want to know more, want to ask questions. Bring your concerns into conversation with the Lord.

Thursday 1st December   Matthew 7:21, 24–27

Jesus said to his disciples, "Not everyone who says to me, 'Lord, Lord,' will enter the kingdom of heaven, but only the one who does the will of my Father in heaven. Everyone then who hears these words of mine and acts on them will be like a wise man who built his house on rock. The rain fell, the floods came, and the winds blew and beat on that house, but it did not fall, because it had been founded on rock. And everyone who hears these words of mine and does not act on them will be like a foolish man who built his house on sand. The rain fell, and the floods came, and the winds blew and beat against that house, and it fell—and great was its fall!"

- Lord, you never let me forget that love is shown in deeds, not words or feelings. I could fill notebooks with resolutions, and in the end be even further from you. As William James put it: *A resolution that is a fine flame of feeling allowed to burn itself out without appropriate action, is not merely a lost opportunity, but a bar to future action.*
- What is my resolution, and how will I act? Today? Tomorrow?

Friday 2nd December — Matthew 9:27–31

As Jesus went on his way, two blind men followed him, crying loudly, "Have mercy on us, Son of David!" When he entered the house, the blind men came to him; and Jesus said to them, "Do you believe that I am able to do this?" They said to him, "Yes, Lord." Then he touched their eyes and said, "According to your faith let it be done to you." And their eyes were opened. Then Jesus sternly ordered them, "See that no one knows of this." But they went away and spread the news about him throughout that district.

- Can I imagine this scene where Jesus is walking along with two very noisy individuals pestering him?
- What happens? What is it like for them?
- Am I blind in any way? Can I put myself in this situation?

Saturday 3rd December, St. Francis Xavier — Matthew 28:16–20

Now the eleven disciples went to Galilee, to the mountain to which Jesus had directed them. When they saw him, they worshipped him; but some doubted. And Jesus came and said to them, "All authority in heaven and on earth has been given to me. Go therefore and make disciples of all nations, baptizing them in the name of the Father and of the Son and of the Holy Spirit, and teaching them to obey everything that I have commanded you. And remember, I am with you always, to the end of the age."

- Lord, you terrify me with this command: "Go, and make disciples of all nations." You were talking to just eleven men, without education, money, or influence, in a despised province of the Roman Empire. But they obeyed you, because they knew you were with them.
- And what of today's Christians, the largest body of believers on this planet? Today's preaching is different. We are educated,

sometimes too well. It is harder than ever to make our voice heard. Yet in *Sacred Space* your word goes out potentially to all nations, and you are still with us.

Something to think and pray about each day this week:

Preparing the space

Did this ever happen to you? A friend invites you to a meal. You arrive on the appointed day in pleasant anticipation. Your friend opens the door, looks at you with a blank face—he has completely forgotten that he invited you. Or you find that he expected you but has made no preparations. "Sit down there and I'll put something together." Family meals are helped by the fact that somebody, mother or father, has made preparations, thought about the event.

Lord, I do not want you to find me with a blank face, or unprepared. I still have three weeks to make ready for you, to think about what it meant that you came as a baby, without a house, a displaced person, in poverty. Christmas cards show us cozy scenes, warm firesides, lights and luxuries. Bethlehem was not like that: no lights, no fire, no furnishings. God wanted to enter the world of the poor and the insecure.

The Presence of God
God is with me, but more,
God is within me, giving me existence.
Let me dwell for a moment on God's life-giving presence
in my body, my mind, my heart
and in the whole of my life.

Freedom
God is not foreign to my freedom.
Instead the Spirit breathes life into my most intimate desires,
gently nudging me towards all that is good.
I ask for the grace to let myself be enfolded by the Spirit.

Consciousness
In God's loving presence I unwind the past day,
starting from now and looking back, moment by moment.
I gather in all the goodness and light, in gratitude.
I attend to the shadows and what they say to me,
seeking healing, courage, forgiveness.

The Word
I read the Word of God slowly, a few times over, and I listen to
what God is saying to me. (Please turn to your scripture on the
following pages. Inspiration points are there should you need
them. When you are ready, return here to continue.)

Conversation
How has God's Word moved me? Has it left me cold?
Has it consoled me or moved me to act in a new way?
I imagine Jesus standing or sitting beside me,
I turn and share my feelings with him.

Conclusion
Glory be to the Father, and to the Son, and to the Holy Spirit,
As it was in the beginning, is now and ever shall be,
World without end. Amen

Sunday 4th December, Second Sunday of Advent
Isaiah 40:1–5

Comfort, O comfort my people, says your God. Speak tenderly to Jerusalem, and cry to her that she has served her term, that her penalty is paid, that she has received from the Lord's hand double for all her sins. A voice cries out: "In the wilderness prepare the way of the Lord, make straight in the desert a highway for our God. Every valley shall be lifted up, and every mountain and hill be made low; the uneven ground shall become level, and the rough places a plain. Then the glory of the Lord shall be revealed, and all people shall see it together, for the mouth of the Lord has spoken."

- There was a time of retribution and punishment, but now is the time for reconciliation. God comes to me in mercy and tenderness.
- How can I prepare the way for the Lord to enter more into my life?
- Is there "uneven ground" or "rough places" in my life, where I don't really want to let God in? Listen to the first couple of sentences again: God comes to me in mercy and tenderness.

Monday 5th December
Isaiah 35:1–4

The wilderness and the dry land shall be glad, the desert shall rejoice and blossom; like the crocus it shall blossom abundantly, and rejoice with joy and singing. The glory of Lebanon shall be given to it, the majesty of Carmel and Sharon. They shall see the glory of the Lord, the majesty of our God. Strengthen the weak hands, and make firm the feeble knees. Say to those who are of a fearful heart, "Be strong, do not fear! Here is your God. He will come with vengeance, with terrible recompense. He will come and save you."

- During Advent the Isaiah passages often bring us to the experiences of parched and lifeless wilderness. Can I bring to prayer a part of me that feels arid and withered?

- Can I let myself go with the promise of glory and majesty? Can I see the flowering of new life in my situation?

Tuesday 6th December　　　　　　　　　Isaiah 40:3–5

A voice cries out: "In the wilderness prepare the way of the Lord, make straight in the desert a highway for our God. Every valley shall be lifted up, and every mountain and hill be made low; the uneven ground shall become level, and the rough places a plain. Then the glory of the Lord shall be revealed, and all people shall see it together, for the mouth of the Lord has spoken."

- "Make straight in the desert a highway for our God." My heart is your highway, Lord, but it is not straight. There are too many hidden byways that I'd rather you did not see. I'll try to prepare a way for you this Christmas.
- First of all, make me more transparent to myself. I know that at the end of the day I will still be a mixture of light and shadow, rough and smooth, crooked and straight. But I can improve.

Wednesday 7th December　　　　　　　Matthew 11:28–30

J esus said, "Come to me, all you that are weary and are carrying heavy burdens, and I will give you rest. Take my yoke upon you, and learn from me; for I am gentle and humble in heart, and you will find rest for your souls. For my yoke is easy, and my burden is light."

- It's important not to rush this precious text just because it is familiar.
- Can I stop and hear Jesus speak these words to me, mulling each phrase over slowly?
- Which phrase—or phrases—are specially meant for me:
  Am I weary and burdened?
  Am I ripe for the challenge of God's yoke?

Do I need God's gentle touch?

Does my soul long for rest?

- Can I allow the Lord to speak to me?

Thursday 8th December, The Immaculate Conception of the Blessed Virgin Mary   Luke 1:26–38

In the sixth month the angel Gabriel was sent by God to a town in Galilee called Nazareth, to a virgin engaged to a man whose name was Joseph, of the house of David. The virgin's name was Mary. And he came to her and said, "Greetings, favored one! The Lord is with you." But she was much perplexed by his words and pondered what sort of greeting this might be. The angel said to her, "Do not be afraid, Mary, for you have found favor with God. And now, you will conceive in your womb and bear a son, and you will name him Jesus. He will be great, and will be called the Son of the Most High, and the Lord God will give to him the throne of his ancestor David. He will reign over the house of Jacob forever, and of his kingdom there will be no end." Mary said to the angel, "How can this be, since I am a virgin?" The angel said to her, "The Holy Spirit will come upon you, and the power of the Most High will overshadow you; therefore the child to be born will be holy; he will be called Son of God. And now, your relative Elizabeth in her old age has also conceived a son; and this is the sixth month for her who was said to be barren. For nothing will be impossible with God." Then Mary said, "Here am I, the servant of the Lord; let it be with me according to your word." Then the angel departed from her.

- I love Mary for her caution. She was perplexed and did not trust visions, so she questioned the message and thought about what the consequences would be. For this, she rose to the greatness which Gerard Manley Hopkins celebrates:

    Mary Immaculate,

    Merely a woman, yet

    Whose presence, power is

Great as no goddess's
Was deemèd, dreamèd; who
This one work has to do—
Let all God's glory through,
God's glory which would go
Through her and from her flow
Off, and no way but so.

Friday 9th December   Matthew 11:16–19

Jesus spoke to the crowds, "But to what will I compare this generation? It is like children sitting in the marketplaces and calling to one another, 'We played the flute for you, and you did not dance; we wailed, and you did not mourn.' For John came neither eating nor drinking, and they say, 'He has a demon'; the Son of Man came eating and drinking, and they say, 'Look, a glutton and a drunkard, a friend of tax collectors and sinners!' Yet wisdom is vindicated by her deeds."

- Who are the commentators in our marketplace? We meet them in what we call the media; always coming up with a story, often a complaint or criticism. News media and journalists, whether in print or TV, want to be noticed and listened to, but we can actually live without them.
- There are times when, for our own peace of mind, we need to ration our exposure to the media. The real world is the one I can do something about—the people around me, those whom I meet and love and fear. How much of my emotional energy do I waste on the world of the media?

Saturday 10th December   Matthew 17:10–13

And the disciples asked him, "Why, then, do the scribes say that Elijah must come first?" He replied, "Elijah is indeed coming and will restore all things; but I tell you that Elijah has already come, and they did not recognize him, but they did to him whatever they pleased. So also the Son of Man is about to suffer at their hands." Then the disciples understood that he was speaking to them about John the Baptist.

- God's messengers, whether it was Elijah, John the Baptist, or even the Son of Man, tend to be rejected and even eliminated.
- This is a very bitter truth about our human condition in the midst of our Advent journey. Advent still calls us to a fulfillment promised and guaranteed by God. In my prayer can I hold together both the promise and the shadow?
- It is good to talk to the Lord about these things.

december 11–17

Something to think and pray about each day this week:

Anticipation

Waiting for someone has its own pleasures: the sound of Dad's car on the driveway, the key turning in the front door. Anticipation is a joy, and at Christmas the Eve is often better than the indulgence of the Day. A great children's doctor noticed that children often dreamed about their first meeting with him on the night before. I think about the people I am to meet, need time to clear my mind and heart.

A good time for asking: "What do I look forward to? What cheers me up?" A friend, a group, a warm fireside, TV, alcohol, the pub, computer games, a lover. For the lucky ones, it is someone we love and who loves us.

Our preparation is for a guest. Life and human history is not just one thing after another. God broke in on human history 2000 years ago and nothing is the same since. The world is young though it may feel old. Christmas is first and foremost a birthday, a memory of Jesus.

The Presence of God
What is present to me is what has a hold on my becoming.
I reflect on the presence of God always there in love,
amidst the many things that have a hold on me.
I pause and pray that I may let God
affect my becoming in this precise moment.

Freedom
There are very few people
who realize what God would make of them
if they abandoned themselves into his hands,
and let themselves be formed by his grace (St. Ignatius).
I ask for the grace to trust myself totally to God's love.

Consciousness
I exist in a web of relationships—links to nature, people, God.
I trace out these links, giving thanks for the life that flows
through them.
Some links are twisted or broken: I may feel regret, anger, disappointment.
I pray for the gift of acceptance and forgiveness.

The Word
God speaks to each one of us individually. I need to listen to
hear what he is saying to me. Read the text a few times, then
listen. (Please turn to your scripture on the following pages.
Inspiration points are there should you need them. When you
are ready, return here to continue.)

Conversation
What is stirring in me as I pray?
Am I consoled, troubled, left cold?
I imagine Jesus himself standing or sitting at my side,
and share my feelings with him.

Conclusion
Glory be to the Father, and to the Son, and to the Holy Spirit,
As it was in the beginning, is now and ever shall be,
World without end. Amen

Sunday 11th December, Third Sunday of Advent
Isaiah 61:1–2,10–11

The spirit of the Lord God is upon me, because the Lord has anointed me; he has sent me to bring good news to the oppressed, to bind up the brokenhearted, to proclaim liberty to the captives, and release to the prisoners; to proclaim the year of the Lord's favor, and the day of vengeance of our God . . . I will greatly rejoice in the Lord, my whole being shall exult in my God; for he has clothed me with the garments of salvation, he has covered me with the robe of righteousness, as a bridegroom decks himself with a garland, and as a bride adorns herself with her jewels. For as the earth brings forth its shoots, and as a garden causes what is sown in it to spring up, so the Lord God will cause righteousness and praise to spring up before all the nations.

- These are the words of Isaiah, God's servant. Jesus applied them to himself. They apply to us, too, as Christians.
- God speaks to us here and asks us to "proclaim the year of the Lord's favor." How am I going to respond? What am I going to do to make 2006 a year when people experience the love of God and are freed from captivity, oppression, and heartbreak?
- If I think I can do nothing, listen to God's promise: the Lord will make justice spring up as surely as what is sown springs up from a garden.

Monday 12th December   Matthew 21:23–27

When Jesus entered the temple, the chief priests and the elders of the people came to him as he was teaching, and said, "By what authority are you doing these things, and who gave you this authority?" Jesus said to them, "I will also ask you one question; if you tell me the answer, then I will also tell you by what authority I do these things. Did the baptism of John come from heaven, or was it of human origin?" And they argued with one another, "If we say, 'From heaven,' he will say to us, 'Why then did you not believe him?' But if we say, 'Of human origin,' we are afraid of the crowd; for all regard John as a prophet." So they answered Jesus, "We do not know." And he said to them, "Neither will I tell you by what authority I am doing these things."

- In this exchange, Jesus might look as if he is playing a cheap trick on the chief priests and elders. But notice the differences between them.
- The chief priests and the elders are motivated both by a desire to protect their own position and authority, and by fear—they are afraid of the crowds. Jesus, on the other hand, always speaks out fearlessly, regardless of how it might jeopardize his popularity.
- Do I let fear run my life? Do I make decisions on the basis of preserving my position and power? Can I talk to Jesus about this, and ask for the grace to be free, as he was?

Tuesday 13th December   Matthew 21:28–32

Jesus said, "What do you think? A man had two sons; he went to the first and said, 'Son, go and work in the vineyard today.' He answered, 'I will not'; but later he changed his mind and went. The father went to the second and said the same; and he answered, 'I go, sir'; but he did not go. Which of the two did the will of his father?" They said, "The first." Jesus said to them, "Truly I tell you, the tax collectors and the prostitutes are going into the kingdom of God ahead of you. For John came to you in the way of righteousness and you did not believe him, but the tax collectors and the prostitutes believed him; and even after you saw it, you did not change your minds and believe him."

- The first son sounds like a grump, hard to live with. His first reaction tended to be *No*. He and others probably suffered from his grumpiness but you could still trust him to help. The second son was a charmer; he flattered but deceived his father. When he should have been working, he found something better to do.
- Lord, I would rather be a grumpy but reliable helper than a sweet-talking charmer.

Wednesday 14th December   Luke 7:19–23

John summoned two of his disciples and sent them to the Lord to ask, "Are you the one who is to come, or are we to wait for another?" When the men had come to him, they said, "John the Baptist has sent us to you to ask, 'Are you the one who is to come, or are we to wait for another?'" Jesus had just then cured many people of diseases, plagues, and evil spirits, and had given sight to many who were blind. And he answered them, "Go and tell John what you have seen and heard: the blind receive their sight, the lame walk, the lepers are cleansed, the deaf hear, the dead are raised, the poor have good news brought to them. And blessed is anyone who takes no offence at me."

- Are you the one, Lord? I am staking my life on it. I am not waiting for anyone else. Trends and fashions come and go but I am sticking with you.
- Show me how to make this world better, by tackling suffering and sickness, and reaching out to the unfortunate. In my doubts and difficulties fill my eyes with the sight of you.

Thursday 15th December   Luke 7:24–30

When John's messengers had gone, Jesus began to speak to the crowds about John: "What did you go out into the wilderness to look at? A reed shaken by the wind? What then did you go out to see? Someone dressed in soft robes? Look, those who put on fine clothing and live in luxury are in royal palaces. What then did you go out to see? A prophet? Yes, I tell you, and more than a prophet. This is the one about whom it is written, 'See, I am sending my messenger ahead of you, who will prepare your way before you.' I tell you, among those born of women no one is greater than John; yet the least in the kingdom of God is greater than he." (And all the people who heard this, including the tax collectors, acknowledged the justice of God, because they had been baptized with John's baptism. But by refusing to be baptized by him, the Pharisees and the lawyers rejected God's purpose for themselves.)

- What an affirmation Jesus gives John! What made John so great was his readiness to take second place and point people towards Jesus.
- Are there situations in my life where I am asked to take "second place," the place that belongs to a person who may be necessary but not prominent?
- Am I happy with "second place" like John the Baptist? Do I feel Jesus' affirmation of me?
- Do I hate "second place"? Is there something I need to talk to the Lord about?

Friday 16th December   John 5:33–36

Jesus said to the Jews: "You sent messengers to John, and he testified to the truth. Not that I accept such human testimony, but I say these things so that you may be saved. He was a burning and shining lamp, and you were willing to rejoice for a while in his light. But I have a testimony greater than John's. The works that the Father has given me to complete, the very works that I am doing, testify on my behalf that the Father has sent me."

- In what ways do I testify to the truth in my daily life? What gifts has the Father given me to help others see the truth and experience light and peace in their lives? Lord, give me the light and the strength to complete the work that you have sent me to do.

Saturday 17th December   Matthew 1:1–17

The book of the genealogy of Jesus Christ, the son of David, the son of Abraham. Abraham was the father of Isaac, and Isaac the father of Jacob, and Jacob the father of Judah and his brothers, and Judah the father of Perez and Zerah by Tamar, and Perez the father of Hezron, and Hezron the father of Aram, and Aram the father of Aminadab, and Aminadab the father of Nahshon, and Nahshon the father of Salmon, and Salmon the father of Boaz by Rahab, and Boaz the father of Obed by Ruth, and Obed the father of Jesse, and Jesse the father of King David the king. And David was the father of Solomon by the wife of Uriah, and Solomon the father of Rehoboam, and Rehoboam the father of Abijah, and Abijah the father of Asaph, and Asaph the father of Jehoshaphat, and Jehoshaphat the father of Joram, and Joram the father of Uzziah, and Uzziah the father of Jotham, and Jotham the father of Ahaz, and Ahaz the father of Hezekiah, and Hezekiah the father of Manasseh, and Manasseh the father of Amos, and Amos the father of Josiah, and Josiah the father of Jechoniah and his brothers, at the time of the deportation to Babylon. And after the deportation to Babylon: Jechoniah was the father of Salathiel, and Salathiel the father of Zerubbabel, and Zerubbabel the father of Abiud, and Abiud the father of Eliakim, and Eliakim the father of Azor, and Azor the father of Zadok, and Zadok the father of Achim, and Achim the father of Eliud, and Eliud the father of Eleazar, and Eleazar the father of Matthan, and Matthan the father of Jacob, and Jacob the father of Joseph the husband of Mary, of whom Jesus was born, who is called the Messiah. So all the generations from Abraham to David are fourteen generations; and from David to the deportation to Babylon, fourteen generations; and from the deportation to Babylon to the Messiah, fourteen generations.

- Today's readings look unsparingly at Jesus' ancestry. Matthew points out that Jesus' forbears included children born of incest (Perez), of mixed races (Boaz), and of adultery (Solomon). This is the way God entered into our human history.
- Lord, teach me to accept my humanity, my genes, my relatives, as you accepted yours.

december 18–24

Something to think and pray about each day this week:

Arriving

Christmas is a birthday. We survive the drabness of daily life by looking forward to the bright spots, when things are special, light at the end of the tunnel. Advent is the tunnel, and it used to have its share of fasting and repentance, sharpening the contrast between anticipation and the event.

Beckett was "waiting for Godot"—who never arrives. Is God different? Does he come? In Innsbruck they re-enact the arrival, putting a live baby and mother on a sleigh drawn through the lighted town. That is lovely, but imaginary. The real arrival is partly in our hearts, partly in our Mass. True, that happens more than once a year. But on this feast, as on a birthday, we celebrate that Bethlehem event which showed (as birthday presents show) that we are the children God wanted, that we matter to him.

The Presence of God
What is present to me is what has a hold on my becoming.
I reflect on the presence of God always there in love,
amidst the many things that have a hold on me.
I pause and pray that I may let God
affect my becoming in this precise moment.

Freedom
There are very few people
who realize what God would make of them
if they abandoned themselves into his hands,
and let themselves be formed by his grace (St. Ignatius).
I ask for the grace to trust myself totally to God's love.

Consciousness
I exist in a web of relationships—links to nature, people, God.
I trace out these links, giving thanks for the life that flows
through them.
Some links are twisted or broken: I may feel regret, anger, disap-
pointment.
I pray for the gift of acceptance and forgiveness.

The Word
God speaks to each one of us individually. I need to listen to
hear what he is saying to me. Read the text a few times, then
listen. (Please turn to your scripture on the following pages.
Inspiration points are there should you need them. When you
are ready, return here to continue.)

Conversation
What is stirring in me as I pray?
Am I consoled, troubled, left cold?
I imagine Jesus himself standing or sitting at my side,
and share my feelings with him.

Conclusion

Glory be to the Father, and to the Son, and to the Holy Spirit,
As it was in the beginning, is now and ever shall be,
World without end. Amen

Sunday 18th December, Fourth Sunday of Advent
Luke 1:26–32, 34–35, 38a

In the sixth month the angel Gabriel was sent by God to a town in Galilee called Nazareth, to a virgin whose name was Mary. And he came to her and said, "Greetings, favored one! The Lord is with you." But she was much perplexed by his words and pondered what sort of greeting this might be. The angel said to her, "Do not be afraid, Mary, for you have found favor with God. And now, you will conceive in your womb and bear a son, and you will name him Jesus. He will be great, and will be called the Son of the Most High, and the Lord God will give to him the throne of his ancestor David." Mary said to the angel, "How can this be, since I am a virgin?" The angel said to her, "The Holy Spirit will come upon you, and the power of the Most High will overshadow you; therefore the child to be born will be holy; he will be called Son of God." Then Mary said, "Here am I, the servant of the Lord; let it be with me according to your word."

- Imagine what Mary felt as she was given this awesome news.
- Mary has questions, and she voices them, but she says "Yes" to God's will for her. Can I learn from her example?

Monday 19th December
Judges 13:2–7, 24–25a

There was a certain man of Zorah, of the tribe of the Danites, whose name was Manoah. His wife was barren, having borne no children. And the angel of the Lord appeared to the woman and said to her, "Although you are barren, having borne no children, you shall conceive and bear a son. Now be careful not to drink wine or strong drink, or to eat anything unclean, for you shall conceive and bear a son. No razor is to come on his head, for the boy shall be a nazirite to God from birth. It is he who shall begin to deliver Israel from the hand of the Philistines." Then the woman came and told her husband, "A man of God came to me, and his appearance was like that of an angel of God, most awe-inspiring; I did not ask him where he came from, and he did not tell me his name; but he said to me, 'You shall conceive and bear a son. So then drink no wine or strong drink, and eat nothing unclean, for the boy shall be a nazirite to God from birth to the day of his death.'" . . . The woman bore a son, and named him Samson. The boy grew, and the Lord blessed him. The spirit of the Lord began to stir him in Mahaneh-dan, between Zorah and Eshtaol.

- God likes us to enjoy stories of his creativity and fruitfulness and power to make up for our shortcomings.
- Can I relate to the wife of Manoah who was stereotyped as barren and unproductive? After years of "failure" how must she have viewed her son Samson?
- Are there areas of "barrenness" in my life where I might be open to being surprised?

Tuesday 20th December   **Isaiah 7:10–14**

Again the Lord spoke to Ahaz, saying, "Ask a sign of the Lord your God; let it be deep as Sheol or high as heaven." But Ahaz said, "I will not ask, and I will not put the Lord to the test." Then Isaiah said: "Hear then, O house of David! Is it too little for you to weary mortals, that you weary my God also? Therefore the Lord himself will give you a sign. Look, the young woman is with child and shall bear a son, and shall name him Immanuel."

- As we build towards the great event of the birth of the Son of God, it is good to remember the prophecy given long before by the Prophet Isaiah: "the young woman is with child. . ."
- Can I situate myself in the great sweep of history where God planned from the beginning to take on flesh and share our lot, my lot?
- Immanuel means God is with us. How is that true for me?

Wednesday 21st December   Luke 1:39–45

In those days Mary set out and went with haste to a Judean town in the hill country, where she entered the house of Zechariah and greeted Elizabeth. When Elizabeth heard Mary's greeting, the child leaped in her womb. And Elizabeth was filled with the Holy Spirit and exclaimed with a loud cry, "Blessed are you among women, and blessed is the fruit of your womb. And why has this happened to me, that the mother of my Lord comes to me? For as soon as I heard the sound of your greeting, the child in my womb leaped for joy. And blessed is she who believed that there would be a fulfillment of what was spoken to her by the Lord."

- Let me be a spectator at this lovely encounter of cousins, the second joyful mystery: the visitation. I will contemplate it as Mary and Elizabeth must have done later, savoring the joy of mutual recognition, and of a shared experience of pregnancy.
- Elizabeth is given the special grace of an intimate insight and appreciation of what is happening and who is really present.
- In life do I always appreciate what is happening and who is really present?

Thursday 22nd December   Luke 1:46–56

And Mary said, "My soul magnifies the Lord, and my spirit rejoices in God my Savior, for he has looked with favor on the lowliness of his servant. Surely, from now on all generations will call me blessed; for the Mighty One has done great things for me, and holy is his name. His mercy is for those who fear him from generation to generation. He has shown strength with his arm; he has scattered the proud in the thoughts of their hearts. He has brought down the powerful from their thrones, and lifted up the lowly; he has filled the hungry with good things, and sent the rich away empty. He has helped his servant Israel, in remembrance of his mercy, according to the promise he made to our ancestors, to Abraham and to his descendants forever." And Mary remained with Elizabeth about three months and then returned to her home.

- Mary's *Magnificat* is a prayer to sit with, quietly. It echoes the song of Hannah in I Samuel 2:1. It places us on the cusp of both the Old and New Testaments, charged with the longing of the Old and savoring the fulfillment of the New. In the whole history of salvation, this is the moment of unalloyed joy.
- Mary is pregnant not merely with her child, but with dreams about a glorious future. A young mother overflows with gratitude for being the channel of God's grace to humankind.
- Can I slowly pray over her words and ask for the grace to share in the vision?

Friday 23rd December   Luke 1:57–66

Now the time came for Elizabeth to give birth, and she bore a son. Her neighbors and relatives heard that the Lord had shown his great mercy to her, and they rejoiced with her. On the eighth day they came to circumcise the child, and they were going to name him Zechariah after his father. But his mother said, "No; he is to be called John." They said to her, "None of your relatives has this name." Then they began motioning to his father to find out what name he wanted to give him. He asked for a writing tablet and wrote, "His name is John." And all of them were amazed. Immediately his mouth was opened and his tongue freed, and he began to speak, praising God. Fear came over all their neighbors, and all these things were talked about throughout the entire hill country of Judea. All who heard them pondered them and said, "What then will this child become?" For, indeed, the hand of the Lord was with him.

- "He is to be called John." The giving of a name was rightly a serious matter. We grow into our names, identify with them, pick them out on a page, hear them above the chatter of conversation. One day my parents and possibly others were choosing a name for me, wondering *What then will this child become?* And indeed the hand of the Lord was with me too.
- Thank you, Lord, for my name and for the dreams that people invested in me.

Saturday 24th December   Luke 1:67–79

Then his father Zechariah was filled with the Holy Spirit and spoke this prophecy: "Blessed be the Lord God of Israel, for he has looked favorably on his people and redeemed them. He has raised up a mighty savior for us in the house of his servant David, as he spoke through the mouth of his holy prophets from of old, that we would be saved from our enemies and from the hand of all who hate us. Thus he has shown the mercy promised to our ancestors, and has remembered his holy covenant, the oath that he swore to our ancestor Abraham, to grant us that we, being rescued from the hands of our enemies, might serve him without fear, in holiness and righteousness before him all our days. And you, child, will be called the prophet of the Most High; for you will go before the Lord to prepare his ways, to give knowledge of salvation to his people by the forgiveness of their sins. By the tender mercy of our God, the dawn from on high will break upon us, to give light to those who sit in darkness and in the shadow of death, to guide our feet into the way of peace."

- The Benedictus is a prayer of prophecy about the coming of the Savior. This "Most High" that Zechariah mentions comes not in a cloud of glory, but as a vulnerable child, with an ordinary family, in a cold stable. That is the kind of God we have.

- This babe in a manger brings light to those in darkness and takes away all my sins, doing away with the power of evil. What do I say to him who loves me beyond all love?

- Am I ready this Christmas to invite Jesus into my heart and my home, giving all that I have over to him?

Something to think and pray about each day this week:

The Gift of Christmas

The Virgin is pale, and she looks at the baby. What I would paint on her face is an anxious wonderment, such as has never before been seen on a human face. For Christ is her baby, flesh of her flesh, and the fruit of her womb. She has carried him for nine months, and she will give him her breast, and her milk will become the blood of God. There are moments when the temptation is so strong that she forgets that he is God. She folds him in her arms and says: "My little one."

But at other moments she feels a stranger, and she thinks: "God is there"—and she finds herself caught by a religious awe before this speechless God, this terrifying infant. All mothers at times are brought up sharp in this way before this fragment of themselves, their baby. They feel themselves in exile at two paces from this new life that they have created from their life, and which is now the province of another's thoughts. But no other baby has been so cruelly and suddenly snatched from his mother, for he is God, and he surpasses in every way anything that she can imagine. It is a hard trial for a mother to be ashamed of herself and her human condition before her son.

The Presence of God
God is with me, but more, God is within me.
Let me dwell for a moment on God's life-giving presence
in my body, in my mind, in my heart,
as I sit here, right now.

Freedom
A thick and shapeless tree-trunk would never believe
that it could become a statue, admired as a miracle of sculpture,
and would never submit itself to the chisel of the sculptor,
who sees by her genius what she can make of it (St. Ignatius).
I ask for the grace to let myself be shaped by my loving Creator.

Consciousness
Knowing that God loves me unconditionally,
I can afford to be honest about how I am.
How has the last day been, and how do I feel now?
I share my feelings openly with the Lord.

The Word
I read the Word of God slowly, a few times over, and I listen to
what God is saying to me. (Please turn to your scripture on the
following pages. Inspiration points are there should you need
them. When you are ready, return here to continue.)

Conversation
Do I notice myself reacting as I pray with the Word of God?
Do I feel challenged, comforted, angry?
Imagining Jesus sitting or standing by me,
I speak out my feelings, as one trusted friend to another.

Conclusion
Glory be to the Father, and to the Son, and to the Holy Spirit,
As it was in the beginning, is now and ever shall be,
World without end. Amen

Sunday 25th December, Feast of the Nativity of the Lord
Luke 2:6–14

While they were in Bethlehem, the time came for Mary to deliver her child. And she gave birth to her firstborn son and wrapped him in bands of cloth, and laid him in a manger, because there was no place for them in the inn. In that region there were shepherds living in the fields, keeping watch over their flock by night. Then an angel of the Lord stood before them, and the glory of the Lord shone around them, and they were terrified. But the angel said to them, "Do not be afraid; for see—I am bringing you good news of great joy for all the people: to you is born this day in the city of David a Savior, who is the Messiah, the Lord. This will be a sign for you: you will find a child wrapped in bands of cloth and lying in a manger." And suddenly there was with the angel a multitude of the heavenly host, praising God and saying, "Glory to God in the highest heaven, and on earth peace among those whom he favors!"

- This baby is the Son of God, the Savior of the world.

    And is it true? And is it true,
    This most tremendous tale of all,
    Seen in a stained-glass window's hue,
    A Baby in an ox's stall?
    The Maker of the stars and sea
    Become a Child on earth for me? (John Betjeman)

Monday 26th December, St. Stephen the first martyr
Acts 6:8–10, 7:54–59

Stephen, full of grace and power, did great wonders and signs among the people. Then some of those who belonged to the synagogue of the Freedmen (as it was called), Cyrenians, Alexandrians, and others of those from Cilicia and Asia, stood up and argued with Stephen. But they could not withstand the wisdom and the Spirit with which he spoke. When they heard these things, they became enraged and ground their teeth at Stephen. But filled with the Holy Spirit, he gazed into heaven and saw the glory of God and Jesus standing at the right hand of God. "Look," he said, "I see the heavens opened and the Son of Man standing at the right hand of God!" But they covered their ears, and with a loud shout all rushed together against him. Then they dragged him out of the city and began to stone him; and the witnesses laid their coats at the feet of a young man named Saul. While they were stoning Stephen, he prayed, "Lord Jesus, receive my spirit." Then he knelt down and cried out in a loud voice, "Lord, do not hold this sin against them." When he had said this, he died.

- On the very day after Christmas we are invited to ponder the first martyrdom of a follower of Jesus.
- What does this event say about the meaning of Christmas? In the blindness and human cruelty here do I see any reflections of my own world?
- How is the Incarnate God present in this scene? How is he present in the broken parts of my world?

Tuesday 27th December, St. John, Apostle and Evangelist
John 20:2–8

So Mary Magdalene ran and went to Simon Peter and the other disciple, the one whom Jesus loved, and said to them, "They have taken the Lord out of the tomb, and we do not know where they have laid him." Then Peter and the other disciple set out and went toward the tomb. The two were running together, but the other disciple outran Peter and reached the tomb first. He bent down to look in and saw the linen wrappings lying there, but he did not go in. Then Simon Peter came, following him, and went into the tomb. He saw the linen wrappings lying there, and the cloth that had been on Jesus' head, not lying with the linen wrappings but rolled up in a place by itself. Then the other disciple, who reached the tomb first, also went in, and he saw and believed.

- John recreates the moment when the world was suddenly changed for him. He remembers the baffling message of Mary Magdalene, the frantic morning race to the tomb, bending down to look into the dark space, seeing the burial clothes doffed and neatly arranged on the stones, allowing Simon Peter to go in first; then the awesome, deepening sense that death had met its victor.
- Lord, for me as for John, the belief in your resurrection changes life. I believe that you conquered death, and promise us the same victory. John saw and believed. I have not seen, but I want to live by that faith.

Wednesday 28th December, Feast of the Holy Innocents
Matthew 2:13–18

Now after the wise men had left, an angel of the Lord appeared to Joseph in a dream and said, "Get up, take the child and his mother, and flee to Egypt, and remain there until I tell you; for Herod is about to search for the child, to destroy him." Then Joseph got up, took the child and his mother by night, and went to Egypt, and remained there until the death of Herod. This was to fulfill what had been spoken by the Lord through the prophet, "Out of Egypt I have called my son." When Herod saw that he had been tricked by the wise men, he was infuriated, and he sent and killed all the children in and around Bethlehem who were two years old or under, according to the time that he had learned from the wise men. Then was fulfilled what had been spoken through the prophet Jeremiah: "A voice was heard in Ramah, wailing and loud lamentation, Rachel weeping for her children; she refused to be consoled, because they are no more."

- There's something about the murder of children that shakes our faith. How could God allow the innocent and unprotected to be killed by evil people when their whole life lies before them? In recent times we saw the massacre of hundreds of Russian children taken hostage in school. We witnessed the parents and families beside themselves with grief and rage. We are driven back to the psalms of rage and protest:

Yahweh, how much longer are the wicked to triumph?
Are these evil men to remain unsilenced,
Boasting and asserting themselves? . . .
No, Yahweh is still my citadel,
My God is a rock where I take shelter;
He will pay them back for all their sins,
He will silence their wickedness,
Yahweh our God will silence them. (Psalm 94)

Thursday 29th December   Luke 2:25–32

Now there was a man in Jerusalem whose name was Simeon; this man was righteous and devout, looking forward to the consolation of Israel, and the Holy Spirit rested on him. It had been revealed to him by the Holy Spirit that he would not see death before he had seen the Lord's Messiah. Guided by the Spirit, Simeon came into the temple; and when the parents brought in the child Jesus, to do for him what was customary under the law, Simeon took him in his arms and praised God, saying, "Master, now you are dismissing your servant in peace, according to your word; for my eyes have seen your salvation, which you have prepared in the presence of all peoples, a light for revelation to the Gentiles and for glory to your people Israel."

- *Nunc dimittis*, the prayer of Simeon, expresses the richness of promises fulfilled, expectations met. What is it that makes this scene so heart-warming? Simeon's sense of God's providence in his life is matched by his happiness in reaching the end of his life, having seen the Messiah. It is a moment of both accomplishment and promise.

- What about my longing and waiting? What am I hoping for deep down? How does the image of the Christ child in his mother's arms speak to my hopes?

Friday 30th December   Luke 2:36–40

There was also a prophet, Anna the daughter of Phanuel, of the tribe of Asher. She was of a great age, having lived with her husband seven years after her marriage, then as a widow to the age of eighty-four. She never left the temple but worshiped there with fasting and prayer night and day. At that moment she came, and began to praise God and to speak about the child to all who were looking for the redemption of Jerusalem. When they had finished everything required by the law of the Lord, they returned to Galilee, to their own town of Nazareth. The child grew and became strong, filled with wisdom; and the favor of God was upon him.

- That last sentence is tantalizing. It sums up 90% of Jesus' life: "The child grew and became strong, filled with wisdom; and the favor of God was with him." Like the prophet Anna, Mary and Joseph watched their child and marveled.
- We watch children with joy and awe as they slowly take on the world. If children are deprived, it is not because we do not give to them, but because we do not treasure what they give to us.

Saturday 31st December   John 1:14–18

And the Word became flesh and lived among us, and we have seen his glory, the glory as of a father's only son, full of grace and truth. (John testified to him and cried out, "This was he of whom I said, 'He who comes after me ranks ahead of me because he was before me.'") From his fullness we have all received, grace upon grace. The law indeed was given through Moses; grace and truth came through Jesus Christ. No one has ever seen God. It is God the only Son, who is close to the Father's heart, who has made him known.

- In this hymn which introduces the fourth gospel, John proclaims the faith that marks us as Christian. We believe that Jesus is the Word of God, his perfect expression. "No one has ever seen God. It is God the only Son, who is close to the Father's heart, who has made him known."
- Lord, in the year that starts tonight, let me grow in the knowledge of God. May I receive of your fullness, grace upon grace. You took on this mortal flesh for me and lived among us. May this coming year bring me closer to you.

Something to think and pray about each day this week:

A peaceful resolution

In recent years, the first day of the new year has been designated World Day of Peace. And the first gospel for this year is filled with a beautiful peace. In fact, it was in response to the angels' song, "Glory to God in the highest and peace to his people on earth," that the shepherds had gone in search of the baby in the manger. On this day, the pope asks all of us to pray for peace and to work for peace. There are many places in the world today where there is a great deal of violence and conflict. Untold millions of innocent people are the victims.

But, when we think of peace, we should not just think of the conflicts which make headlines in our news. Conflict on a wide scale happens because of the conflicts on the small scale: in single nations, in single communities, in neighborhoods, and within families. We may not be able to do much about peace in Iraq or Israel or Sudan or in some other troubled spot (if we do not live there), but we can all do something about peace in our immediate surroundings.

All of us can and need to be agents of forgiveness and reconciliation. We can all be peacemakers. "Blessed are the peacemakers for they shall be called the children of God." We could hardly make a better resolution at the beginning of this new year.

The Presence of God
As I sit here, the beating of my heart,
the ebb and flow of my breathing, the movements of my mind
are all signs of God's ongoing creation of me.
I pause for a moment, and become aware
of this presence of God within me.

Freedom
I ask for the grace
to let go of my own concerns
and be open to what God is asking of me,
to let myself be guided and formed by my loving Creator.

Consciousness
In the presence of my loving Creator,
I look honestly at my feelings over the last day,
the highs, the lows and the level ground.
Can I see where the Lord has been present?

The Word
I take my time to read the Word of God, slowly, a few times,
allowing myself to dwell on anything that strikes me. (Please
turn to your scripture on the following pages. Inspiration points
are there should you need them. When you are ready, return
here to continue.)

Conversation
Remembering that I am still in God's presence,
I imagine Jesus himself standing or sitting beside me,
and say whatever is on my mind, whatever is in my heart,
speaking as one friend to another.

Conclusion
Glory be to the Father, and to the Son, and to the Holy Spirit,
As it was in the beginning, is now and ever shall be,
World without end. Amen

Sunday 1st January, Solemnity of Mary, Mother of God
Luke 2:15–21

When the angels had left them and gone into heaven, the shepherds said to one another, "Let us go now to Bethlehem and see this thing that has taken place, which the Lord has made known to us." So they went with haste and found Mary and Joseph, and the child lying in the manger. When they saw this, they made known what had been told them about this child; and all who heard it were amazed at what the shepherds told them. But Mary treasured all these words and pondered them in her heart. The shepherds returned, glorifying and praising God for all they had heard and seen, as it had been told them. After eight days had passed, it was time to circumcise the child; and he was called Jesus, the name given by the angel before he was conceived in the womb.

- Can I imagine myself as one of the shepherds who have just heard extraordinary news? We head off quickly towards Bethlehem.
- What do we find? What is happening? Who do I see here? How are they reacting?
- Can I simply allow this scene to touch me deeply?

Monday 2nd January
John 1:19–28

This is the testimony given by John when the Jews sent priests and Levites from Jerusalem to ask him, "Who are you?" He confessed and did not deny it, but confessed, "I am not the Messiah." And they asked him, "What then? Are you Elijah?" He said, "I am not." "Are you the prophet?" He answered, "No." Then they said to him, "Who are you? Let us have an answer for those who sent us. What do you say about yourself?" He said, "I am the voice of one crying out in the wilderness, 'Make straight the way of the Lord,'" as the prophet Isaiah said. Now they had been sent from the Pharisees. They asked him, "Why then are you baptizing if you are neither the

Messiah, nor Elijah, nor the prophet?" John answered them, "I baptize with water. Among you stands one whom you do not know, the one who is coming after me; I am not worthy to untie the thong of his sandal." This took place in Bethany across the Jordan where John was baptizing.

- John the Baptist has appeared on the scene. Can I imagine myself as one of those sent by the Pharisees to find out who he is and what is going on?
- What do I find?

Tuesday 3rd January   **John 1:29–34**

The next day John saw Jesus coming toward him and declared, "Here is the Lamb of God who takes away the sin of the world! This is he of whom I said, 'After me comes a man who ranks ahead of me because he was before me.' I myself did not know him; but I came baptizing with water for this reason, that he might be revealed to Israel." And John testified, "I saw the Spirit descending from heaven like a dove, and it remained on him. I myself did not know him, but the one who sent me to baptize with water said to me, 'He on whom you see the Spirit descend and remain is the one who baptizes with the Holy Spirit.' And I myself have seen and have testified that this is the Son of God."

- This is the culminating moment of John's life, the arrival of the One for whom he prepared the way.
- Can I hear John's account of himself? He knew he was to prepare the way, but until now, he didn't know the identity of the one he was preparing for.
- How do I understand John? Does he move me to look towards the one who was to come?

Wednesday 4th January   **John 1:35–42**

The next day John again was standing with two of his disciples, and as he watched Jesus walk by, he exclaimed, "Look, here is the Lamb of God!" The two disciples heard him say this, and they followed Jesus. When Jesus turned and saw them following, he said to them, "What are you looking for?" They said to him, "Rabbi" (which translated means Teacher), "where are you staying?" He said to them, "Come and see." They came and saw where he was staying, and they remained with him that day. It was about four o'clock in the afternoon. One of the two who heard John speak and followed him was Andrew, Simon Peter's brother. He first found his brother Simon and said to him, "We have found the Messiah" (which is translated Anointed). He brought Simon to Jesus, who looked at him and said, "You are Simon son of John. You are to be called Cephas" (which is translated Peter).

- Can I imagine myself as one of these two disciples? What is the scene like? How does Jesus look?
- Do I hear him address me: "What are you looking for?"
- When he says "come and see," what does he show me?

Thursday 5th January   **John 1:43–51**

The next day Jesus decided to go to Galilee. He found Philip and said to him, "Follow me." Now Philip was from Beth-saida, the city of Andrew and Peter. Philip found Nathanael and said to him, "We have found him about whom Moses in the law and also the prophets wrote, Jesus son of Joseph from Nazareth." Nathanael said to him, "Can anything good come out of Nazareth?" Philip said to him, "Come and see." When Jesus saw Nathanael coming toward him, he said of him, "Here is truly an Israelite in whom there is no deceit!" Nathanael asked him, "Where did you get to know me?" Jesus answered, "I saw you under the fig tree before Philip called you." Nathanael replied,

"Rabbi, you are the Son of God! You are the King of Israel!" Jesus answered, "Do you believe because I told you that I saw you under the fig tree? You will see greater things than these." And he said to him, "Very truly, I tell you, you will see heaven opened and the angels of God ascending and descending upon the Son of Man."

- We see two disciples move all the way from narrow-minded prejudice to acceptance and worship.
- How did Nathanael almost miss recognizing the one in front of him? How did Jesus help him see?
- Are there parallels here with my life experiences?

Friday 6th January   Mark 1:6–11

Now John was clothed with camel's hair, with a leather belt around his waist, and he ate locusts and wild honey. He proclaimed, "The one who is more powerful than I is coming after me; I am not worthy to stoop down and untie the thong of his sandals. I have baptized you with water; but he will baptize you with the Holy Spirit." In those days Jesus came from Nazareth of Galilee and was baptized by John in the Jordan. And just as he was coming up out of the water, he saw the heavens torn apart and the Spirit descending like a dove on him. And a voice came from heaven, "You are my Son, the Beloved; with you I am well pleased."

- Do I recognize the One who is more powerful than myself at work in my life? My actions are but external signs of his presence at work in me. Unworthy though I am, Lord, you have called me to be a member of your family and a witness to your love.

Saturday 7th January   Matthew 4:12–17

Now when Jesus heard that John had been arrested, he withdrew to Galilee. He left Nazareth and made his home in Capernaum by the sea, in the territory of Zebulun and

Naphtali, so that what had been spoken through the prophet Isaiah might be fulfilled: "Land of Zebulun, land of Naphtali, on the road by the sea, across the Jordan, Galilee of the Gentiles—the people who sat in darkness have seen a great light, and for those who sat in the region and shadow of death light has dawned." From that time Jesus began to proclaim, "Repent, for the kingdom of heaven has come near."

- Over the past few weeks we have been watching the gradual unfolding of God's plans in the Word made flesh.
- Now we see Jesus come of age and realize that the plans have a purpose.
- How does this purpose affect me?

january 8–14

Something to think and pray about each day this week:

Patient love
"A bruised reed he will not break, and a dimly burning wick he will not quench." Thank you, Lord, I need that. There are times when I feel bruised and easily broken, smoldering and easily quenched. You will have patience with me as I labor through my darkest days, and keep the flame and the promise alive. You will not lose hope for me, though I myself may falter.

The Presence of God
I pause for a moment
and reflect on God's life-giving presence
in every part of my body, in everything around me,
in the whole of my life.

Freedom
I ask for the grace to believe
in what I could be and do
if I only allowed God, my loving Creator,
to continue to create me, guide me and shape me.

Consciousness
Knowing that God loves me unconditionally,
I look honestly over the last day, its events and my feelings.
Do I have something to be grateful for? Then I give thanks.
Is there something I am sorry for? Then I ask forgiveness.

The Word
God speaks to each one of us individually. I need to listen to
hear what he is saying to me. Read the text a few times, then
listen. (Please turn to your scripture on the following pages.
Inspiration points are there should you need them. When you
are ready, return here to continue.)

Conversation
How has God's Word moved me? Has it left me cold?
Has it consoled me or moved me to act in a new way?
I imagine Jesus standing or sitting beside me,
I turn and share my feelings with him.

Conclusion
Glory be to the Father, and to the Son, and to the Holy Spirit,
As it was in the beginning, is now and ever shall be,
World without end. Amen

Sunday 8th January, The Epiphany of the Lord
Matthew 2:1–12

In the time of King Herod, after Jesus was born in Bethlehem of Judea, wise men from the East came to Jerusalem, asking, "Where is the child who has been born king of the Jews? For we observed his star at its rising, and have come to pay him homage." When King Herod heard this, he was frightened, and all Jerusalem with him; and calling together all the chief priests and scribes of the people, he inquired of them where the Messiah was to be born. They told him, "In Bethlehem of Judea; for so it has been written by the prophet: 'And you, Bethlehem, in the land of Judah, are by no means least among the rulers of Judah; for from you shall come a ruler who is to shepherd my people Israel.'" Then Herod secretly called for the wise men and learned from them the exact time when the star had appeared. Then he sent them to Bethlehem, saying, "Go and search diligently for the child; and when you have found him, bring me word so that I may also go and pay him homage." When they had heard the king, they set out; and there, ahead of them, went the star that they had seen at its rising, until it stopped over the place where the child was. When they saw that the star had stopped, they were overwhelmed with joy. On entering the house, they saw the child with Mary his mother; and they knelt down and paid him homage. Then, opening their treasure chests, they offered him gifts of gold, frankincense, and myrrh. And having been warned in a dream not to return to Herod, they left for their own country by another road.

- Epiphany means the showing of God to all nations. The Magi follow a star. They are not deterred by the evil scheming of Herod; like many good people they hardly seem to perceive his wickedness, but make good use of the information he offers. They bring gifts: the gold of Gaspar, the myrrh of Melchior, the frankincense of Balthasar. And in the Christian tradition they symbolize all nations and every race.

There were three kings, and O what a sight!
One was yellow and one was white,
And one was black as Epiphany night
On Christmas day in the morning.

- Twelfth Night, Little Christmas, the end of festivities, now we go back to everyday life like the Magi, their magic hour over, their gifts presented. Lord, may I keep my eyes on your star to sustain my hope in a world that is sometimes indifferent or evil. *Sacred Space* is a new epiphany, showing you to the nations.

Monday 9th January, The Baptism of the Lord
Mark 1:7–11

John proclaimed, "The one who is more powerful than I is coming after me; I am not worthy to stoop down and untie the thong of his sandals. I have baptized you with water; but he will baptize you with the Holy Spirit." In those days Jesus came from Nazareth of Galilee and was baptized by John in the Jordan. And just as he was coming up out of the water, he saw the heavens torn apart and the Spirit descending like a dove on him. And a voice came from heaven, "You are my Son, the Beloved; with you I am well pleased."

- This passage falls into two definite halves: John's proclamation, and the baptism of Jesus.
- The baptism can be a powerful scene as an imaginative contemplation—picturing the scene in your imagination and allowing it to unfold—but first spend some time listening to John's proclamation, the sense of expectation, the hopes that were pinned on this Messiah.
- Imagine yourself witnessing the scene, perhaps standing in the shallows, the water flowing around your ankles. What is it like?

Tuesday 10th January   **Mark 1:21b–28**

When the sabbath came, Jesus entered the synagogue and taught. They were astounded at his teaching, for he taught them as one having authority, and not as the scribes. Just then there was in their synagogue a man with an unclean spirit, and he cried out, "What have you to do with us, Jesus of Nazareth? Have you come to destroy us? I know who you are, the Holy One of God." But Jesus rebuked him, saying, "Be silent, and come out of him!" And the unclean spirit, convulsing him and crying with a loud voice, came out of him. They were all amazed, and they kept on asking one another, "What is this? A new teaching—with authority! He commands even the unclean spirits, and they obey him." At once his fame began to spread throughout the surrounding region of Galilee.

- Authority is mentioned a lot in this passage. What do you think Jesus has that makes his listeners feel he has authority?
- Try and imagine Jesus speaking to them. Does he have fine clothes? money? a puffed-up self-importance? What is it about him that makes it so clear he is for real?
- The possessed man tells Jesus, "I know who you are." Can I say the same to him? What would I say next?

Wednesday 11th January   **Mark 1:35–39**

In the morning, while it was still very dark, Jesus got up and went out to a deserted place, and there he prayed. And Simon and his companions hunted for him. When they found him, they said to him, "Everyone is searching for you." He answered, "Let us go on to the neighboring towns, so that I may proclaim the message there also; for that is what I came out to do." And he went throughout Galilee, proclaiming the message in their synagogues and casting out demons.

- Picture the scene when Jesus gets up early and goes to a quiet place to pray on his own. Does he sit or kneel or stand? What is the expression on his face? How does he pray?
- Notice how, for Jesus, the prayer leads to mission, and is a source of strength and guidance for that mission.
- Do I let my prayer lead me into mission, into doing something for God and for others? Does it make me more aware of the needs of people around me? Or do I use it as a cocoon, to insulate myself from the real world?

Thursday 12th January   Mark 1:40–45

A leper came to Jesus and begging him, and kneeling he said to him, "If you choose, you can make me clean." Moved with pity, Jesus stretched out his hand and touched him, and said to him, "I do choose. Be made clean!" Immediately the leprosy left him, and he was made clean. After sternly warning him he sent him away at once, saying to him, "See that you say nothing to anyone; but go, show yourself to the priest, and offer for your cleansing what Moses commanded, as a testimony to them." But he went out and began to proclaim it freely, and to spread the word, so that Jesus could no longer go into a town openly, but stayed out in the country; and people came to him from every quarter.

- The grace the leper asked for was to be made clean. What grace do I most need from the Lord right now? It might be to be washed clean of something, or the strength to face some difficulty, or to overcome some grudge or resentment.
- Whatever it is, can I ask the Lord for it? "If you choose, you can … "
- Can I listen to the reply, "I do choose"?

Friday 13th January   Mark 2:1–5

When Jesus returned to Capernaum after some days, it was reported that he was at home. So many gathered around that there was no longer room for them, not even in front of the door; and he was speaking the word to them. Then some people came, bringing to him a paralyzed man, carried by four of them. And when they could not bring him to Jesus because of the crowd, they removed the roof above him; and after having dug through it, they let down the mat on which the paralytic lay. When Jesus saw their faith, he said to the paralytic, "Son, your sins are forgiven."

- Think what friends the paralyzed man had. They cared so much about him and believed so strongly in Jesus' power to heal him that they went onto the roof, dug a big hole in it, and lowered their friend down to get him to Jesus.
- Imagine what this group was like. What kind of people were they? What were they saying to each other?
- When Jesus saw their faith, he told the man, "your sins are forgiven." It is not through his own effort or virtue, but that of his friends, that this man is healed. So, what can I do for people I know to bring them healing? And what can I receive from them to help heal me?

Saturday 14th January   Mark 2:13–17

Jesus went out again beside the sea; the whole crowd gathered around him, and he taught them. As he was walking along, he saw Levi son of Alphaeus sitting at the tax booth, and he said to him, "Follow me." And he got up and followed him. And as he sat at dinner in Levi's house, many tax collectors and sinners were also sitting with Jesus and his disciples—for there were many who followed him. When the scribes of the Pharisees saw that he was eating with sinners and tax collectors, they said to his disciples, "Why does he eat with tax collectors and sinners?" When Jesus heard this, he said to them, "Those who are well have no need of a physician, but those who are sick; I have come to call not the righteous but sinners."

- Levi just ups and follows Jesus at his word; a sure sign of a dynamic leader with a magnetic presence, people want to follow him.
- Jesus calls everyone to follow him. The Pharisees didn't get this and wondered why he favored the marginalized in society.
- Jesus calls each one of us, not only me but the "have-nots" as well, with equal love. How am I going to let this affect my attitude?

january 15–21

Something to think and pray about each day this week:

Challenging the call

We might think that we are the ones who should be asking, what does God want? But when John the Baptist's disciples began to go after Jesus, they find they are challenged by Jesus with the question: "What do you want?"

And what do we really want from life, from God? It is not such an easy question to answer, but it tells us where we really are. It is a question that challenges us for an answer at different stages in our life.

What is the disciples' response? They have another question but also an answer to Jesus' query: "Teacher (source of wisdom), where do you stay?" They are asking, "Jesus, where are you to be found? Where in our lives do we encounter you, where can we be with you?" If that were to be OUR answer to Jesus' question, "What do you want?", we would be doing very well.

Then Jesus comes back and builds on their question with his warm invitation: "Come and see." Knowing Jesus and where he stays is not a matter of knowing information, like knowing an address. It is not a question of knowing all the scripture or theology, nor is it a question of being an expert in religious teaching or rules: Pharisees of all times are good at that.

God is calling me now, today. What is he saying to me? Am I really listening?

The Presence of God
The world is charged with the grandeur of God (Gerard Manley Hopkins).
I dwell for a moment on the presence of God
around me, in every part of my body,
and deep within my being.

Freedom
"In these days, God taught me
as a schoolteacher teaches a pupil" (St. Ignatius).
I remind myself that there are things God has to teach me yet,
and ask for the grace to hear them and let them change me.

Consciousness
How do I find myself today?
Where am I with God? With others?
Do I have something to be grateful for? Then I give thanks.
Is there something I am sorry for? Then I ask forgiveness.

The Word
I read the Word of God slowly, a few times over, and I listen to what God is saying to me. (Please turn to your scripture on the following pages. Inspiration points are there should you need them. When you are ready, return here to continue.)

Conversation
What feelings are rising in me
as I pray and reflect on God's Word?
I imagine Jesus himself sitting or standing near me
and open my heart to him.

Conclusion
Glory be to the Father, and to the Son, and to the Holy Spirit,
As it was in the beginning, is now and ever shall be,
World without end. Amen

Sunday 15th January, Second Sunday in Ordinary Time
John 1:35–42

The next day John again was standing with two of his disciples, and as he watched Jesus walk by, he exclaimed, "Look, here is the Lamb of God!" The two disciples heard him say this, and they followed Jesus. When Jesus turned and saw them following, he said to them, "What are you looking for?" They said to him, "Rabbi" (which translated means Teacher), "where are you staying?" He said to them, "Come and see." They came and saw where he was staying, and they remained with him that day. It was about four o'clock in the afternoon. One of the two who heard John speak and followed him was Andrew, Simon Peter's brother. He first found his brother Simon and said to him, "We have found the Messiah" (which is translated Anointed). He brought Simon to Jesus, who looked at him and said, "You are Simon son of John. You are to be called Cephas" (which is translated Peter).

- As yesterday, we see the willingness of people to follow Jesus. They are drawn to him, recognize something different in him.
- Not only were they impressed and ready to say this is someone special, but they were ready to tell others to follow him too. Andrew went and found his brother, because he knew this Jesus person was important, and he loved his brother enough to share the news with him.
- Does getting to know Jesus make me want to tell those I love about him? Does my time with him lead to actively encouraging others to get to know him?

Monday 16th January   Mark 2:18–22

Now John's disciples and the Pharisees were fasting; and people came and said to him, "Why do John's disciples and the disciples of the Pharisees fast, but your disciples do not fast?" Jesus said to them, "The wedding guests cannot fast while the bridegroom is with them, can they? As long as they have the bridegroom with them, they cannot fast.

The days will come when the bridegroom is taken away from them, and then they will fast on that day. No one sews a piece of unshrunk cloth on an old cloak; otherwise, the patch pulls away from it, the new from the old, and a worse tear is made. And no one puts new wine into old wineskins; otherwise, the wine will burst the skins, and the wine is lost, and so are the skins; but one puts new wine into fresh wineskins."

- The Pharisees are well known for their strict observance of the law, perhaps to the point of foolishness. Those who didn't observe the dietary laws and customs, for example, weren't considered as holy and wise as the Pharisees themselves.
- They are blind to the fact of who Jesus really is, the Son of God. Jesus tries to tell them that things are a little different now that he is among us. A new era has begun.
- It's like having Windows 98, and suddenly you upgrade to the latest operating system; you don't want anything to do with Windows 98 ever again!

Tuesday 17th January   **Mark 2:23–28**

One sabbath Jesus was going through the grainfields; and as they made their way his disciples began to pluck heads of grain. The Pharisees said to him, "Look, why are they doing what is not lawful on the sabbath?" And he said to them, "Have you never read what David did when he and his companions were hungry and in need of food? He entered the house of God, when Abiathar was high priest, and ate the bread of the Presence, which it is not lawful for any but the priests to eat, and he gave some to his companions." Then he said to them, "The sabbath was made for humankind, and not humankind for the sabbath; so the Son of Man is lord even of the sabbath."

- The Pharisees—quite conscientiously—believe that observing the rules is what God asks of them. This is the be-all and end-all for them.

- Jesus knows that God does not want to make our lives more difficult, and does not impose arbitrary rules on us. For him, the be-all and end-all is the law of love.
- Do I believe in a God who only wants what is good for me? Can I talk to Jesus about this?
- What rules govern my life? Would people who know me be able to say that I follow the law of love?

Wednesday 18th January   Mark 3:1–6

Again he entered the synagogue, and a man was there who had a withered hand. They watched him to see whether he would cure him on the sabbath, so that they might accuse him. And he said to the man who had the withered hand, "Come forward." Then he said to them, "Is it lawful to do good or to do harm on the sabbath, to save life or to kill?" But they were silent. He looked around at them with anger; he was grieved at their hardness of heart and said to the man, "Stretch out your hand." He stretched it out, and his hand was restored. The Pharisees went out and immediately conspired with the Herodians against him, how to destroy him.

- Jesus puts the needs of the man with the withered hand before "the rules," and he is fearless in challenging an unjust law.
- There is nothing that scares the powerful more than fearless love. Anyone who is courageous and has a passion for justice is a threat to them. They conspire because they are frightened.
- Where do "the rules" and the needs of people around me come in my list of priorities?
- Can I ask the Lord for the grace to love fearlessly?

Thursday 19th January   Mark 3:7–12

Jesus departed with his disciples to the sea, and a great multitude from Galilee followed him; hearing all that he was doing, they came to him in great numbers from Judea,

Jerusalem, Idumea, beyond the Jordan, and the region around Tyre and Sidon. He told his disciples to have a boat ready for him because of the crowd, so that they would not crush him; for he had cured many, so that all who had diseases pressed upon him to touch him. Whenever the unclean spirits saw him, they fell down before him and shouted, "You are the Son of God!" But he sternly ordered them not to make him known.

- In this passage, Jesus is acclaimed and recognized for who he is. Even the unclean spirits acknowledge him as the Son of God.
- All these people want to be in his presence, to touch him, to be healed by him.
- Do I recognize Jesus for who he is? Do I want to be in is presence, to touch him and be healed by him? The invitation is there, now.

Friday 20th January   Mark 3:13–19

He went up the mountain and called to him those whom he wanted, and they came to him. And he appointed twelve, whom he also named apostles, to be with him, and to be sent out to proclaim the message, and to have authority to cast out demons. So he appointed the twelve: Simon (to whom he gave the name Peter); James son of Zebedee and John the brother of James (to whom he gave the name Boanerges, that is, Sons of Thunder); and Andrew, and Philip, and Bartholomew, and Matthew, and Thomas, and James son of Alphaeus, and Thaddaeus, and Simon the Cananaean, and Judas Iscariot, who betrayed him.

- I may think I have chosen Jesus, but he has chosen me. Like the apostles, I am chosen to be part of his mission. How do I feel about that? Can I talk to Jesus about it?
- Imagine the apostles, having been chosen, looking at each other, and James and John turning to Andrew and asking, "Who's this Thaddeus guy?"

- I may be surprised by the others the Lord chooses, and at times I may have difficulties with them, but they are chosen, with their faults, just as I am.

Saturday 21st January   Mark 3:20–21

Then Jesus went home; and the crowd came together again, so that they could not even eat. When his family heard it, they went out to restrain him, for people were saying, "He has gone out of his mind."

- Early on in his public life Jesus was saying and doing things that people—even those close to him—couldn't understand.
- Can I imagine Jesus' close relatives worrying that he was losing it?
- What feelings does this evoke in me?
- Does this man who stands out, even in the face of misunderstanding, have anything to teach me?

Something to think and pray about each day this week:

Walking out into the deep

Four fishermen are called: "Follow me and I will make you fishers of people." At once, we are told, Peter and Andrew left their nets and their occupation behind, and followed after Jesus. Just as quickly, leaving their father Zebedee and his hired men, James and John also went after him.

It was a complete act of trust and a total surrender of themselves. To what? Actually, they had no idea; no idea of where they were going or of what the future held. This was the extent of their great trust in this man who came suddenly into their lives, challenging them to leave behind their security and to walk away with him. They would, in fact, go through many unexpected experiences, some of them joyful, some of them full of pain.

The call is still going out to each one of us. Am I ready to answer? To follow? What limits my freedom to follow? What are the nets that still entangle me? What personal relationships are blocking my way? What anxieties? What self-centered ambitions?

The Presence of God
As I sit here, God is present,
breathing life into me and into everything around me.
For a few moments, I sit silently,
and become aware of God's loving presence.

Freedom
If God were trying to tell me something, would I know?
If God were reassuring me or challenging me, would I notice?
I ask for the grace to be free of my own preoccupations
and open to what God may be saying to me.

Consciousness
In God's loving presence I unwind the past day,
starting from now and looking back, moment by moment.
I gather in all the goodness and light, in gratitude.
I attend to the shadows and what they say to me,
seeking healing, courage, forgiveness.

The Word
I take my time to read the Word of God, slowly, a few times,
allowing myself to dwell on anything that strikes me. (Please
turn to your scripture on the following pages. Inspiration points
are there should you need them. When you are ready, return
here to continue.)

Conversation
What is stirring in me as I pray?
Am I consoled, troubled, left cold?
I imagine Jesus himself standing or sitting at my side,
and share my feelings with him.

Conclusion
Glory be to the Father, and to the Son, and to the Holy Spirit,
As it was in the beginning, is now and ever shall be,
World without end. Amen

Sunday 22nd January, Third Sunday in Ordinary Time
Mark 1:14–20

Now after John was arrested, Jesus came to Galilee, proclaiming the good news of God, and saying, "The time is fulfilled, and the kingdom of God has come near; repent, and believe in the good news." As Jesus passed along the Sea of Galilee, he saw Simon and his brother Andrew casting a net into the sea—for they were fishermen. And Jesus said to them, "Follow me and I will make you fish for people." And immediately they left their nets and followed him. As he went a little farther, he saw James son of Zebedee and his brother John, who were in their boat mending the nets. Immediately he called them; and they left their father Zebedee in the boat with the hired men, and followed him.

- This passage came up a few weeks ago. It is a "here-and-now" text, full of immediacy. If I am a bit impatient by nature, this text may give me some consolation.
- The commercial slogan, "just do it" seems to be the theme of this passage. Jesus tells us that now is the time. Simon, Andrew, James, and John drop everything and follow when Jesus calls them.
- Do I find myself looking forward to a time in the future when I will be less busy and can spend more time with God? Or is there something else that I keep meaning to do and never get around to? Something important but not urgent. That time won't come unless I make it come. Now is the time.

Monday 23rd January
Mark 3:22–30

And the scribes who came down from Jerusalem said, "He has Beelzebul, and by the ruler of the demons he casts out demons." And he called them to him, and spoke to them in parables, "How can Satan cast out Satan? If a kingdom is divided against itself, that kingdom cannot stand. And if a house is divided against itself, that house will not be able to stand. And if Satan has risen up against himself and is divided, he cannot stand, but his end has come. But no one can enter a strong man's house and plunder his property without first tying up the strong man; then indeed the house can be plundered. Truly I tell you, people will be forgiven for their sins and whatever blasphemies they utter; but whoever blasphemes against the Holy Spirit can never have forgiveness, but is guilty of an eternal sin"—for they had said, "He has an unclean spirit."

- The One who is utterly innocent is accused of being an agent of the Devil. How could something be so badly misinterpreted?
- Do I know of situations in which the good is sidelined and where misunderstanding reigns?
- Can I ask the Spirit of truth to enlighten me about some situation?

Tuesday 24th January, St. Francis de Sales   John 15:9–17

Jesus said to his disciples, "As the Father has loved me, so I have loved you; abide in my love. If you keep my commandments, you will abide in my love, just as I have kept my Father's commandments and abide in his love. I have said these things to you so that my joy may be in you, and that your joy may be complete. This is my commandment, that you love one another as I have loved you. No one has greater love than this, to lay down one's life for one's friends. You are my friends if you do what I command you. I do not call you servants any longer, because the servant does not know what the master is doing; but I have called you friends, because I have made known to you everything that I have heard from my Father. You did not choose me but I chose you. And I appointed you to go and bear fruit, fruit that will last, so that the Father will give you whatever you ask him in my name. I am giving you these commands so that you may love one another."

- Can I relate to Jesus as my friend, as he invites me to do here, or do I feel it is disrespectful? Listen to him saying to you, "I call you my friend … "

- Jesus has chosen me. But it's not like a job interview, where I'm kind of hoping they'll think I'm better than I really am. He knows all my strengths—and weaknesses—and still chooses me. Listen to him saying, to you, "I chose you ..."
- Jesus has chosen me to be part of his mission. Can I talk to him about what it is he wants me to do?

Wednesday 25th January, Conversion of St. Paul
Acts 22:4–11

"I persecuted this Way up to the point of death by binding both men and women and putting them in prison, as the high priest and the whole council of elders can testify about me. From them I also received letters to the brothers in Damascus, and I went there in order to bind those who were there and to bring them back to Jerusalem for punishment. While I was on my way and approaching Damascus, about noon a great light from heaven suddenly shone about me. I fell to the ground and heard a voice saying to me, 'Saul, Saul, why are you persecuting me?' I answered, 'Who are you, Lord?' Then he said to me, 'I am Jesus of Nazareth whom you are persecuting.' Now those who were with me saw the light but did not hear the voice of the one who was speaking to me. I asked, 'What am I to do, Lord?' The Lord said to me, 'Get up and go to Damascus; there you will be told everything that has been assigned to you to do.' Since I could not see because of the brightness of that light, those who were with me took my hand and led me to Damascus."

- Conversion means a turning, moving round a corner. It can be a sharp, sudden bend, as was Paul's on the road to Damascus, or a gentle, open curve through which we change gradually. It is the Holy Spirit who does the work of sanctification, pulling us round the bend. *Come, Holy Spirit, fill the hearts of your faithful, and enkindle in them the fire of your love.*

Thursday 26th January — Mark 4:21–25

He said to them, "Is a lamp brought in to be put under the bushel basket, or under the bed, and not on the lampstand? For there is nothing hidden, except to be disclosed; nor is anything secret, except to come to light. Let anyone with ears to hear listen!" And he said to them, "Pay attention to what you hear; the measure you give will be the measure you get, and still more will be given you. For to those who have, more will be given; and from those who have nothing, even what they have will be taken away."

- *To the one who has, more will be given.* Jesus quotes a proverb about economics: The rich get richer and the poor get poorer. His message is to be generous: "The measure you give will be the measure you get." As Francis of Assisi prayed, "It is in giving that we receive."

Friday 27th January — Mark 4:26–34

Jesus said to the crowd, "The kingdom of God is as if someone would scatter seed on the ground, and would sleep and rise night and day, and the seed would sprout and grow, he does not know how. The earth produces of itself, first the stalk, then the head, then the full grain in the head. But when the grain is ripe, at once he goes in with his sickle, because the harvest has come." He also said, "With what can we compare the kingdom of God, or what parable will we use for it? It is like a mustard seed, which, when sown upon the ground, is the smallest of all the seeds on earth; yet when it is sown it grows up and becomes the greatest of all shrubs, and puts forth large branches, so that the birds of the air can make nests in its shade." With many such parables he spoke the word to them, as they were able to hear it; he did not speak to them except in parables, but he explained everything in private to his disciples.

- Will I take time and allow this beautiful parable of God sowing seeds to speak to me? The fact that I am sitting here means that I am involved with the Divine Sower.
- I don't know how the seed grows nor have I any control over how it works. Still, can I recognize instances of God's seeds growing in me or through me or around me?
- What are these instances? Who are the other people involved? Can I see their faces in my mind's eye and give praise and thanks to God?

Saturday 28th January, St. Thomas Aquinas
Matthew 23:8–12

Jesus said to the crowds, "But you are not to be called rabbi, for you have one teacher, and you are all students. And call no one your father on earth, for you have one Father—the one in heaven. Nor are you to be called instructors, for you have one instructor, the Messiah. The greatest among you will be your servant. All who exalt themselves will be humbled, and all who humble themselves will be exalted."

- If another person is my teacher, or father, or instructor, it seems right that I should have respect for them and for their position. So, what is Jesus saying here? That we shouldn't respect our teachers, fathers, and instructors?
- The second part of the passage helps to clarify the point. The best teacher, father, or instructor is one who does not rely on his or her position, one who does not demand respect, but earns it through humble service and devotion to those in their care.
- Have you ever met anyone like that? A teacher, or a boss, or someone else in authority who had no regard for their office or rank, and would just muck in and try to help wherever they could?
- Do I want to have that kind of humility? Can I ask the Lord for that grace?

january 29–february 4

Something to think and pray about each day this week:

Possibilities

While there is an ancient Christian tradition of the Purification of Jesus on 2nd February, there is also an ancient Irish tradition of the beginning of the northern spring on 1st February, the feast of St. Brigid. The start of spring is a time of possibilities, of risky ventures, of blessed mistakes. That is the mood of St. Brigid's feast. At the ceremony of her final vows, St. Patrick mistakenly used the form for ordaining priests. When told of it he replied, "So be it, my son, she is destined for great things." There is a prayer attributed to her which ends:

> I would like cheerfulness to preside over all. I would like
> a great lake of beer for the King of Kings. I would like to
> be watching Heaven's family drinking it through all
> eternity.

The Presence of God
As I sit here with my book, God is here.
Around me, in my sensations, in my thoughts and deep within me.
I pause for a moment, and become aware
of God's life-giving presence.

Freedom
I need to close out the noise, to rise above the noise;
The noise that interrupts, that separates,
The noise that isolates.
I need to listen to God again.

Consciousness
I exist in a web of relationships—links to nature, people, God.
I trace out these links, giving thanks for the life that flows through them.
Some links are twisted or broken: I may feel regret, anger, disappointment.
I pray for the gift of acceptance and forgiveness.

The Word
God speaks to each one of us individually. I need to listen to what he is saying to me. (Please turn to your scripture on the following pages. Inspiration points are there should you need them. When you are ready, return here to continue.)

Conversation
Do I notice myself reacting as I pray with the Word of God?
Do I feel challenged, comforted, angry?
Imagining Jesus sitting or standing by me,
I speak out my feelings, as one trusted friend to another.

Conclusion
Glory be to the Father, and to the Son, and to the Holy Spirit,
As it was in the beginning, is now and ever shall be,
World without end. Amen

Sunday 29th January, Fourth Sunday in Ordinary Time
Mark 1:21–28

When the sabbath came, Jesus entered the synagogue and taught. They were astounded at his teaching, for he taught them as one having authority, and not as the scribes. Just then there was in their synagogue a man with an unclean spirit, and he cried out, "What have you to do with us, Jesus of Nazareth? Have you come to destroy us? I know who you are, the Holy One of God." But Jesus rebuked him, saying, "Be silent, and come out of him!" And the unclean spirit, convulsing him and crying with a loud voice, came out of him. They were all amazed, and they kept on asking one another, "What is this? A new teaching—with authority! He commands even the unclean spirits, and they obey him." At once his fame began to spread throughout the surrounding region of Galilee.

- The people recognize Jesus as one who teaches with authority, even before he drives out the unclean spirit.
- Imagine the scene as Jesus teaches. What is it about him that makes his authority clear? Is he a high-ranking member of society? Does he dress in expensive clothes?
- What kind of people do I have respect for? Whose opinions do I listen to? The "big cheeses," the rich and powerful? Or am I looking for some other quality?

Monday 30th January   **Mark 5:1–13**

Jesus and his disciples came to the other side of the sea, to the country of the Gerasenes. And when he had stepped out of the boat, immediately a man out of the tombs with an unclean spirit met him. He lived among the tombs; and no one could restrain him any more, even with a chain; for he had often been restrained with shackles and chains, but the chains he wrenched apart, and the shackles he broke in pieces; and no one had the strength to subdue him. Night and day among the tombs and on the mountains he was always howling and bruising himself with stones. When he saw Jesus from a distance, he ran and bowed down before him; and he shouted at the top of his voice, "What have you to do with me, Jesus, Son of the Most High God? I adjure you by God, do not torment me." For he had said to him, "Come out of the man, you unclean spirit!" Then Jesus asked him, "What is your name?" He replied, "My name is Legion; for we are many." He begged him earnestly not to send them out of the country. Now there on the hillside a great herd of swine was feeding; and the unclean spirits begged him, "Send us into the swine; let us enter them." So he gave them permission. And the unclean spirits came out and entered the swine; and the herd, numbering about two thousand, rushed down the steep bank into the sea, and were drowned in the sea.

- Mark wants us to see this event not as the cure of mental illness but as a manifestation of the power of Jesus over evil.
- Am I aware of evil in my world in dramatic or subtle forms?
- Does the power of Jesus give me confidence?

Tuesday 31st January, St. John Bosco   Matthew 18:1–5

At that time the disciples came to Jesus and asked, "Who is the greatest in the kingdom of heaven?" He called a child, whom he put among them, and said, "Truly I tell you, unless you change and become like children, you will never enter the kingdom of heaven. Whoever becomes humble like this child is the greatest in the kingdom of heaven. Whoever welcomes one such child in my name welcomes me."

- Jesus is counter-cultural in this passage. He challenges the values of his listeners and of their society by prizing humility and simple trust above wealth, power, and conventional greatness.
- It is just as much a challenge today to the priorities of our society.
- It is also a challenge to me. Why would I want to have child-like humility? Can I talk to the Lord about this?

Wednesday 1st February, St. Brigid   Mark 5:21–43

When Jesus had crossed again in the boat to the other side, a great crowd gathered around him; and he was by the sea. Then one of the leaders of the synagogue named Jairus came and, when he saw him, fell at his feet and begged him repeatedly, "My little daughter is at the point of death. Come and lay your hands on her, so that she may be made well, and live." So he went with him. And a large crowd followed him and pressed in on him. Now there was a woman who had been suffering from hemorrhages for twelve years. She had endured much under many physicians, and had spent all that she had; and she was no better, but rather grew worse. She had heard about Jesus, and came up behind him in the crowd and touched his cloak, for she said, "If I but touch his clothes, I will be made well." Immediately her hemorrhage stopped; and she felt in her body that she was healed of her disease. Immediately aware that power had gone forth from him, Jesus turned about in the crowd and said, "Who touched my clothes?" And his disciples said to him, "You see the crowd pressing in on you; how can you say, 'Who touched me?'" He looked all around to see who had done it. But the woman, knowing what had happened to her, came in fear and trembling, fell down before him, and told him the whole truth. He said to her, "Daughter, your faith has made you well; go in peace, and be healed of your disease." While he was still speaking, some people came from the leader's house to say, "Your daughter is dead. Why trouble the teacher any further?" But overhearing what they said, Jesus said to the leader of the synagogue, "Do not fear, only believe." He allowed no one to follow him except Peter, James, and John, the brother of James. When they came to the house of the leader of the synagogue, he saw a commotion, people weeping and wailing loudly. When he had entered, he said to them, "Why do you make a commotion and weep? The child is not dead but sleeping." And they laughed at him. Then he put them all outside, and took the child's father and mother and those who were with him, and went in where the child was. He took her by the hand and said to her, "Talitha cum," which means, "Little girl, get up!" And immediately the girl got up and began to walk about (she was twelve years of age). At this they were overcome with amazement. He strictly ordered them that no one should know this, and told them to give her something to eat.

- Here are two healings by Jesus, of a girl dying after twelve years of life, and of a woman sick for twelve years. In both there is physical contact with Jesus. The woman reaches out through the crowd to touch him. Jesus takes the little girl by the hand.

- Lord, I cannot touch you, but I reach out to you in faith. You said of the little girl: "She is not dead but sleeping." And you woke her up. I am waiting for your hand on me, to make me more fully alive. Let me hear you say to me: "Talitha cum."

Thursday 2nd February, The Presentation of the Lord
Luke 2:22–24

When the time came for their purification according to the law of Moses, they brought him up to Jerusalem to present him to the Lord (as it is written in the law of the Lord, "Every firstborn male shall be designated as holy to the Lord"), and they offered a sacrifice according to what is stated in the law of the Lord, "a pair of turtledoves or two young pigeons."

- The Purification is the feast of the Lord coming to his temple, a feast that links the Old Testament and God's promises to the Jews, with the fulfilment of those promises in Jesus. He comes not in splendour, but as a baby in his mother's arms. He is not merely the glory of his people Israel, but a light for revelation to the Gentiles.
- Lord, I am one of those Gentiles, a glorious company reaching backwards and forward in time. You share my humanity in every

way. Like you, I want to grow and become strong, filled with wisdom. May the favor of God be with me as with you.

Friday 3rd February   1 Kings 2:1–4

When David's time to die drew near, he charged his son Solomon, saying: "I am about to go the way of all the earth. Be strong, be courageous, and keep the charge of the Lord your God, walking in his ways and keeping his statutes, his commandments, his ordinances, and his testimonies, as it is written in the law of Moses, so that you may prosper in all that you do and wherever you turn. Then the Lord will establish his word that he spoke concerning me: 'If your heirs take heed to their way, to walk before me in faithfulness with all their heart and with all their soul, there shall not fail you a successor on the throne of Israel.'"

- Listen to David's words, "Be strong, be courageous." Are there situations in my life where I need strength and courage at the moment? Can I ask the Lord for that grace?
- Do I walk in faithfulness to God, with all my heart and all my soul? Or am I keeping something back? Are there parts of my life that are no-go areas for God?

Saturday 4th February   1 Kings 3:5–13

At Gibeon the Lord appeared to Solomon in a dream by night; and God said, "Ask what I should give you." And Solomon said, "You have shown great and steadfast love to your servant my father David, because he walked before you in faithfulness, in righteousness, and in uprightness of heart toward you; and you have kept for him this great and steadfast love, and have given him a son to sit on his throne today. And now, O Lord my God, you have made your servant king in place of my father David, although I am only a little child; I do not know how to go out or come in. And your servant is in the midst of the people whom you have chosen, a great people, so numerous they cannot be numbered or counted. Give your servant therefore an understanding mind to govern your people, able to discern between good and evil; for who can govern this your great people?" It pleased the Lord that Solomon had asked this. God said to him, "Because you have asked this, and have not asked for yourself long life or riches, or for the life of your enemies, but have asked for yourself understanding to discern what is right, I now do according to your word. Indeed I give you a wise and discerning mind; no one like you has been before you and no one like you shall arise after you. I give you also what you have not asked, both riches and honour all your life; no other king shall compare with you."

- Often, if I am asked what I want, I think first of the immediate things, the superficial things: a better printer, perhaps, or a new laptop, or even some new car I have my eye on.
- It can take longer to get in touch with what I desire most deeply.
- But God makes that invitation to me, to search my soul and to say what it is that I really want. God is listening and wants to grant me my desire.

february 5–11

Something to think and pray about each day this week:

Working for life

When Jesus cures the sick, Jesus is at work—but it is work that is so full of meaning. He is using his energies to bring healing and wholeness into the lives of people. The difference comes from his radical approach: Jesus is there to serve, to give, to share. He is not thinking, "How much am I going to get for doing this?" or "When can I finish so I can leave and go home, or go out to enjoy myself?"

Jesus is not just making a living for himself. He is not out for power, status, promotion, wealth . . . he is working for others.

Let me consider less what I can squeeze for myself out of my society and consider how much I am putting into it—to be like Jesus, finding myself in sharing what I have and what I am with others. A person for others. That is life-giving, that gives work meaning and value. And it can give meaning and value to my work and life.

The Presence of God

I pause for a moment, aware that God is here.
I think of how everything around me,
the air I breathe, my whole body,
is tingling with the presence of God.

Freedom

I will ask God's help,
to be free from my own preoccupations,
to be open to God in this time of prayer,
to come to love and serve him more.

Consciousness

How am I really feeling? Light-hearted? Heavy-hearted?
I may be very much at peace, happy to be here.
Equally, I may be frustrated, worried or angry.
I acknowledge how I really am. It is the real me that the Lord loves.

The Word

I read the Word of God slowly, a few times over, and I listen to what God is saying to me. (Please turn to your scripture on the following pages. Inspiration points are there should you need them. When you are ready, return here to continue.)

Conversation

Remembering that I am still in God's presence,
I imagine Jesus himself standing or sitting beside me,
and say whatever is on my mind, whatever is in my heart,
speaking as one friend to another.

Conclusion

Glory be to the Father, and to the Son, and to the Holy Spirit,
As it was in the beginning, is now and ever shall be,
World without end. Amen

Sunday 5th February, Fifth Sunday in Ordinary Time
Mark 1:29–31

As soon as they left the synagogue, they entered the house of Simon and Andrew, with James and John. Now Simon's mother-in-law was in bed with a fever, and they told Jesus about her at once. He came and took her by the hand and lifted her up. Then the fever left her, and she began to serve them.

- Imagine this scene, perhaps from the point of view of Simon's mother-in-law. What does the house look, smell, feel like?
- Does Jesus say anything to me as he lifts me up? Do I have anything to say to him?
- Can I imagine the feeling as the fever leaves me? How do I respond to this experience?

Monday 6th February
Mark 6:53–56

When Jesus and the disciples had crossed over, they came to land at Gennesaret and moored the boat. When they got out of the boat, people at once recognized him, and rushed about that whole region and began to bring the sick on mats to wherever they heard he was. And wherever he went, into villages or cities or farms, they laid the sick in the marketplaces, and begged him that they might touch even the fringe of his cloak; and all who touched it were healed.

- Is there any sickness or disquiet that I want Jesus to heal me of?
- Can I put myself among all those in this scene who need healing?
- Jesus is offering that healing. Can I accept it from him?

Tuesday 7th February
Mark 7:1–2,5–8

Now when the Pharisees and some of the scribes who had come from Jerusalem gathered around him, they noticed that some of his disciples were eating with defiled hands, that is, without washing them. So the Pharisees and the scribes asked him, "Why do your disciples not live according to the tradition of the elders, but eat with defiled hands?" He said to them, "Isaiah prophesied rightly about you hypocrites, as it is written, 'This people honors me with their lips, but their hearts are far from me; in vain do they worship me, teaching human precepts as doctrines.' You abandon the commandment of God and hold to human tradition."

- "This people honors me with their lips, but their hearts are far from me." Is my service of God just lip-service? Or do I put my heart into it?
- Jesus tells us here that worship is worthless if its main concern is to follow some human tradition, or some ritual or rubric of our own invention.
- God does not look to my outward conformity. God looks to my heart. It is there that my real relationship with God goes on.

Wednesday 8th February   Mark 7:14–23

Then he called the crowd again and said to them, "Listen to me, all of you, and understand: there is nothing outside a person that by going in can defile, but the things that come out are what defile." When he had left the crowd and entered the house, his disciples asked him about the parable. He said to them, "Then do you also fail to understand? Do you not see that whatever goes into a person from outside cannot defile, since it enters, not the heart but the stomach, and goes out into the sewer?" (Thus he declared all foods clean.) And he said, "It is what comes out of a person that defiles. For it is from within, from the human heart, that evil intentions come: fornication, theft, murder, adultery, avarice, wickedness, deceit, licentiousness, envy, slander, pride, folly. All these evil things come from within, and they defile a person."

- Dirt and germs may be unhygienic, but what defiles me as a human being is doing things that are unworthy of a person made in the image and likeness of God.

- If I can remember just one time when I did or said something I felt ashamed of afterwards—something mean, hurtful, dishonest, lewd, or arrogant—then I already know what Jesus is talking about.
- Perhaps I can ask myself, "What comes out of me?" and notice, over the next day or so, what does.

Thursday 9th February   Mark 7:24–30

From there Jesus set out and went away to the region of Tyre. He entered a house and did not want anyone to know he was there. Yet he could not escape notice, but a woman whose little daughter had an unclean spirit immediately heard about him, and she came and bowed down at his feet. Now the woman was a Gentile, of Syrophoenician origin. She begged him to cast the demon out of her daughter. He said to her, "Let the children be fed first, for it is not fair to take the children's food and throw it to the dogs." But she answered him, "Sir, even the dogs under the table eat the children's crumbs." Then he said to her, "For saying that, you may go—the demon has left your daughter." So she went home, found the child lying on the bed, and the demon gone.

- It was very much against the conventions of the time for Jesus, a Jew, to even speak to a gentile, especially a woman. Jesus breaks these conventions for the sake of the child's need for healing.
- In this scene, the woman answers Jesus back, and he responds positively. Can I imagine myself as the woman in this scene? What does it feel like to be her?
- When I pray, do I speak my mind like this woman does, or do I feel I have to be polite and deferential? Jesus wants me to be honest with him, even if I am full of bad feelings. It is the real me that he loves and wants to talk to.

Friday 10th February   **Mark 7:31–37**

Then Jesus returned from the region of Tyre, and went by way of Sidon towards the Sea of Galilee, in the region of the Decapolis. They brought to him a deaf man who had an impediment in his speech; and they begged him to lay his hand on him. He took him aside in private, away from the crowd, and put his fingers into his ears, and he spat and touched his tongue. Then looking up to heaven, he sighed and said to him, "Ephphatha," that is, "Be opened." And immediately his ears were opened, his tongue was released, and he spoke plainly. Then Jesus ordered them to tell no one; but the more he ordered them, the more zealously they proclaimed it. They were astounded beyond measure, saying, "He has done everything well; he even makes the deaf to hear and the mute to speak."

- The stories of Jesus healing deaf people (and blind people) have a pretty clear symbolic meaning. They are not just about physical infirmity, but about the senses. Notice all the references to spitting, the tongue, the ears, touching.
- Jesus repeatedly urges us to use our senses, to be sensitive to what is around us, to have eyes to see and ears to hear.
- Are there things around me that I ignore, that I block out of my senses, that I am closed to? Can I imagine Jesus speaking those words, "Be opened," to me?

Saturday 11th February   **Mark 8:1–8**

In those days when there was again a great crowd without anything to eat, Jesus called his disciples and said to them, "I have compassion for the crowd, because they have been with me now for three days and have nothing to eat. If I send them away hungry to their homes, they will faint on the way—and some of them have come from a great distance." His disciples replied, "How can one feed these people with bread here in the desert?" He asked them, "How many loaves do you have?" They said,

"Seven." Then he ordered the crowd to sit down on the ground; and he took the seven loaves, and after giving thanks he broke them and gave them to his disciples to distribute; and they distributed them to the crowd. They had also a few small fish; and after blessing them, he ordered that these too should be distributed. They ate and were filled; and they took up the broken pieces left over, seven baskets full.

- Jesus is not just concerned about some remote spiritual realm. He is in touch with the real needs of these people, and responds to them.
- The disciples' first reaction is "that's not possible." Jesus is determined to find a way.
- How do I react to this story? disbelief? uncertainty? wonder? Can I talk to Jesus about this?

february 12–18

Something to think and pray about each day this week:

Touching our depths

Apart from the appalling physical disintegration of body and limbs, leprosy meant social ostracism, contempt, and fear. This was real pain and suffering.

When the leper approaches Jesus, he is desperate, at the end of the line. But he comes with a marvelous faith: "If you choose, you can make me clean." It expresses the man's faith in the power of Jesus, who has only to wish for his healing for it to happen. The leper has already seen it at work in other people.

Jesus then does something very significant: He physically touches the leper to indicate his compassion. It sent a strong message of affirmation to the sick person—and to the rest of us. "I do choose," says Jesus to the man. "Be made clean!"

And we can ask ourselves today, what has our experience of knowing Jesus been like? How is it we do not have the enthusiasm of this man, this leper, this social outcast?

The Presence of God

For a few moments, I think of God's veiled presence in things:
in the elements, giving them existence;
in plants, giving them life; in animals, giving them sensation;
and finally, in me, giving me all this and more,
making me a temple, a dwelling-place of the Spirit.

Freedom

God is not foreign to my freedom.
Instead the Spirit breathes life into my most intimate desires,
gently nudging me towards all that is good.
I ask for the grace to let myself be enfolded by the Spirit.

Consciousness

Knowing that God loves me unconditionally,
I can afford to be honest about how I am.
How has the last day been, and how do I feel now?
I share my feelings openly with the Lord.

The Word

I take my time to read the Word of God, slowly, a few times,
allowing myself to dwell on anything that strikes me. (Please
turn to your scripture on the following pages. Inspiration points
are there should you need them. When you are ready, return
here to continue.)

Conversation

How has God's Word moved me? Has it left me cold?
Has it consoled me or moved me to act in a new way?
I imagine Jesus standing or sitting beside me,
I turn and share my feelings with him.

Conclusion

Glory be to the Father, and to the Son, and to the Holy Spirit,
As it was in the beginning, is now and ever shall be,
World without end. Amen

Sunday 12th February, Sixth Sunday in Ordinary Time
Mark 1:40–45

A leper came to Jesus begging him, and kneeling he said to him, "If you choose, you can make me clean." Moved with pity, Jesus stretched out his hand and touched him, and said to him, "I do choose. Be made clean!" Immediately the leprosy left him, and he was made clean. After sternly warning him he sent him away at once, saying to him, "See that you say nothing to anyone; but go, show yourself to the priest, and offer for your cleansing what Moses commanded, as a testimony to them." But he went out and began to proclaim it freely, and to spread the word, so that Jesus could no longer go into a town openly, but stayed out in the country; and people came to him from every quarter.

- The grace the leper asked for was to be made clean. What grace do I most need from the Lord right now? It might be to be washed clean of something, or the strength to face some difficulty, or to overcome some grudge or resentment.
- Whatever it is, can I ask the Lord for it? "Lord, if you choose, you can …"
- I am in the Lord's presence. Can I watch him looking me straight in the eye and saying, "I do choose"?

Monday 13th February
Mark 8:11–13

The Pharisees came and began to argue with Jesus, asking him for a sign from heaven, to test him. And he sighed deeply in his spirit and said, "Why does this generation ask for a sign? Truly I tell you, no sign will be given to this generation." And he left them, and getting into the boat again, he went across to the other side.

- The Pharisees were asking for a sign when in fact the Sign was standing in front of them.

- What did they really want? If they got it, would it have satisfied them?
- And me? What sign do I crave?

Tuesday 14th February, Sts. Cyril and Methodius
Luke 10:1–9

After this the Lord appointed seventy others and sent them on ahead of him in pairs to every town and place where he himself intended to go. He said to them, "The harvest is plentiful, but the laborers are few; therefore ask the Lord of the harvest to send out laborers into his harvest. Go on your way. See, I am sending you out like lambs into the midst of wolves. Carry no purse, no bag, no sandals; and greet no one on the road. Whatever house you enter, first say, 'Peace to this house!' And if anyone is there who shares in peace, your peace will rest on that person; but if not, it will return to you. Remain in the same house, eating and drinking whatever they provide, for the laborer deserves to be paid. Do not move about from house to house. Whenever you enter a town and its people welcome you, eat what is set before you; cure the sick who are there, and say to them, 'The kingdom of God has come near to you.'"

- Can I imagine myself being sent on ahead by Jesus as one of a pair? The instructions before setting out suggest a good deal of insecurity ahead and a big need for trust.
- He wants us to announce two messages especially: "Peace to this house" and "the Kingdom of God has come near to you."
- Do I feel prepared to proclaim those two realities? What do I need to say to Jesus about this mission?
- Can I imagine myself as one of these seventy, being missioned by Jesus?
- Can I ask the Lord what mission he has for me?
- We are not sent alone. Who are my partners in this mission? Do I look to them for help, and do I give them support?

Wednesday 15th February   Mark 8:22–25

They came to Bethsaida. Some people brought a blind man to Jesus and begged him to touch him. He took the blind man by the hand and led him out of the village; and when he had put saliva on his eyes and laid his hands on him, he asked him, "Can you see anything?" And the man looked up and said, "I can see people, but they look like trees, walking." Then Jesus laid his hands on his eyes again; and he looked intently and his sight was restored, and he saw everything clearly.

* Can I imagine myself in this scene, as the blind man? What are the sounds and smells around me? What does it feel like, being unable to see?
* How do I want to respond to Jesus when he asks me, "Can you see anything?"
* What is it like when my sight is restored? What do I want to say to Jesus now?
* Is there any blindness in my life? Are there things I fail to see or refuse to face? Can I ask the Lord for the grace to see them?

Thursday 16th February   Mark 8:27–33

Jesus went on with his disciples to the villages of Caesarea Philippi; and on the way he asked his disciples, "Who do people say that I am?" And they answered him, "John the Baptist; and others, Elijah; and still others, one of the prophets." He asked them, "But who do you say that I am?" Peter answered him, "You are the Messiah." And he sternly ordered them not to tell anyone about him. Then he began to teach them that the Son of Man must undergo great suffering, and be rejected by the elders, the chief priests, and the scribes, and be killed, and after three days rise again. He said all this quite openly. And Peter took him aside and began to rebuke him. But turning and looking at his disciples, he rebuked Peter and said, "Get behind me, Satan! For you are setting your mind not on divine things but on human things."

- Imagine the conversation as the disciples talk about the villagers. Perhaps they were even laughing and making fun of people's reactions. But Jesus puts them on the spot when he asks them, "Who do you say I am?"
- Imagine yourself as a disciple in this scene. How do you respond to Jesus?
- Jesus talks openly about expecting to suffer and be rejected, and Peter cannot stomach this. He thinks the Messiah must be mighty, glorious, all-conquering, not a "loser."
- Jesus makes it pretty clear that self-sacrificing love is his way, not "might-is-right." How do I feel about this?

Friday 17th February   Mark 8:34–9:1

Jesus called the crowd with his disciples, and said to them, "If any want to become my followers, let them deny themselves and take up their cross and follow me. For those who want to save their life will lose it, and those who lose their life for my sake, and for the sake of the gospel, will save it. For what will it profit them to gain the whole world and forfeit their life? Indeed, what can they give in return for their life? Those who are ashamed of me and of my words in this adulterous and sinful generation, of them the Son of Man will also be ashamed when he comes in the glory of his Father with the holy angels." And he said to them, "Truly I tell you, there are some standing here who will not taste death until they see that the kingdom of God has come with power."

- These words may sound pretty tough, but in fact Jesus is offering me a choice here, and telling me the plain truth about what that choice will mean.
- I can live for myself. I can concentrate on my life, my ambitions, my pleasures, so much that I become closed up in my own—fairly

comfortable—little world. I can choose that if I want to, and nobody is going to stop me.

- Or I can choose to be a person for others. This does not mean making myself a "doormat" or neglecting my real needs, but giving of myself for others, wanting other people's lives to have been better because I have lived.
- If I choose living for others (and it's not a one-off decision, but one I'll need to renew again from time to time) then my relationships take on a new quality. It is then that I am fully alive.

Saturday 18th February   Mark 9:2–8

Six days later, Jesus took with him Peter and James and John, and led them up a high mountain apart, by themselves. And he was transfigured before them, and his clothes became dazzling white, such as no one on earth could bleach them. And there appeared to them Elijah with Moses, who were talking with Jesus. Then Peter said to Jesus, "Rabbi, it is good for us to be here; let us make three dwellings, one for you, one for Moses, and one for Elijah." He did not know what to say, for they were terrified. Then a cloud overshadowed them, and from the cloud there came a voice, "This is my Son, the Beloved; listen to him!" Suddenly when they looked around, they saw no one with them any more, but only Jesus.

- You might find it helpful to contemplate a picture of this scene.
- Imagine yourself to be present. What is it like? (What are Elijah, Moses and Jesus talking to each other about?)
- How do you imagine the voice that says, "This is my Son . . ."?
- At the end of the scene, when Jesus is standing there alone, what do you want to say to him?

Something to think and pray about each day this week:

Crippled no more
Four men carrying their paralytic friend are anxious to get to Jesus. Blocked by the crowd they go up by the outside staircase of the house on to the flat roof, remove a few tiles, and let the man down right at the feet of Jesus. Jesus is touched by their determination which is a measure of their faith, trust, and confidence in him.

Jesus surprised them by saying, "Child, your sins are forgiven." The man came for healing of his disability, not forgiveness. But Jesus teaches us that there can be no healing of the body without inner healing.

At the same time, the scribes present are shocked and say to themselves, "The man is blaspheming. Only God can forgive sins." But their eyes are closed to the logic of their own remark. They refuse to draw the obvious conclusion; they don't see because they do not want to see.

Lord, how often do I recognize your presence and gifts, how often do I thank you and praise you? I can imagine the exhilaration of the paralytic as he rose and walked. As paralysis cripples the body, so sin incapacitates us too. Do I feel the same excitement and want to give thanks at being freed from sin?

The Presence of God
I pause for a moment
and think of the love and the grace that God showers on me,
creating me in his image and likeness, making me his temple.

Freedom
Everything has the potential to draw forth from me a fuller love
and life.
Yet my desires are often fixed, caught, on illusions of fulfillment.
I ask that God, through my freedom, may orchestrate
my desires in a vibrant loving melody rich in harmony.

Consciousness
In the presence of my loving Creator,
I look honestly at my feelings over the last day,
the highs, the lows and the level ground.
Can I see where the Lord has been present?

The Word
God speaks to each one of us individually. I need to listen to
what he is saying to me. (Please turn to your scripture on the
following pages. Inspiration points are there should you need
them. When you are ready, return here to continue.)

Conversation
What feelings are rising in me
as I pray and reflect on God's Word?
I imagine Jesus himself sitting or standing beside me,
and open my heart to him.

Conclusion
Glory be to the Father, and to the Son, and to the Holy Spirit,
As it was in the beginning, is now and ever shall be,
World without end. Amen

Sunday 19th February, Seventh Sunday in Ordinary Time
Mark 2:1–5

When he returned to Capernaum after some days, it was reported that he was at home. So many gathered around that there was no longer room for them, not even in front of the door; and he was speaking the word to them. Then some people came, bringing to him a paralyzed man, carried by four of them. And when they could not bring him to Jesus because of the crowd, they removed the roof above him; and after having dug through it, they let down the mat on which the paralytic lay. When Jesus saw their faith, he said to the paralytic, "Son, your sins are forgiven."

- This passage came up about a month ago. If you prayed with it then, see if your reactions to it are different this time.
- Think what friends the paralyzed man had. They cared so much about him and believed so strongly in Jesus' power to heal him that they went onto the roof, dug a big hole in it, and lowered their friend down to get him to Jesus.
- Imagine what this group was like. What kind of people were they? What were they saying to each?
- When Jesus saw their faith, he told the man, "your sins are forgiven." It is not through his own effort or virtue, but that of his friends, that this man is healed. So, what can I do for people I know to bring them healing? And what can I receive from them to help heal me?

Monday 20th February James 3:13–18

Who is wise and understanding among you? Show by your good life that your works are done with gentleness born of wisdom. But if you have bitter envy and selfish ambition in your hearts, do not be boastful and false to the truth. Such wisdom does not come down from above, but is earthly, unspiritual, devilish. For where there is envy and selfish ambition, there will also be disorder and wickedness of every kind. But the wisdom from above is first pure, then peaceable, gentle, willing to yield, full of mercy and good fruits, without a trace of partiality or hypocrisy. And a harvest of righteousness is sown in peace for those who make peace.

- Do I find these words challenging, obvious, judgmental, clichéd?
- Sometimes the truth is hard to accept, or perhaps it is so obvious that it doesn't seem worth mentioning. Do I recognize the truth in these words?
- Do they make me think of anything in my own life?

Tuesday 21st February   Mark 9:30–37

Jesus and his disciples went on from there and passed through Galilee. He did not want anyone to know it; for he was teaching his disciples, saying to them, "The Son of Man is to be betrayed into human hands, and they will kill him, and three days after being killed, he will rise again." But they did not understand what he was saying and were afraid to ask him. Then they came to Capernaum; and when he was in the house he asked them, "What were you arguing about on the way?" But they were silent, for on the way they had argued with one another who was the greatest. He sat down, called the twelve, and said to them, "Whoever wants to be first must be last of all and servant of all." Then he took a little child and put it among them; and taking it in his arms, he said to them, "Whoever welcomes one such child in my name welcomes me, and whoever welcomes me welcomes not me but the one who sent me."

- This is a classic case of "crossed wires." It would be good to revisit each stage of this scene and see what was concerning Jesus and, on the other hand, what various things were filling the minds of the disciples.
- Jesus is challenging the disciples about what is really important for them. Can I let him challenge me?

Wednesday 22nd February, The See of St. Peter
Matthew 16:13–19

Now when Jesus came into the district of Caesarea Philippi, he asked his disciples, "Who do people say that the Son of Man is?" And they said, "Some say John the Baptist, but others Elijah, and still others Jeremiah or one of the prophets." He said to them, "But who do you say that I am?" Simon Peter answered, "You are the Messiah, the Son of the living God." And Jesus answered him, "Blessed are you, Simon son of Jonah! For flesh and blood has not revealed this to you, but my Father in heaven. And I tell you, you are Peter, and on this rock I will build my church, and the gates of Hades will not prevail against it. I will give you the keys of the kingdom of heaven, and whatever you bind on earth will be bound in heaven, and whatever you loose on earth will be loosed in heaven."

- The disciples are happy enough to talk about what other people say and think about Jesus. However, they become quiet (except Peter), when he asks them to put themselves on the line.
- Imagine yourself in the group of disciples. When Jesus asks this question, do you merge into the background, or do you speak up? What do you want to say?
- Now imagine Jesus speaking these words, "Blessed are you … I will give you the keys of the kingdom of heaven," to you. What do you think he means? What does it feel like? How do you want to respond?

Thursday 23rd February
Mark 9:41–42,50

Jesus said to the disciples, "For truly I tell you, whoever gives you a cup of water to drink because you bear the name of Christ will by no means lose the reward. If any of you put a stumbling block before one of these little ones who believe in me, it would be better for you if a great millstone were hung around your neck and you were thrown into the sea. Salt is good; but if salt has lost its saltiness, how can you season it? Have salt in yourselves, and be at peace with one another."

- There are three strong and distinct points in what Jesus says here. There is a connection between the second (about being the cause of others' stumbling) and the third (about losing our saltiness). The connection is cynicism.
- Cynicism is a pervasive and destructive force, and can be a real "stumbling block" for believers. It is very difficult to believe in something and stand up for it when people around me are cynical about it ... "The Bible is just made up" "the Resurrection was a stunt" "Church leaders are only in it for the money."
- If "saltiness" is my faith and zeal, then it is when I begin to lose it that I become more cynical. Jesus warns me not to undermine the faith of others with cynicism.

Friday 24th February   Mark 10:1–9

Jesus left that place and went to the region of Judea and beyond the Jordan. And crowds again gathered around him; and, as was his custom, he again taught them. Some Pharisees came, and to test him they asked, "Is it lawful for a man to divorce his wife?" He answered them, "What did Moses command you?" They said, "Moses allowed a man to write a certificate of dismissal and to divorce her." But Jesus said to them, "Because of your hardness of heart he wrote this commandment for you. But from the beginning of creation, 'God made them male and female.' 'For this reason a man shall leave his father and mother and be joined to his wife, and the two shall become one flesh.' So they are no longer two, but one flesh. Therefore what God has joined together, let no one separate."

- Under the law of Moses, a man could divorce his wife (but not vice-versa) for the slightest of reasons.

- It is quite rare for Jesus to contradict the law openly, but here he does so quite emphatically.
- Jesus takes a strong stand against this casual attitude to marriage and to women. How does hearing his words make me feel? Can I talk to him about it?

Saturday 25th February   Mark 10:13–16

People were bringing little children to Jesus in order that he might touch them; and the disciples spoke sternly to them. But when Jesus saw this, he was indignant and said to them, "Let the little children come to me; do not stop them; for it is to such as these that the kingdom of God belongs. Truly I tell you, whoever does not receive the kingdom of God as a little child will never enter it." And he took them up in his arms, laid his hands on them, and blessed them.

- Jesus is not mildly annoyed when his disciples try to stop the children from approaching him; he is indignant. Jesus is passionately concerned to be approachable and available to everyone.
- That everyone includes me. Whatever I may think of myself, however I may feel, Jesus wants me to talk to him and is overjoyed when I say, Yes.
- I may have all sorts of questions and doubts as I approach him, and those may be reasonable enough, but it is openness and child-like trust—not intellectual rigor—that I need first.

february 26–march 4

Something to think and pray about each day this week:

Exploring the wilderness

Ash Wednesday speaks to us of the "wilderness" of our human existence: our mortality, the mystery of suffering, the temptation to sin, the reality of evil. Jesus speaks words of hope to all this. He emerges from the wilderness "proclaiming the Good News from God," telling us that "the kingdom of God is close at hand" and calling us to "repent and believe in the Good News." These are not just high-sounding, prophetic words of advice: They are life-giving words that draw us into Jesus' own trust and confidence in the Father's love; they are living words which give us a share in Jesus' hope, his peace, his victorious struggle over all that threatens to defeat and destroy us. Let's open our hearts in prayer to the True Vine this Lent and allow Jesus' spirit to course through the dark corners of our human experience. This will bring us true peace and the deepest consolation.

The Presence of God

I reflect for a moment on God's presence around me and in me.
Creator of the universe, the sun and the moon, the earth,
every molecule, every atom, everything that is:
God is in every beat of my heart. God is with me, now.

Freedom

If God were trying to tell me something, would I know?
If God were reassuring me or challenging me, would I notice?
I ask for the grace to be free of my own preoccupations
and open to what God may be saying to me.

Consciousness

How do I find myself today?
Where am I with God? With others?
Do I have something to be grateful for? Then I give thanks.
Is there something I am sorry for? Then I ask forgiveness.

The Word

I read the Word of God slowly, a few times over, and I listen to
what God is saying to me. (Please turn to your scripture on the
following pages. Inspiration points are there should you need
them. When you are ready, return here to continue.)

Conversation

What is stirring in me as I pray?
Am I consoled, troubled, left cold?
I imagine Jesus himself standing or sitting at my side,
and share my feelings with him.

Conclusion

Glory be to the Father, and to the Son, and to the Holy Spirit,
As it was in the beginning, is now and ever shall be,
World without end. Amen

Sunday 26th February, Eighth Sunday in Ordinary Time
Mark 2:18–22

Now John's disciples and the Pharisees were fasting; and people came and said to Jesus, "Why do John's disciples and the disciples of the Pharisees fast, but your disciples do not fast?" Jesus said to them, "The wedding guests cannot fast while the bridegroom is with them, can they? As long as they have the bridegroom with them, they cannot fast. The days will come when the bridegroom is taken away from them, and then they will fast on that day. No one sews a piece of unshrunk cloth on an old cloak; otherwise, the patch pulls away from it, the new from the old, and a worse tear is made. And no one puts new wine into old wineskins; otherwise, the wine will burst the skins, and the wine is lost, and so are the skins; but one puts new wine into fresh wineskins."

- The Pharisees' concern was for religious observance—they thought real virtue was about following the tiniest points of the law, rather than putting love into practice as Jesus exemplified.
- The Pharisees also failed to recognize Jesus for who he really is. His coming into the world is the start of a new era, a new opportunity, a new chance for humankind.
- Nobody puts wine—old or new—into skins these days. But if Jesus had said, "You don't try to run Windows XP on an old 386," what point would you have thought he was making?

Monday 27th February   Mark 10:17–22

As he was setting out on a journey, a man ran up and knelt before him, and asked him, "Good Teacher, what must I do to inherit eternal life?" Jesus said to him, "Why do you call me good? No one is good but God alone. You know the commandments: 'You shall not murder; You shall not commit adultery; You shall not steal; You shall not bear false witness; You shall not defraud; Honor your father and mother.'" He said to him,

"Teacher, I have kept all these since my youth." Jesus, looking at him, loved him and said, "You lack one thing; go, sell what you own, and give the money to the poor, and you will have treasure in heaven; then come, follow me." When he heard this, he was shocked and went away grieving, for he had many possessions.

- Imagine yourself in this scene, having this dialogue with Jesus. What is the scene like? Is the road bumpy or even? Is it sunny or overcast? What is Jesus wearing? Who else is around? What are they doing and saying?
- Let the scene unfold in your imagination. What does Jesus say to you when he begins, "You lack one thing . . . "?
- Is there something I am very attached to that stops me from being a better follower of Jesus? Is he asking me to do something about it?
- Do I go away grieving? Or can I respond in a different way?

Tuesday 28th February   Mark 10:28–31

Peter began to say to Jesus, "Look, we have left everything and followed you." Jesus said, "Truly I tell you, there is no one who has left house or brothers or sisters or mother or father or children or fields, for my sake and for the sake of the good news, who will not receive a hundredfold now in this age—houses, brothers and sisters, mothers and children, and fields with persecutions—and in the age to come eternal life. But many who are first will be last, and the last will be first."

- Sacrifice is not a fashionable word in many circles today, but it is what Jesus is talking about here, and he doesn't just talk about it—his own self-sacrifice is the supreme example.
- If I look at it selfishly and superficially, making real sacrifices for the sake of the gospel looks like a bad deal, a deal where I play the fool.

116

- But when my relationship with Jesus is important to me, and I care about the well-being of others, I see it differently, and my only satisfaction is in being of service to God and to people.
- Can I ask God for this grace, this conversion of heart? And can I ask for the grace to hear and discern what sacrifices—big or small—I might be called to make?

Wednesday 1st March, Ash Wednesday   Joel 2:12–14

Yet even now, says the Lord, return to me with all your heart, with fasting, with weeping, and with mourning; rend your hearts and not your clothing. Return to the Lord, your God, for he is gracious and merciful, slow to anger, and abounding in steadfast love, and relents from punishing. Who knows whether he will not turn and relent, and leave a blessing behind him, a grain offering and a drink offering for the Lord, your God?

- We are at that time of the year when we are invited to test our inner freedom and to question the notion: *I can take it, or leave it.* Try that with pornography, alcohol, complaining, gossiping, anger, gambling. What habits make me hard to live with?
- Lent is about regaining self-control, especially in those areas that damage others. We don't admire those whose appetites or habits lead them by the nose. *A pure heart create for me, O God. Put a steadfast spirit within me.*

Thursday 2nd March   Deuteronomy 30:15–16,19–20

See, I have set before you today life and prosperity, death and adversity. If you obey the commandments of the Lord your God that I am commanding you today, by loving the Lord your God, walking in his ways, and observing his commandments, decrees, and ordinances, then you shall live and become numerous, and the Lord your God will bless you in the land that you are entering to possess. . . . Choose life so that you and your descendants may live, loving the Lord your God, obeying him, and holding fast to him; for that means life to you and length of days, so that you may live in the land that the Lord swore to give to your ancestors, to Abraham, to Isaac, and to Jacob.

- Today, Lord, you remind me that it is a small profit to gain the whole world if I lose my own soul. Today you set before me life and good, death and evil.
- Can I use this Lent to make more choices that are life-giving?

Friday 3rd March   Isaiah 58:5–9

Is such the fast that I choose, a day to humble oneself? Is it to bow down the head like a bulrush, and to lie in sackcloth and ashes? Will you call this a fast, a day acceptable to the Lord? Is not this the fast that I choose: to loose the bonds of injustice, to undo the thongs of the yoke, to let the oppressed go free, and to break every yoke? Is it not to share your bread with the hungry, and bring the homeless poor into your house; when you see the naked, to cover them, and not to hide yourself from your own kin? Then your light shall break forth like the dawn, and your healing shall spring up quickly; your vindicator shall go before you, the glory of the Lord shall be your rear guard. Then you shall call, and the Lord will answer; you shall cry for help, and he will say, Here I am.

- "Is not this the fast that I choose," says the Lord, "… to share your bread with the hungry, and bring the homeless poor into your house? … Then you shall call, and the Lord will answer."
- Lord, I am looking for a change in myself this Lent. Help me to find the sort of generosity you speak of.

Saturday 4th March   Luke 5:27–32

After this he went out and saw a tax collector named Levi, sitting at the tax booth; and he said to him, "Follow me." And he got up, left everything, and followed him. Then Levi gave a great banquet for him in his house; and there was a large crowd of tax collectors and others sitting at the table with them. The Pharisees and their scribes were complaining to his disciples, saying, "Why do you eat and drink with tax collectors and sinners?" Jesus answered, "Those who are well have no need of a physician, but those who are sick; I have come to call not the righteous but sinners to repentance."

- In Caravaggio's painting of the call of Levi, the tax-collector is stunned and incredulous when he sees the beckoning finger of Jesus: *Who? Me! There must be some mistake!* But Jesus knew this man. Levi left everything, his cash-filled table and his moneyed friends, and followed the Lord. The grace of God's call is free, but not cheap. A change of life is required.
- Jesus, may I share your feast, answer your call, and change my life.

march 5–11

Something to think and pray about each day this week:

Lenten listening

Can you imagine sailing against a head wind on a stormy sea? Tension is high. You've got to be alert, concentrated, steadfast, and energetic in setting yourself against the ongoing challenge. It's tough but it's also exhilarating, exciting, and deeply satisfying to know you're on course despite the elements' efforts to upturn you!

Lent invites us to re-engage with the Christian struggle, to face the enemy within (our tendency to sin) and without (elements of our culture that are un-loving, un-Christian) and boldly fix our eyes on the goal, the prize of true freedom.

The struggle can be tough and demanding, but it brings with it a wonderful sense of well-being and fulfillment. God confirms our efforts and encourages us along the way—his way, the way of truth.

Let us be attentive to the voice of our Captain this Lent. Let us listen to his Word, his advice, his instruction. It will surely bring wisdom, courage, consolation, and great joy into our lives.

The Presence of God

For a few moments, I think of God's veiled presence in things:
in the elements, giving them existence;
in plants, giving them life; in animals, giving them sensation;
and finally, in me, giving me all this and more,
making me a temple, a dwelling-place of the Spirit.

Freedom

God is not foreign to my freedom.
Instead the Spirit breathes life into my most intimate desires,
gently nudging me towards all that is good.
I ask for the grace to let myself be enfolded by the Spirit.

Consciousness

Knowing that God loves me unconditionally,
I can afford to be honest about how I am.
How has the last day been, and how do I feel now?
I share my feelings openly with the Lord.

The Word

I take my time to read the Word of God, slowly, a few times,
allowing myself to dwell on anything that strikes me. (Please
turn to your scripture on the following pages. Inspiration points
are there should you need them. When you are ready, return
here to continue.)

Conversation

How has God's Word moved me? Has it left me cold?
Has it consoled me or moved me to act in a new way?
I imagine Jesus standing or sitting beside me,
I turn and share my feelings with him.

Conclusion

Glory be to the Father, and to the Son, and to the Holy Spirit,
As it was in the beginning, is now and ever shall be,
World without end. Amen

Sunday 5th March, First Sunday of Lent   Mark 1:12–15

And the Spirit immediately drove him out into the wilderness. He was in the wilderness forty days, tempted by Satan; and he was with the wild beasts; and the angels waited on him. Now after John was arrested, Jesus came to Galilee, proclaiming the good news of God, and saying, "The time is fulfilled, and the kingdom of God has come near; repent, and believe in the good news."

- There is a time for every activity under the sun—a time to act and a time to pray.
- Sometimes the need is to act, and God calls me to go out and do something.
- At other times, I just need to spend time alone with God, and that will give me the strength and the wisdom to do the right thing when it is the time for doing.
- Can I speak to the Lord and ask him where he is calling me now?

Monday 6th March   Matthew 25:34–40

Jesus said to his disciples "Then the king will say to those at his right hand, 'Come, you that are blessed by my Father, inherit the kingdom prepared for you from the foundation of the world; for I was hungry and you gave me food, I was thirsty and you gave me something to drink, I was a stranger and you welcomed me, I was naked and you gave me clothing, I was sick and you took care of me, I was in prison and you visited me.' Then the righteous will answer him, 'Lord, when was it that we saw you hungry and gave you food, or thirsty and gave you something to drink? And when was it that we saw you a stranger and welcomed you, or naked and gave you clothing? And when was it that we saw you sick or in prison and visited you?' And the king will answer them, 'Truly I tell you, just as you did it to one of the least of these who are members of my family, you did it to me.'"

- Jesus challenges us to put our treatment of other people on par with our treatment of him.
- It is said that you can judge a society by the way it treats its weakest members. Jesus tells me I can judge myself too by the way I treat "the least" of people I meet.
- How do I feel when I hear this? Disbelieving? Guilty? Inspired? Challenged? Can I talk to the Lord about it?
- When I meet people today, can I treat them as I would treat Jesus?

Tuesday 7th March   Isaiah 55:10–12

For as the rain and the snow come down from heaven, and do not return there until they have watered the earth, making it bring forth and sprout, giving seed to the sower and bread to the eater, so shall my word be that goes out from my mouth; it shall not return to me empty, but it shall accomplish that which I purpose, and succeed in the thing for which I sent it. For you shall go out in joy, and be led back in peace; the mountains and the hills before you shall burst into song, and all the trees of the field shall clap their hands.

- Isaiah has no doubt about the strength of purpose behind everything that God does, and God's confidence that this purpose will be fulfilled.
- What purpose does God have for me? What does God want me to accomplish? Can I talk to the Lord about this?
- Transforming the world through love may sound an ambitious mission to be a part of. Am I daunted by it? Can I ask the Lord for the grace of confidence and hope, for the kind of joy that Isaiah describes in this passage?

Wednesday 8th March   Psalm 51:1–3, 10–11, 16–17

Have mercy on me, O God, according to your steadfast love; according to your abundant mercy blot out my transgressions. Wash me thoroughly from my iniquity, and cleanse me from my sin. For I know my transgressions, and my sin is ever before me. . . . Create in me a clean heart, O God, and put a new and right spirit within me. Do not cast me away from your presence, and do not take your holy spirit from me. . . . For you have no delight in sacrifice; if I were to give a burnt offering, you would not be pleased. The sacrifice acceptable to God is a broken spirit; a broken and contrite heart, O God, you will not despise.

- "A broken and contrite heart, O God, you will not despise." Save me, Lord, from a religious hysteria that blinds me to the uglier side of myself. I want not merely to acknowledge the truth about my own sins, but to keep a habitual sense of my weakness, which may save me from arrogance.
- I pray with St. Francis de Sales: *It is good to have a crevice in the soul and fill it with repentance; then you can grow there any virtue you please.*

Thursday 9th March   Matthew 7:7–11

Jesus said to the crowds, "Ask, and it will be given you; search, and you will find; knock, and the door will be opened for you. For everyone who asks receives, and everyone who searches finds, and for everyone who knocks, the door will be opened. Is there anyone among you who, if your child asks for bread, will give a stone? Or if the child asks for a fish, will give a snake? If you then, who are evil, know how to give good gifts to your children, how much more will your Father in heaven give good things to those who ask him!"

- Jesus illustrates the Golden Rule, *Whatever you wish that people would do to you, do so to them.* The Rabbi Hillel used to say about this: "The rest is commentary. Now go and study."
- I study myself. How do I wish people would treat me? Lord, show me where I fall down on this.

Friday 10th March   **Matthew 5:20–26**

J esus said to his disciples, "For I tell you, unless your righteousness exceeds that of the scribes and Pharisees, you will
never enter the kingdom of heaven. You have heard that it was
said to those of ancient times, 'You shall not murder'; and
'whoever murders shall be liable to judgment.' But I say to you
that if you are angry with a brother or sister, you will be liable
to judgment; and if you insult a brother or sister, you will be
liable to the council; and if you say, 'You fool,' you will be liable
to the hell of fire. So when you are offering your gift at the altar,
if you remember that your brother or sister has something
against you, leave your gift there before the altar and go; first be
reconciled to your brother or sister, and then come and offer
your gift. Come to terms quickly with your accuser while you
are on the way to court with him, or your accuser may hand you
over to the judge, and the judge to the guard, and you will be
thrown into prison. Truly I tell you, you will never get out until
you have paid the last penny."

• The listeners knew their Bible and the law of Moses. Jesus takes
  the law and makes it deeper, more interior. The root of the act of
  killing is in the angry hatred of the killer's heart. Tackle the evil at
  its source.
• Does that mean that I must repress and deny all anger? You might
  as well deny feeling hot in the Sahara desert. The feeling is
  innocent; the evil arises when I act out my anger and injure my
  neighbour, when I give way to hatred, to anger.
• Lord, I come before your altar. Help me to work on the seeds of
  hatred in my heart. You tell me that there can be no true worship
  of God without justice.

Saturday 11th March   **Matthew 5:43–48**

J esus said to the disciples, "You have heard that it was said,
'You shall love your neighbour and hate your enemy.' But I

say to you, Love your enemies and pray for those who persecute you, so that you may be children of your Father in heaven; for he makes his sun rise on the evil and on the good, and sends rain on the righteous and on the unrighteous. For if you love those who love you, what reward do you have? Do not even the tax collectors do the same? And if you greet only your brothers and sisters, what more are you doing than others? Do not even the Gentiles do the same? Be perfect, therefore, as your heavenly Father is perfect."

- Lord, you warn us against tribal or racial exclusiveness, where we love only kith and kin, and reject outsiders. For you there are no outsiders. Your sun shines and your rain falls on all alike. We are to open our hearts even to those who hate us.
- Is this hopeless idealism or a wise strategy for overcoming the persecutor? Teach me to change aggression into a strategy for winning through the wisdom of love.

march 12–18

Something to think and pray about each day this week:

God's dependents

St. Paul tells us that "the body is for the Lord." And so it is—destined to be transfigured like Christ's. But the body is also subject to sin, suffering, and death. Illness or bereavement brings home to us in stark fashion the misery of our human condition while at the same time heightening our nostalgia for the destiny intended for us, eternal life.

Lent is a time to take stock of our true situation, to remember that we are creatures, not gods, and thus utterly dependent on God's gratuitous love and mercy. This should not frighten or dismay us but rather fill us with gratitude for the miracle of salvation which God has wrought in our lives.

"Come, let us bow and do reverence; kneel before Yahweh who made us."

The Presence of God
I pause for a moment
and think of the love and the grace that God showers on me,
creating me in his image and likeness, making me his temple.

Freedom
Everything has the potential to draw forth from me a fuller love
and life.
Yet my desires are often fixed, caught, on illusions of fulfillment.
I ask that God, through my freedom, may orchestrate
my desires in a vibrant loving melody rich in harmony.

Consciousness
In the presence of my loving Creator,
I look honestly at my feelings over the last day,
the highs, the lows and the level ground.
Can I see where the Lord has been present?

The Word
God speaks to each one of us individually. I need to listen to
what he is saying to me. (Please turn to your scripture on the
following pages. Inspiration points are there should you need
them. When you are ready, return here to continue.)

Conversation
What feelings are rising in me
as I pray and reflect on God's Word?
I imagine Jesus himself sitting or standing beside me,
and open my heart to him.

Conclusion
Glory be to the Father, and to the Son, and to the Holy Spirit,
As it was in the beginning, is now and ever shall be,
World without end. Amen

Sunday 12th March, Second Sunday of Lent   Mark 9:2–10

Six days later, Jesus took with him Peter and James and John, and led them up a high mountain apart, by themselves. And he was transfigured before them, and his clothes became dazzling white, such as no one on earth could bleach them. And there appeared to them Elijah with Moses, who were talking with Jesus. Then Peter said to Jesus, "Rabbi, it is good for us to be here; let us make three dwellings, one for you, one for Moses, and one for Elijah." He did not know what to say, for they were terrified. Then a cloud overshadowed them, and from the cloud there came a voice, "This is my Son, the Beloved; listen to him!" Suddenly when they looked around, they saw no one with them any more, but only Jesus. As they were coming down the mountain, he ordered them to tell no one about what they had seen, until after the Son of Man had risen from the dead. So they kept the matter to themselves, questioning what this rising from the dead could mean.

- Imagine yourself to be present. What is it like? What are Elijah, Moses, and Jesus talking to each other about?
- How do you imagine the voice that says, "This is my Son . . ."?
- At the end of the scene, when Jesus is standing there alone, what do you want to say to him?

Monday 13th March   Luke 6:36–38

Jesus said to the disciples, "Be merciful, just as your Father is merciful. Do not judge, and you will not be judged; do not condemn, and you will not be condemned. Forgive, and you will be forgiven; give, and it will be given to you. A good measure, pressed down, shaken together, running over, will be put into your lap; for the measure you give will be the measure you get back."

- Lord, my lap and my hands are open to receive from you. You tell me they will be able to contain the cascade of good things from your hand, provided my hands are open to give as well as to receive. Can I open my hands? Does my trust have limits?

Tuesday 14th March   **Matthew 23:8–12**

Jesus said to the crowds and to his disciples, "You are not to be called rabbi, for you have one teacher, and you are all students. And call no one your father on earth, for you have one Father—the one in heaven. Nor are you to be called instructors, for you have one instructor, the Messiah. The greatest among you will be your servant. All who exalt themselves will be humbled, and all who humble themselves will be exalted."

• Do I have the openness and humility to accept instruction, to learn new lessons, or do I exalt myself and think I know it all at this stage?
• Saint Ignatius writes in his autobiography of times in his adult life when God dealt with him "as a schoolteacher deals with a pupil." What lessons might God have to teach me? Would I be listening?
• Can I ask for the grace to be attentive and listening, and to be able to discern what God is trying to tell me?

Wednesday 15th March   **Matthew 20:17–23**

While Jesus was going up to Jerusalem, he took the twelve disciples aside by themselves, and said to them on the way, "See, we are going up to Jerusalem, and the Son of Man will be handed over to the chief priests and scribes, and they will condemn him to death; then they will hand him over to the Gentiles to be mocked and flogged and crucified; and on the third day he will be raised. Then the mother of the sons of Zebedee came to him with her sons, and kneeling before him, she asked a favor of him. And he said to her, "What do you want?" She said to him, "Declare that these two sons of mine will sit, one at your right hand and one at your left, in your kingdom." But Jesus answered, "You do not know what you are

asking. Are you able to drink the cup that I am about to drink?"
They said to him, "We are able." He said to them, "You will
indeed drink my cup, but to sit at my right hand and at my left,
this is not mine to grant, but it is for those for whom it has been
prepared by my Father."

- Lord, you listened to the pushy Mrs. Zebedee. Her sons James
  and John said yes, they could drink from your cup. But when the
  time for suffering came, James at least went into hiding.
- Among your followers, there is no place for lording it over others.
  The only dignity lies in being a servant. Am I slow to learn this
  lesson, Lord? Am I listening?

Thursday 16th March   Jeremiah 17:5–8

Thus says the Lord: Cursed are those who trust in mere
mortals and make mere flesh their strength, whose hearts
turn away from the Lord. They shall be like a shrub in the
desert, and shall not see when relief comes. They shall live in the
parched places of the wilderness, in an uninhabited salt land.
Blessed are those who trust in the Lord, whose trust is the Lord.
They shall be like a tree planted by water, sending out its roots
by the stream. It shall not fear when heat comes, and its leaves
shall stay green; in the year of drought it is not anxious, and it
does not cease to bear fruit.

- The one who trusts in the Lord is like a tree planted by water, that
  sends out its roots to the stream and does not fear when the heat
  comes. I know, Lord, what dryness, desolation, and sterility feel
  like. Let me pray with you.

Friday 17th March, St. Patrick   Isaiah 52:7–10

How beautiful upon the mountains are the feet of the
messenger who announces peace, who brings good news,
who announces salvation, who says to Zion, "Your God reigns."
Listen! Your sentinels lift up their voices, together they sing for

joy; for in plain sight they see the return of the Lord to Zion. Break forth together into singing, you ruins of Jerusalem; for the Lord has comforted his people, he has redeemed Jerusalem. The Lord has bared his holy arm before the eyes of all the nations; and all the ends of the earth shall see the salvation of our God.

- As a teenager, St. Patrick was kidnapped and lived the life of a slave herding swine on a hillside. In that isolation he turned to God in prayer; that was his nourishment and protection. He left us *The Deer's Cry.*
   Christ as a light, illumine and guide me
   Christ as a shield, o'ershadow and cover me.
   Christ be under me, Christ be over me,
   Christ be beside me, on left hand and right.
   Christ be before me, behind me, around me.
   Christ this day be within and without me. Amen.

Saturday 18th March   Micah 7:14–15, 18–20

Shepherd your people with your staff, the flock that belongs to you, which lives alone in a forest in the midst of a garden land; let them feed in Bashan and Gilead as in the days of old. As in the days when you came out of the land of Egypt, show us marvellous things. Who is a God like you, pardoning iniquity and passing over the transgression of the remnant of your possession? He does not retain his anger forever, because he delights in showing clemency. He will again have compassion upon us; he will tread our iniquities under foot. You will cast all our sins into the depths of the sea. You will show faithfulness to Jacob and unswerving loyalty to Abraham, as you have sworn to our ancestors from the days of old.

- He does not retain his anger forever, because he delights in steadfast love. The parable of the prodigal son gives me a picture of that steadfast love. There, Lord, you show how your heavenly father would appear in human form. When he welcomes back his lost son with tears of delight, kills the fatted calf, brings out the best robe, and throws a great party, it is not to please other people, but to give expression to his own overwhelming pleasure that his child has come home. You delight in me.

march 19–25

Something to think and pray about each day this week:

The loving fire of purification

Dante Alighieri's *Inferno* paints an ugly picture of hell's torments. Nor was the author shy of naming some of his contemporaries who would, by virtue of their behavior, find themselves there! Hyperbole, perhaps, but nevertheless a salutary jolt reminding us all that sparks from hell can and do take root in our hearts, with bilious results! In Galatians, Paul lists them out: antagonisms, rivalry, jealousy, bad temper, quarrels, disagreements, factions, malice. We might do well to review them.

Lent is a time of purification. We resolve to let the fire of love—heaven's spark—clear out any pathogenic toxins (resentment, bitterness, greed, lust, etc.) that reside unchallenged in our system. Like Jesus, we need to clear out the Temple so that love holds sway over all selfish tendencies.

The Presence of God
I reflect for a moment on God's presence around me and in me.
Creator of the universe, the sun and the moon, the earth,
every molecule, every atom, everything that is:
God is in every beat of my heart. God is with me, now.

Freedom
A thick and shapeless tree-trunk would never believe
that it could become a statue, admired as a miracle of sculpture,
and would never submit itself to the chisel of the sculptor,
who sees by her genius what she can make of it (St. Ignatius).
I ask for the grace to let myself be shaped by my loving Creator.

Consciousness
Knowing that God loves me unconditionally,
I look honestly over the last day, its events and my feelings.
Do I have something to be grateful for? Then I give thanks.
Is there something I am sorry for? Then I ask forgiveness.

The Word
I read the Word of God slowly, a few times over, and I listen to
what God is saying to me. (Please turn to your scripture on the
following pages. Inspiration points are there should you need
them. When you are ready, return here to continue.)

Conversation
What is stirring in me as I pray?
Am I consoled, troubled, left cold?
I imagine Jesus himself standing or sitting at my side,
and share my feelings with him.

Conclusion
Glory be to the Father, and to the Son, and to the Holy Spirit,
As it was in the beginning, is now and ever shall be,
World without end. Amen

138

Sunday 19th March, Third Sunday of Lent
1 Corinthians 1:25–30

For God's foolishness is wiser than human wisdom, and God's weakness is stronger than human strength. Consider your own call, brothers and sisters: not many of you were wise by human standards, not many were powerful, not many were of noble birth. But God chose what is foolish in the world to shame the wise; God chose what is weak in the world to shame the strong; God chose what is low and despised in the world, things that are not, to reduce to nothing things that are, so that no one might boast in the presence of God. He is the source of your life in Christ Jesus, who became for us wisdom from God, and righteousness and sanctification and redemption.

- You could not ask for a clearer expression of the revolutionary character of Christianity than these lines from St. Paul.
- How do I feel when I read these lines? Inspired? Ashamed? Challenged?
- What might I do differently if I was putting into practice the standard spelt out here?
- What do I really want? To live my life by this standard, or to be "somebody," to be influential and important? Can I talk to the Lord about this?

Monday 20th March, St. Joseph
Matthew 1:18–25

Now the birth of Jesus the Messiah took place in this way. When his mother Mary had been engaged to Joseph, but before they lived together, she was found to be with child from the Holy Spirit. Her husband Joseph, being a righteous man and unwilling to expose her to public disgrace, planned to dismiss her quietly. But just when he had resolved to do this, an angel of the Lord appeared to him in a dream and said, "Joseph, son of David, do not be afraid to take Mary as your wife, for the child conceived in her is from the Holy Spirit. She will bear a son, and you are to name him Jesus, for he will save his people from their sins." All this took place to fulfill what had been spoken by the Lord through the prophet: "Look, the virgin shall conceive and bear a son, and they shall name him Emmanuel," which means, "God is with us." When Joseph awoke from sleep, he did as the angel of the Lord commanded him; he took her as his wife, but had no marital relations with her until she had borne a son; and he named him Jesus.

- What do we know about St. Joseph? We know that he loved Mary so much that he suppressed his doubts about her chastity and allowed himself to be regarded as the father of her child, knowing that he wasn't; that he brought up that child as his own, despite great difficulties and dangers, particularly at the start; that he taught him his trade; that he loved him; and that Jesus' virile health as an adult (physical stamina, courage, strength of purpose, and attractiveness to women, men, and children) is proof of good parenting by his foster-father. Joseph is the obvious patron of adoptive fathers.

Tuesday 21st March   Matthew 18:21–35

Then Peter came and said to him, "Lord, if another member of the church sins against me, how often should I forgive? As many as seven times?" Jesus said to him, "Not seven times, but, I tell you, seventy-seven times. For this reason the kingdom of heaven may be compared to a king who wished to settle accounts with his slaves. When he began the reckoning, one who owed him ten thousand talents was brought to him; and, as he could not pay, his lord ordered him to be sold, together with his wife and children and all his possessions, and payment to be made. So the slave fell on his knees before him, saying, 'Have patience with me, and I will pay you everything.' And out of pity for him, the lord of that slave released him and forgave him the debt. But that same slave, as he went out, came upon one of his fellow slaves who owed him a hundred denarii; and seizing him by the throat, he said, 'Pay what you owe.' Then his fellow slave fell down and pleaded with him, 'Have patience with me, and I will pay you.' But he refused; then he went and threw him into prison until he would pay the debt. When his fellow slaves saw what had happened, they were greatly distressed, and they went and reported to their lord all that had taken place. Then his lord summoned him and said to him, 'You wicked slave! I forgave you all that debt because you pleaded with me. Should you not have had mercy on your fellow slave, as I had mercy on you?' And in anger his lord handed him over to be tortured until he would pay his entire debt. So my heavenly Father will also do to every one of you, if you do not forgive your brother or sister from your heart."

- A warlord begs foreign donors to bring water to his desert land; then he entertains journalists in his palace, with its six swimming pools. Like the unforgiving creditor in the gospel, he probably did not notice the inconsistency.
- Lord, I show understanding and sympathy with my own desires, but apply different standards to others. Can I look hard at my behavior? Will I find hypocrisy there?

Wednesday 22nd March   **Matthew 5:17–19**

Do not think that I have come to abolish the law or the prophets; I have come not to abolish but to fulfill. For truly I tell you, until heaven and earth pass away, not one letter, not one stroke of a letter, will pass from the law until all is accomplished. Therefore, whoever breaks one of the least of these commandments, and teaches others to do the same, will be called least in the kingdom of heaven; but whoever does them and teaches them will be called great in the kingdom of heaven.

- Jesus did not reject the Old Testament of the Jews, but brought it back to its basics: love God and love your neighbor.

- It is harder to live one sermon than to preach a dozen. Lord, help me to make my life whole, so that other people learn Christian principles from my behavior.

Thursday 23rd March   Jeremiah 7:23–28

But this command I gave them, "Obey my voice, and I will be your God, and you shall be my people; and walk only in the way that I command you, so that it may be well with you." Yet they did not obey or incline their ear, but, in the stubbornness of their evil will, they walked in their own counsels, and looked backward rather than forward. From the day that your ancestors came out of the land of Egypt until this day, I have persistently sent all my servants the prophets to them, day after day; yet they did not listen to me, or pay attention, but they stiffened their necks. They did worse than their ancestors did. So you shall speak all these words to them, but they will not listen to you. You shall call to them, but they will not answer you. You shall say to them: This is the nation that did not obey the voice of the Lord their God, and did not accept discipline; truth has perished; it is cut off from their lips.

- "The stubbornness of their evil will." Lord, I know what you mean by my heart hardening. I have felt that in the past, when I was unwilling to be open to the fact of my cruelty or ignoring others' needs. I harden into a selfish shell.
- Your heart remained loving in face of hostility and injustice. Open my heart to your love.

Friday 24th March   Mark 12:28–34

One of the scribes came near and heard them disputing with one another, and seeing that he answered them well, he asked him, "Which commandment is the first of all?" Jesus answered, "The first is, 'Hear, O Israel: the Lord our God, the Lord is one; you shall love the Lord your God with all your heart, and with all your soul, and with all your mind, and with all your strength.' The second is this, 'You shall love your neighbor as yourself.' There is no other commandment greater than these." Then the scribe said to him, "You are right, Teacher; you have truly said that 'he is one, and besides him there is no other'; and 'to love him with all the heart, and with all the understanding, and with all the strength,' and 'to love one's neighbor as oneself,'—this is much more important than all whole burnt offerings and sacrifices." When Jesus saw that he answered wisely, he said to him, "You are not far from the kingdom of God." After that no one dared to ask him any question.

- "The Lord our God, the Lord is one." As I hear Jesus' answer to the scribe, I think how a Moslem would agree warmly with all that he hears, and how Jesus might well say of many a Moslem, Jew and Christian equally: "You are not far from the kingdom of God." Lord, let me not put barriers where you put windows.

Saturday 25th March, The Annunciation
Luke 1:26–32, 34–35, 38a

In the sixth month the angel Gabriel was sent by God to a town in Galilee called Nazareth, to a virgin engaged to a man whose name was Joseph, of the house of David. The virgin's name was Mary. And he came to her and said, "Greetings, favored one! The Lord is with you." But she was much perplexed by his words and pondered what sort of greeting this might be. The angel said to her, "Do not be afraid, Mary, for you have found favor with God. And now, you will conceive in your womb and bear a son, and you will name him Jesus. He will be great, and will be called the Son of the Most High, and the Lord God will give to him the throne of his ancestor David." Mary said to the angel, "How can this be, since I am a virgin?" The angel said to her, "The Holy Spirit will come upon you, and the power of the Most High will overshadow you; therefore the child to be born will be holy; he will be called Son of God." Then Mary said, "Here am I, the servant of the Lord; let it be with me according to your word."

- You might find it helpful to contemplate a picture of this scene.
- Imagine what Mary felt as she was given this awesome news.
- Mary has questions and she voices them, but she says "Yes" to God's will for her. Can I learn from her example?

march 26–april 1

Something to think and pray about each day this week:

The sense of God's love

"Then he came to his senses." This deceptively simple statement about the prodigal son poses a profound challenge to us all. None of us can claim to be without sin. "We all fall short of the glory of God." Lent can be that moment in which we come to our senses, face facts about ourselves, and make the appropriate adjustments.

After a brief romantic affair which threatened to destroy his marriage and alienate his family and friends, John came to his senses. Before matters got worse, he had the courage to face his fault, admit his sin, and turn back. He was fortunate to receive his wife's understanding, love, and forgiveness.

During Lent we turn back to God and entrust ourselves once again to his immense mercy. We allow the Father to embrace us in our sinfulness and sorrow. In being forgiven much, we discover the depths of God's love.

The Presence of God
In the silence of my innermost being,
in the fragments of my yearned-for wholeness,
can I hear the whispers of God's presence?
Can I remember when I felt God's nearness?
When we walked together and I let myself be embraced by God's love.

Freedom
There are very few people
who realize what God would make of them
if they abandoned themselves into his hands,
and let themselves be formed by his grace (St. Ignatius).
I ask for the grace to trust myself totally to God's love.

Consciousness
How do I find myself today?
Where am I with God? With others?
Do I have something to be grateful for? Then I give thanks.
Is there something I am sorry for? Then I ask forgiveness.

The Word
I take my time to read the Word of God, slowly, a few times, allowing myself to dwell on anything that strikes me. (Please turn to your scripture on the following pages. Inspiration points are there should you need them. When you are ready, return here to continue.)

Conversation
Do I notice myself reacting as I pray with the Word of God?
Do I feel challenged, comforted, angry?
Imagining Jesus sitting or standing by me,
I speak out my feelings, as one trusted friend to another.

Conclusion
Glory be to the Father, and to the Son, and to the Holy Spirit,
As it was in the beginning, is now and ever shall be,
World without end. Amen

Sunday 26th March, Fourth Sunday of Lent

John 3:14–18

Jesus said to Nicodemus, "And just as Moses lifted up the serpent in the wilderness, so must the Son of Man be lifted up, that whoever believes in him may have eternal life. For God so loved the world that he gave his only Son, so that everyone who believes in him may not perish but may have eternal life. Indeed, God did not send the Son into the world to condemn the world, but in order that the world might be saved through him. Those who believe in him are not condemned; but those who do not believe are condemned already, because they have not believed in the name of the only Son of God."

- With Moses in the desert, the people looked up at the serpent and were healed. Jesus wants me to look up at him and be healed.
- Our lives are serious and can go very badly wrong. In the times of greatest chaos the Son is there for me.
- Can I open my heart to accept that all God's love is there for me?

Monday 27th March

John 4:46b–54

Now there was a royal official whose son lay ill in Capernaum. When he heard that Jesus had come from Judea to Galilee, he went and begged him to come down and heal his son, for he was at the point of death. Then Jesus said to him, "Unless you see signs and wonders you will not believe." The official said to him, "Sir, come down before my little boy dies." Jesus said to him, "Go; your son will live." The man believed the word that Jesus spoke to him and started on his way. As he was going down, his slaves met him and told him that his child was alive. So he asked them the hour when he began to recover, and they said to him, "Yesterday at one in the afternoon the fever left him." The father realized that this was the hour when Jesus had said to him, "Your son will live." So he himself believed, along with his whole household. Now this was the second sign that Jesus did after coming from Judea to Galilee.

- At first Jesus recoils; what he treasures is the company of those who want to know God for himself, not for what he can deliver. The father returns as a believer, and Jesus welcomes him.
- Lord, forgive me for the times I have turned to you in a crisis, begging a favor. When the crisis passes, I go back to living as though you did not exist. I want to find time for you.

Tuesday 28th March   John 5:1–8

After this there was a festival of the Jews, and Jesus went up to Jerusalem. Now in Jerusalem by the Sheep Gate there is a pool, called in Hebrew Beth-zatha, which has five porticoes. In these lay many invalids—blind, lame, and paralyzed. One man was there who had been ill for thirty-eight years. When Jesus saw him lying there and knew that he had been there a long time, he said to him, "Do you want to be made well?" The sick man answered him, "Sir, I have no one to put me into the pool when the water is stirred up; and while I am making my way, someone else steps down ahead of me." Jesus said to him, "Stand up, take your mat and walk."

- Jesus asks the crippled man a curious question: "Do you want to be healed?" Surely that much was obvious.
- But the question does makes sense, if a cure would change his life and push him back into the daily grind. If sickness becomes a way of life, it is hard to face this change. Save me, Lord, from making excuses, from pleading my special circumstances.

Wednesday 29th March   Isaiah 49:13–15

For the Lord has comforted his people, and will have compassion on his suffering ones. But Zion said, "The Lord has forsaken me, my Lord has forgotten me. "Can a woman forget her nursing child, or show no compassion for the child of her womb? Even these may forget, yet I will not forget you."

- Here is a reminder of the motherhood of God: "Can a woman forget her nursing child, or show no compassion for the child of her womb? Even these may forget, yet I will not forget you."
- My God, you tell me that for you I am unique, and that I have a place in your mind which nobody else can fill. You regard me with the delight and tenderness of a mother with her baby.

Thursday 30th March   John 5:44–47

Jesus said to the Jews, "How can you believe when you accept glory from one another and do not seek the glory that comes from the one who alone is God? Do not think that I will accuse you before the Father; your accuser is Moses, on whom you have set your hope. If you believed Moses, you would believe me, for he wrote about me. But if you do not believe what he wrote, how will you believe what I say?"

- This reading reflects the age-old struggle between God and his chosen people, the Jews. It says something to us, too: "How can you believe, who receive glory from one another, and do not seek the glory that comes from the only God?"
- Lord, I often hunger for ego-massage, for the good feeling when other people accept and approve of me. Do I make too much of it? Does it turn me from seeking you. Let me sniff the sweet air of flattery, but not inhale.

Friday 31st March   Wisdom 2:1, 12–15

For the godless reasoned unsoundly, saying to themselves, "Short and sorrowful is our life, and there is no remedy when a life comes to its end, and no one has been known to return from Hades. Let us lie in wait for the righteous man, because he is inconvenient to us and opposes our actions; he reproaches us for sins against the law, and accuses us of sins against our training. He professes to have knowledge of God, and calls himself a child of the Lord. He became to us a reproof of our thoughts; the very sight of him is a burden to us, because his manner of life is unlike that of others, and his ways are strange."

- You touch me where it hurts, Lord, when you describe the jealousy we often feel for somebody whose life is different and pulls us up sharply. "He became to us a reproof of our thoughts; the very sight of him is a burden to us."

- Do we ever get over sibling rivalry? It is a sign of grace to be happy at the sight of somebody close to us who outshines us, whether in conversation, friendship, or work. Lord, make my heart more generous, so that I rejoice in the success of others.

Saturday 1st April   John 7:50–53

Nicodemus, who had gone to Jesus before, and who was one of the Pharisees, asked, "Our law does not judge people without first giving them a hearing to find out what they are doing, does it?" They replied, "Surely you are not also from Galilee, are you? Search and you will see that no prophet is to arise from Galilee." Then each of them went home.

- They went each to his own house. They retreated to safety; at their own table they would not face disagreement, there they could indulge their prejudices at will.

- Lord, I do it myself; I turn away from people with different viewpoints, I do not engage with them, but retreat into the company of those who share my prejudices. Give me the blessed gift of listening and answering, especially when I am feeling uncomfortable.

april 2–8

Something to think and pray about each day this week:

Seeing the real Jesus

Jesus excited curiosity so that people like Zacchaeus (Luke 19:1) and Greek visitors to the festival (John 12:20) wanted to see him, to know what he looked like.

But Jesus had other ideas, confronting and revolutionary ideas. To "see" him was to enter totally into his way of thinking, to understand why he had to suffer and die and rise again. Like the grain of wheat, Jesus has to let go of everything, including his own life, in order to bring life to himself and many others. This is the "emptying," the *kenosis*, that the Letter to the Philippians speaks about. In the process, both Jesus and we will be transformed, just as the grain of wheat, apparently annihilated, becomes something altogether greater and enriching for others.

Are we ready for that? Are we afraid to let everything go? Is Jesus asking too much? Lead us to see and accept this as the core of Jesus' life, so that we really see Him.

The Presence of God
I remind myself that, as I sit here now,
God is gazing on me with love and holding me in being.
I pause for a moment and think of this.

Freedom
I ask for the grace   ·
to let go of my own concerns
and be open to what God is asking of me,
to let myself be guided and formed by my loving Creator.

Consciousness
In God's loving presence I unwind the past day,
starting from now and looking back, moment by moment.
I gather in all the goodness and light, in gratitude.
I attend to the shadows and what they say to me,
seeking healing, courage, forgiveness.

The Word
God speaks to each one of us individually. I need to listen to
what he is saying to me. (Please turn to your scripture on the
following pages. Inspiration points are there should you need
them. When you are ready, return here to continue.)

Conversation
Remembering that I am still in God's presence,
I imagine Jesus himself standing or sitting beside me,
and say whatever is on my mind, whatever is in my heart,
speaking as one friend to another.

Conclusion
Glory be to the Father, and to the Son, and to the Holy Spirit,
As it was in the beginning, is now and ever shall be,
World without end. Amen

Sunday 2nd April, Fifth Sunday of Lent   **John 12:20–24**

Now among those who went up to worship at the festival were some Greeks. They came to Philip, who was from Bethsaida in Galilee, and said to him, "Sir, we wish to see Jesus." Philip went and told Andrew; then Andrew and Philip went and told Jesus. Jesus answered them, "The hour has come for the Son of Man to be glorified. Very truly, I tell you, unless a grain of wheat falls into the earth and dies, it remains just a single grain; but if it dies, it bears much fruit."

- Imagine the scene. Some Greeks, complete newcomers, went to meet Jesus. What attracted them?
- They immediately hear ominous predictions about suffering and death. We don't even know if they understood or were frightened off.
- How do I react to Jesus' talk of coming trials?
- Remember that I am told these things not to frighten me but to strengthen me.

Monday 3rd April   **Daniel 13:55–56, 60–62**
                       (New Jerusalem Bible)

Daniel said, "Indeed! Your lie recoils on you own head: the angel of God has already received from him your sentence and will cut you in half." He dismissed the man, ordered the other to be brought and said to him, "Son of Canaan, not of Judah, beauty has seduced you, lust has led your heart astray!" ... Then the whole assembly shouted, blessing God, the Savior of those who trust in him. And they turned on the two elders whom Daniel had convicted of false evidence out of their own mouths. As the Law of Moses prescribes, they were given the same punishment as they had schemed to inflict on their neighbor. They were put to death. And thus, that day, an innocent life was saved.

- These are not happy characters. Dissipation and addiction are forms of imprisonment in which the chains are inside you, not outside, so the pain is greater. The German ("God is dead") philosopher Nietzsche stated the downside of lust: "The mother of dissipation is not joy, but joylessness." Thomas Aquinas put it more positively: "A joyful heart is a sure sign of temperance and self-control." Do I show that sign?

Tuesday 4th April   Numbers 21:4–9

From Mount Hor they set out by the way to the Red Sea, to go around the land of Edom; but the people became impatient on the way. The people spoke against God and against Moses, "Why have you brought us up out of Egypt to die in the wilderness? For there is no food and no water, and we detest this miserable food." Then the Lord sent poisonous serpents among the people, and they bit the people, so that many Israelites died. The people came to Moses and said, "We have sinned by speaking against the Lord and against you; pray to the Lord to take away the serpents from us." So Moses prayed for the people. And the Lord said to Moses, "Make a poisonous serpent, and set it on a pole; and everyone who is bitten shall look at it and live." So Moses made a serpent of bronze, and put it upon a pole; and whenever a serpent bit someone, that person would look at the serpent of bronze and live.

- The Book of Numbers tells a story of people complaining, being punished, turning to God, and finding relief.
- Lord, you have often taught me like a strict parent, and when I look back on the periods of punishment, they sometimes brought me greater blessings and wisdom than times of consolation. You lead me to more abundant life through pruning and pain.

Wednesday 5th April John 8:31–32

Then Jesus said to the Jews who had believed in him, "If you continue in my word, you are truly my disciples; and you will know the truth, and the truth will make you free."

- "The truth will make you free." But at a cost. The man who acknowledges that he cannot control his drinking, the mother who admits that her darling son is a bully at school, the girl who accepts that her shop-lifting is a form of stealing, they are all liberated by seeing the truth, but they have to pay a price.
- Are there issues in my life which I fear to face, where I dodge the truth? Who can tell me the truth—my friends, or my enemies? It is often the remarks that rankle with us, that push us to face unwelcome truths.

Thursday 6th April Genesis 17:3–8

Then Abram fell on his face; and God said to him, "As for me, this is my covenant with you: You shall be the ancestor of a multitude of nations. No longer shall your name be Abram, but your name shall be Abraham; for I have made you the ancestor of a multitude of nations. I will make you exceedingly fruitful; and I will make nations of you, and kings shall come from you. I will establish my covenant between me and you, and your offspring after you throughout their generations, for an everlasting covenant, to be God to you and to your offspring after you. And I will give to you, and to your offspring after you, the land where you are now an alien, all the land of Canaan, for a perpetual holding; and I will be their God."

- God made a covenant with Abraham. What sort of special choosing, planning, and missioning is that?
- The covenant was not just for an individual. It is meant to embrace and involve a great community.
- How does God's covenant with humankind embrace and engage me?

Friday 7th April   **Psalm 18:1–3** •

Ilove you, O Lord, my strength. The Lord is my rock, my fortress, and my deliverer, my God, my rock in whom I take refuge, my shield, and the horn of my salvation, my stronghold. I call upon the Lord, who is worthy to be praised, so I shall be saved from my enemies.

- The author of the Psalms knew good times and bad. In my own situation can I make these words my own?

Saturday 8th April   **Ezekiel 37:26–28**

Iwill make a covenant of peace with them; it shall be an ever-lasting covenant with them; and I will bless them and multiply them, and will set my sanctuary among them forever-more. My dwelling place shall be with them; and I will be their God, and they shall be my people. Then the nations shall know that I the Lord sanctify Israel, when my sanctuary is among them forevermore.

- This is the renewal of God's loving plan with a people who have abandoned and betrayed him.
- There is a plan for my good no matter what has happened.
- What does this say to me?

april 9–15

Something to think and pray about each day this week:

Forsaken, yet transformed

"My God, my God, why have you forsaken me?" This cry of almost total desperation rings out across the centuries from the very bowels of suffering humanity. In our own time, we have witnessed the agony of innocent people's lives blown apart by terrorist bombs. We have seen the tortuous faces of the wounded and bereaved on our television screens. God's Kingdom of justice, love, and peace can seem totally remote and meaning-less—just a pipe dream.

And yet the one who seems "forsaken" says that God is not indifferent. The God-Man Jesus absorbs and embraces all human suffering and transforms it into an act of love. His—and our—forsakenness is not the last word. By divine alchemy, on Calvary, all human suffering is transformed into love.

During this week our *Sacred Space* brings us to the foot of the Cross. As we hear once again Christ's words, "Why have you forsaken me?" we may be drawn to pray with and for the count-less women and men who continue to cry out for an explana-tion, a meaning, to their suffering. We may begin to understand the suffering in our own lives.

The Presence of God
God is with me, but more,
God is within me, giving me existence.
Let me dwell for a moment on God's life-giving presence
in my body, my mind, my heart
and in the whole of my life.

Freedom
I ask for the grace to believe
in what I could be and do
if I only allowed God, my loving Creator,
to continue to create me, guide me and shape me.

Consciousness
I exist in a web of relationships—links to nature, people, God.
I trace out these links, giving thanks for the life that flows
through them.
Some links are twisted or broken: I may feel regret, anger, disappointment.
I pray for the gift of acceptance and forgiveness.

The Word
I read the Word of God slowly, a few times over, and I listen to
what God is saying to me. (Please turn to your scripture on the
following pages. Inspiration points are there should you need
them. When you are ready, return here to continue.)

Conversation
How has God's Word moved me? Has it left me cold?
Has it consoled me or moved me to act in a new way?
I imagine Jesus standing or sitting beside me,
I turn and share my feelings with him.

Conclusion
Glory be to the Father, and to the Son, and to the Holy Spirit,
As it was in the beginning, is now and ever shall be,
World without end. Amen

Sunday 9th April, Palm Sunday   Philippians 2:6–11

Let the same mind be in you that was in Christ Jesus, who, though he was in the form of God, did not regard equality with God as something to be exploited, but emptied himself, taking the form of a slave, being born in human likeness. And being found in human form, he humbled himself and became obedient to the point of death—even death on a cross. Therefore God also highly exalted him and gave him the name that is above every name, so that at the name of Jesus every knee should bend, in heaven and on earth and under the earth, and every tongue should confess that Jesus Christ is Lord, to the glory of God the Father.

- Lord, give me the grace to celebrate this occasion. Palm Sunday did not last—what does? But while we dance together, it is a foretaste of heaven.

Monday 10th April   Isaiah 42:1–4

Here is my servant, whom I uphold, my chosen, in whom my soul delights; I have put my spirit upon him; he will bring forth justice to the nations. He will not cry or lift up his voice, or make it heard in the street; a bruised reed he will not break, and a dimly burning wick he will not quench; he will faithfully bring forth justice. He will not grow faint or be crushed until he has established justice in the earth; and the coastlands wait for his teaching.

- "My servant will not cry or lift up his voice, or make it heard in the street ... he will faithfully bring forth justice."
- That is our mission too, Lord: not by force or violence, but by gentle, faithful persistence, to bring forth justice on the earth.

Tuesday 11th April   **Isaiah 49:1–4**

L isten to me, O coastlands, pay attention, you peoples from far away! The Lord called me before I was born, while I was in my mother's womb he named me. He made my mouth like a sharp sword, in the shadow of his hand he hid me; he made me a polished arrow, in his quiver he hid me away. And he said to me, "You are my servant, Israel, in whom I will be glorified." But I said, "I have labored in vain, I have spent my strength for nothing and vanity; yet surely my cause is with the Lord, and my reward with my God."

- God knows me intimately, even from my first moments. He has a plan for me; whatever talents I have he can put to use.
- Do I stand in the Lord's way, with my own plan? I worked hard, I tried my best but now I have nothing left to give. Is this now the Lord's time when my way seems blocked?

Wednesday 12th April   **Matthew 26:14–16**

T hen one of the twelve, who was called Judas Iscariot, went to the chief priests and said, "What will you give me if I betray him to you?" They paid him thirty pieces of silver. And from that moment he began to look for an opportunity to betray him.

- There were two treacheries. Judas went out to grab his money, betrayed Jesus, and then killed himself in despair. Peter, despite his protests, would deny his Lord; he faced his own appalling guilt, then wept bitterly. His failure was not the end of his mission, but the beginning.
- Success is what I do with my failures. Teach me to trust in your love Lord, no matter what I have done, and to learn from my mistakes and even from treachery.

Thursday 13th April, Holy Thursday   John 13:12–16

After Jesus had washed their feet, had put on his robe, and had returned to the table, he said to them, "Do you know what I have done to you? You call me Teacher and Lord—and you are right, for that is what I am. So if I, your Lord and Teacher, have washed your feet, you also ought to wash one another's feet. For I have set you an example, that you also should do as I have done to you. Very truly, I tell you, servants are not greater than their master, nor are messengers greater than the one who sent them."

- John's gospel describes the Last Supper without mentioning the Eucharist. Instead it describes Jesus washing his friends' feet.
- On his knees like a servant, Jesus turned human status upside down. Do I celebrate with the community of those who serve?

Friday 14th April, Good Friday   Isaiah 53:1–5

Who has believed what we have heard? And to whom has the arm of the Lord been revealed? For he grew up before him like a young plant, and like a root out of dry ground; he had no form or majesty that we should look at him, nothing in his appearance that we should desire him. He was despised and rejected by others; a man of suffering and acquainted with infirmity; and as one from whom others hide their faces he was despised, and we held him of no account. Surely he has borne our infirmities and carried our diseases; yet we accounted him stricken, struck down by God, and afflicted. But he was wounded for our transgressions, crushed for our iniquities; upon him was the punishment that made us whole, and by his bruises we are healed.

- Now we are at the heart of Jesus' mission: to suffer appallingly and to die without faltering in his love for us. This is where the gospel begins and ends. Yet it is hard to contemplate. We shy away from the pain and injustice of the passion.

- I carry the nail-marks in my hands from baptism. I may wander far from the cross, but at the end I am drawn back to it.

Saturday 15th April, Holy Saturday   Romans 6:3–11

Do you not know that all of us who have been baptized into Christ Jesus were baptized into his death? Therefore we have been buried with him by baptism into death, so that, just as Christ was raised from the dead by the glory of the Father, so we too might walk in newness of life. For if we have been united with him in a death like his, we will certainly be united with him in a resurrection like his. We know that our old self was crucified with him so that the body of sin might be destroyed, and we might no longer be enslaved to sin. For whoever has died is freed from sin. But if we have died with Christ, we believe that we will also live with him. We know that Christ, being raised from the dead, will never die again; death no longer has dominion over him. The death he died, he died to sin, once for all; but the life he lives, he lives to God. So you also must consider yourselves dead to sin and alive to God in Christ Jesus.

- Tonight we reaffirm our ancient faith: Christ has robbed death of its ultimate sting and has invigorated this sweet, precious, precarious, once-only life that is slipping away from us with every hour and day and year.
- When we breath the evening air, when we catch the sweet smells of the new season, we have hints of a day that knows no ending, a light that will not yield to darkness, and a life in these weary bodies that even creeping death will not be able to frustrate or despoil. We yearn for new life.

april 16–22

Something to think and pray about each day this week:

The consolation of the Risen Christ

St. Ignatius says that the Risen Christ comes to us first of all as a "Consoler." On that first Easter morning he appeared to his friends who were still reeling from the ordeal of his passion and death and brought them unimagined consolation and joy.

In these Easter days can I allow Jesus to come close enough to me to be my Consoler in any sorrow that I experience? Am I open to being a consoler for others?

His consolation, of course, is not a warm fuzzy feeling, but a deep trust in God's love, which is a gift of the Spirit. With that deep consolation I will be able to be a true consoler of others in my turn. As I pray in *Sacred Space* in these days, let me be open to receive this wonderful Easter gift.

The Presence of God
To be present is to arrive as one is and open up to the other.
At this instant, as I arrive here, God is present waiting for me.
God always arrives before me, desiring to connect with me
even more than my most intimate friend.
I take a moment and greet my loving God.

Freedom
"In these days, God taught me
as a schoolteacher teaches a pupil" (St. Ignatius).
I remind myself that there are things God has to teach me yet,
and ask for the grace to hear them and let them change me.

Consciousness
How am I really feeling? Light-hearted? Heavy-hearted?
I may be very much at peace, happy to be here.
Equally, I may be frustrated, worried or angry.
I acknowledge how I really am. It is the real me that the Lord
loves.

The Word
I take my time to read the Word of God, slowly, a few times,
allowing myself to dwell on anything that strikes me. (Please
turn to your scripture on the following pages. Inspiration points
are there should you need them. When you are ready, return
here to continue.)

Conversation
What feelings are rising in me
as I pray and reflect on God's Word?
I imagine Jesus himself sitting or standing beside me,
and open my heart to him.

Conclusion
Glory be to the Father, and to the Son, and to the Holy Spirit,
As it was in the beginning, is now and ever shall be,
World without end. Amen

Sunday 16th April, Easter Sunday   John 20:1–9

Early on the first day of the week, while it was still dark, Mary Magdalene came to the tomb and saw that the stone had been removed from the tomb. So she ran and went to Simon Peter and the other disciple, the one whom Jesus loved, and said to them, "They have taken the Lord out of the tomb, and we do not know where they have laid him." Then Peter and the other disciple set out and went toward the tomb. The two were running together, but the other disciple outran Peter and reached the tomb first. He bent down to look in and saw the linen wrappings lying there, but he did not go in. Then Simon Peter came, following him, and went into the tomb. He saw the linen wrappings lying there, and the cloth that had been on Jesus' head, not lying with the linen wrappings but rolled up in a place by itself. Then the other disciple, who reached the tomb first, also went in, and he saw and believed; for as yet they did not understand the scripture, that he must rise from the dead.

- Jesus has risen, and we have risen with him to new life.
- Where do I seek him now?

Monday 17th April   Matthew 28:8–10

So the women left the tomb quickly with fear and great joy, and ran to tell his disciples. Suddenly Jesus met them and said, "Greetings!" And they came to him, took hold of his feet, and worshiped him. Then Jesus said to them, "Do not be afraid; go and tell my brothers to go to Galilee; there they will see me."

- Does a happy Easter mean three days in an armchair, or deep joy in the knowledge that the best part of us will cheat the grave? Our weary bones, heavy flesh, addled brain already hold the seeds of that resurrection. We are none of us mortal.

Tuesday 18th April   **John 20:11–17**

As Mary Magdalene wept, she bent over to look into the tomb; and she saw two angels in white, sitting where the body of Jesus had been lying, one at the head and the other at the feet. They said to her, "Woman, why are you weeping?" She said to them, "They have taken away my Lord, and I do not know where they have laid him." When she had said this, she turned around and saw Jesus standing there, but she did not know that it was Jesus. Jesus said to her, "Woman, why are you weeping? Whom are you looking for?" Supposing him to be the gardener, she said to him, "Sir, if you have carried him away, tell me where you have laid him, and I will take him away." Jesus said to her, "Mary!" She turned and said to him in Hebrew, "Rabbouni!" (which means Teacher). Jesus said to her, "Do not hold on to me, because I have not yet ascended to the Father. But go to my brothers and say to them, 'I am ascending to my Father and your Father, to my God and your God.'"

- Jesus called her Mary. That was enough. You know my name and my body, Lord. You see my lived-in face, shaped by my history, showing the lines of love, excesses, suffering, humor, gentleness.
- Teach me to love my face and body, my temple of the Holy Spirit. It will grow old and die with me, but that is not the end. My body is sacred, and Easter opens a window for it and me onto a mysterious but endless vista.

Wednesday 19th April   **Luke 24:13–27**

Now on that same day two of them were going to a village called Emmaus, about seven miles from Jerusalem, and talking with each other about all these things that had happened. While they were talking and discussing, Jesus himself came near and went with them, but their eyes were kept from recognizing him. And he said to them, "What are you discussing with each other while you walk along?" They stood still, looking sad. Then one of them, whose name was Cleopas, answered him, "Are you the only stranger in Jerusalem who does not know the things that have taken place there in these days?" He asked them, "What things?" They replied, "The things about Jesus of Nazareth, who was a prophet mighty in deed and word before God and all the people, and how our chief priests and leaders handed him over to be condemned to death and crucified him. But we had hoped that he was the one to redeem Israel. Yes, and besides all this, it is now the third day since these things took place. Moreover, some women of our group astounded us. They were at the tomb early this morning, and when they did not find his body there, they came back and told us that they had indeed seen a vision of angels who said that he was alive. Some of those who were with us went to the tomb and found it just as the women had said; but they did not see him." Then he said to them, "Oh, how foolish you are, and how slow of heart to believe all that the prophets have declared! Was it not necessary that the Messiah should suffer these things and then enter into his glory?" Then beginning with Moses and all the prophets, he interpreted to them the things about himself in all the scriptures.

- Like Cleopas I walk with you, Lord, in all sorts of shapes; but I do not always recognize you. Open the scriptures to me, show me your face in those I walk with, put some warmth into my heart.

Thursday 20th April   Luke 24:36–43

While they were talking about this, Jesus himself stood among them and said to them, "Peace be with you." They were startled and terrified, and thought that they were seeing a ghost. He said to them, "Why are you frightened, and why do doubts arise in your hearts? Look at my hands and my feet; see that it is I myself. Touch me and see; for a ghost does not have flesh and bones as you see that I have." And when he had said this, he showed them his hands and his feet. While in their joy they were disbelieving and still wondering, he said to them, "Have you anything here to eat?" They gave him a piece of broiled fish, and he took it and ate in their presence.

- An ancient tradition, based not on scripture but on a sense of their bond, is that the risen Jesus must have appeared first to his blessed mother. The old Irish poem addresses her:

  > Queen of all queens, oh wonder of the loveliness of women
  > Heart that has held in check for us the righteous wrath of God,
  > Strong staff of light and fosterer of the Bright Child of heaven,
  > Pray thou for us as we now pray that we may be forgiven.

Friday 21st April   John 21:2–8

Gathered there together were Simon Peter, Thomas called the Twin, Nathanael of Cana in Galilee, the sons of Zebedee, and two others of his disciples. Simon Peter said to them, "I am going fishing." They said to him, "We will go with you." They went out and got into the boat, but that night they caught nothing. Just after daybreak, Jesus stood on the beach; but the disciples did not know that it was Jesus. Jesus said to them, "Children, you have no fish, have you?" They answered him, "No." He said to them, "Cast the net to the right side of the boat, and you will find some." So they cast it, and now they were not able to haul it in because there were so many fish. That disciple whom Jesus loved said to Peter, "It is the Lord!" When Simon Peter heard that it was the Lord, he put on some clothes, for he was naked, and jumped into the sea. But the other disciples came in the boat, dragging the net full of fish, for they were not far from the land, only about a hundred yards off.

- It is dawn. Peter and his companions are weary from the night's fishing, but wake up sharply at the sight of this familiar figure. They dared not ask him: "Who are you?" How did they know it

168

was Jesus? Perhaps from the care he showed for them in preparing breakfast and involving them in the preparation.

- Lord, may I recognize you in those I meet. You cross my path many times a day, and you care for me. You also ask me to contribute what I can.

Saturday 22nd April   Mark 16:9–15

Now after he rose early on the first day of the week, he appeared first to Mary Magdalene, from whom he had cast out seven demons. She went out and told those who had been with him, while they were mourning and weeping. But when they heard that he was alive and had been seen by her, they would not believe it. After this he appeared in another form to two of them, as they were walking into the country. And they went back and told the rest, but they did not believe them. Later he appeared to the eleven themselves as they were sitting at the table; and he upbraided them for their lack of faith and stubbornness, because they had not believed those who saw him after he had risen. And he said to them, "Go into all the world and proclaim the good news to the whole creation."

- What an extraordinary command to slow-witted and faint-hearted fishermen, to preach the gospel "to the whole creation."
- Yet they started the work which today sees in Christians the largest body of believers on this planet. God's hand is evident. The best preaching does not involve words. As the holy Brazilian bishop Helder Camara used to warn his catechists: "Watch how you live. Your lives may be the only gospel your sisters and brothers will ever read."

april 23–29

Something to think and pray about each day this week:

Meeting doubt, with Jesus

"Doubt no longer, but believe." There are many scenes in the gospel which illustrate how Jesus patiently approaches us in our doubt and assists us in our struggle to believe.

Think of Nicodemus who came to Jesus under cover of darkness; he wrestled hard with the notion of being "born from above." Think of the woman at the well whose secular world-view blinded her to her deepest thirst and the true source of its satisfaction, Jesus—"the spring of water gushing up to eternal life." Think of Thomas who, refusing to be taken in by the majority view, sought personal confirmation of Jesus' authenticity.

All these represent our own struggle to believe. When I doubt, Jesus does not judge or condemn us but meets us halfway. More than half-way. He longs for my faith. As I go to pray today, can I open my heart to Jesus who longs for my faith?

The Presence of God
What is present to me is what has a hold on my becoming.
I reflect on the presence of God always there in love,
amidst the many things that have a hold on me.
I pause and pray that I may let God
affect my becoming in this precise moment.

Freedom
If God were trying to tell me something, would I know?
If God were reassuring me or challenging me, would I notice?
I ask for the grace to be free of my own preoccupations
and open to what God may be saying to me.

Consciousness
Knowing that God loves me unconditionally,
I can afford to be honest about how I am.
How has the last day been, and how do I feel now?
I share my feelings openly with the Lord.

The Word
God speaks to each one of us individually. I need to listen to
what he is saying to me. (Please turn to your scripture on the
following pages. Inspiration points are there should you need
them. When you are ready, return here to continue.)

Conversation
What is stirring in me as I pray?
Am I consoled, troubled, left cold?
I imagine Jesus himself standing or sitting at my side,
and share my feelings with him.

Conclusion
Glory be to the Father, and to the Son, and to the Holy Spirit,
As it was in the beginning, is now and ever shall be,
World without end. Amen

Sunday 23rd April, Second Sunday of Easter
John 20:24–29

But Thomas (who was called the Twin), one of the twelve, was not with them when Jesus came. So the other disciples told him, "We have seen the Lord." But he said to them, "Unless I see the mark of the nails in his hands, and put my finger in the mark of the nails and my hand in his side, I will not believe." A week later his disciples were again in the house, and Thomas was with them. Although the doors were shut, Jesus came and stood among them and said, "Peace be with you." Then he said to Thomas, "Put your finger here and see my hands. Reach out your hand and put it in my side. Do not doubt but believe." Thomas answered him, "My Lord and my God!" Jesus said to him, "Have you believed because you have seen me? Blessed are those who have not seen and yet have come to believe."

- In this scene, who do you identify with? Thomas? Or one of the other apostles? (It's instructive to know which you identify with.)
- Enter into the scene and see where it leads you.

Monday 24th April
John 3:1–8

Now there was a Pharisee named Nicodemus, a leader of the Jews. He came to Jesus by night and said to him, "Rabbi, we know that you are a teacher who has come from God; for no one can do these signs that you do apart from the presence of God." Jesus answered him, "Very truly, I tell you, no one can see the kingdom of God without being born from above." Nicodemus said to him, "How can anyone be born after having grown old? Can one enter a second time into the mother's womb and be born?" Jesus answered, "Very truly, I tell you, no one can enter the kingdom of God without being born of water and Spirit. What is born of the flesh is flesh, and what is born of the Spirit is spirit. Do not be astonished that I said to you,

'You must be born from above.' The wind blows where it chooses, and you hear the sound of it, but you do not know where it comes from or where it goes. So it is with everyone who is born of the Spirit."

- Do I identify with the person who comes to Jesus under cover of darkness?
- When I hear Jesus speak, what is my honest response? Am I inspired? Am I confused? Am I intrigued?
- Where might this "being born from above" be real for me?

Tuesday 25th April, St. Mark the Evangelist
Mark 16:15–20

And Jesus said to the disciples, "Go into all the world and proclaim the good news to the whole creation. The one who believes and is baptized will be saved; but the one who does not believe will be condemned. And these signs will accompany those who believe: by using my name they will cast out demons; they will speak in new tongues; they will pick up snakes in their hands, and if they drink any deadly thing, it will not hurt them; they will lay their hands on the sick, and they will recover." So then the Lord Jesus, after he had spoken to them, was taken up into heaven and sat down at the right hand of God. And they went out and proclaimed the good news everywhere, while the Lord worked with them and confirmed the message by the signs that accompanied it.

- If I read this passage slowly I could, by turns, be challenged, frightened, amazed, distorted, inspired, consoled ...
- Which reactions do I rest with spontaneously? Does that tell me something about myself?
- Both the first and the last sentence of the passage tell of good news. Can I situate my reactions within the context of this good news?

Wednesday 26th April   **John 3:16–17**

Jesus said to Nicodemus, "For God so loved the world that he gave his only Son, so that everyone who believes in him may not perish but may have eternal life. Indeed, God did not send the Son into the world to condemn the world, but in order that the world might be saved through him."

- God gave his son, only-begotten, the only son of the eternal father. The words "father," "son," and "begetting" are human metaphors for the mysterious dynamic of the Blessed Trinity.
- Here is the core of our belief: God intervened in human history and gave his only son for us; Jesus, our brother; God, our loving parent.

Thursday 27th April   **Acts 5:27–33**

When they had brought the apostles, they had them stand before the council. The high priest questioned them, saying, "We gave you strict orders not to teach in this name, yet here you have filled Jerusalem with your teaching and you are determined to bring this man's blood on us." But Peter and the apostles answered, "We must obey God rather than any human authority. The God of our ancestors raised up Jesus, whom you had killed by hanging him on a tree. God exalted him at his right hand as Leader and Saviour that he might give repentance to Israel and forgiveness of sins. And we are witnesses to these things, and so is the Holy Spirit whom God has given to those who obey him." When they heard this, they were enraged and wanted to kill them.

- "We must obey God rather than men." This was the response of the early martyrs, when called on to offer sacrifice to idols. Modern states try to avoid making martyrs, yet Christians still have to make costly choices. In political, in business, and in family life, what choices have I made about remaining honest, truthful, faithful to my commitments?

- Lord, when your voice is calling in another direction, may I obey you rather than men, whether in the form of the boss or the crowd. Give me courage like St. Peter's.

Friday 28th April   Acts 5:34–42

But a Pharisee in the council named Gamaliel, a teacher of the law, respected by all the people, stood up and ordered the men to be put outside for a short time. Then he said to them, "Fellow Israelites, consider carefully what you propose to do to these men. For some time ago Theudas rose up, claiming to be somebody, and a number of men, about four hundred, joined him; but he was killed, and all who followed him were dispersed and disappeared. After him Judas the Galilean rose up at the time of the census and got people to follow him; he also perished, and all who followed him were scattered. So in the present case, I tell you, keep away from these men and let them alone; because if this plan or this undertaking is of human origin, it will fail; but if it is of God, you will not be able to overthrow them—in that case you may even be found fighting against God!" They were convinced by him, and when they had called in the apostles, they had them flogged. Then they ordered them not to speak in the name of Jesus, and let them go. As they left the council, they rejoiced that they were considered worthy to suffer dishonor for the sake of the name. And every day in the temple and at home they did not cease to teach and proclaim Jesus as the Messiah.

- "Leave these men alone. If this undertaking is of men, it will fail. If it is of God, you will not be able to overthrow them." Gamaliel's words seem wise in retrospect. The undertaking of Christ's followers was not of men.
- The good news drew people from a pantheon of half-human gods to the unimaginable Trinity.
- Lord, I am still part of this undertaking, still seeking you.

Saturday 29th April   **John 6:16–21**

When evening came, his disciples went down to the sea, got into a boat, and started across the sea to Capernaum. It was now dark, and Jesus had not yet come to them. The sea became rough because a strong wind was blowing. When they had rowed about three or four miles, they saw Jesus walking on the sea and coming near the boat, and they were terrified. But he said to them, "It is I; do not be afraid." Then they wanted to take him into the boat, and immediately the boat reached the land toward which they were going.

- "It is I; do not be afraid." When things are bad, I become fearful, I feel I am liable to sink at any moment, I am not grounded. Let me put my hand in the hand of the man who walked on the water.
- Lord, you always calm me, tell me not to fear. Give me the courage to put one foot in front of another, to move forward and not go into hiding.

Something to think and pray about each day this week:

Leaving the shallows

"Put out into the deep." This is a call to dig deep within ourselves in order to rediscover the treasure we possess and have to share with others.

As Christians we are challenged to rekindle in ourselves the ardor of the apostles at Pentecost. We can be part of a new evangelization, which will be truly effective if it proclaims from the rooftops what it has first lived in intimacy with the Lord.

Putting out into the deep calls me to challenge all forms of shallowness in myself and in our culture which can encourage me to avoid the deeper questions or accept too-easy answers to the human quest for meaning.

Jesus, who searches the human heart, invites me to explore the depths of human experience with him, not apart from him. Can I let him, Master and Teacher, be my guide and our inspiration?

The Presence of God

God is with me, but more, God is within me.
Let me dwell for a moment on God's life-giving presence
in my body, in my mind, in my heart,
as I sit here, right now.

Freedom

I need to close out the noise, to rise above the noise;
The noise that interrupts, that separates,
The noise that isolates.
I need to listen to God again.

Consciousness

In the presence of my loving Creator,
I look honestly at my feelings over the last day,
the highs, the lows and the level ground.
Can I see where the Lord has been present?

The Word

I read the Word of God slowly, a few times over, and I listen to
what God is saying to me. (Please turn to your scripture on the
following pages. Inspiration points are there should you need
them. When you are ready, return here to continue.)

Conversation

Do I notice myself reacting as I pray with the Word of God?
Do I feel challenged, comforted, angry?
Imagining Jesus sitting or standing by me,
I speak out my feelings, as one trusted friend to another.

Conclusion

Glory be to the Father, and to the Son, and to the Holy Spirit,
As it was in the beginning, is now and ever shall be,
World without end. Amen

Sunday 30th April, Third Sunday of Easter Luke 24:36–43

While they were talking about this, Jesus himself stood among them and said to them, "Peace be with you." They were startled and terrified, and thought that they were seeing a ghost. He said to them, "Why are you frightened, and why do doubts arise in your hearts? Look at my hands and my feet; see that it is I myself. Touch me and see; for a ghost does not have flesh and bones as you see that I have." And when he had said this, he showed them his hands and his feet. While in their joy they were disbelieving and still wondering, he said to them, "Have you anything here to eat?" They gave him a piece of broiled fish, and he took it and ate in their presence.

- Ironic that when they see the one they long for, they are startled and terrified. The risen Lord always takes us by surprise.
- He brings them to reality by inviting them to touch his hands and feet which had suffered wounds. It is direct and tangible.
- How, in my own life, can I reach out in faith and touch the hands and feet of Christ?

Monday 1st May   John 6:26–29

Jesus answered them, "Very truly, I tell you, you are looking for me, not because you saw signs, but because you ate your fill of the loaves. Do not work for the food that perishes, but for the food that endures for eternal life, which the Son of Man will give you. For it is on him that God the Father has set his seal." Then they said to him, "What must we do to perform the works of God?" Jesus answered them, "This is the work of God, that you believe in him whom he has sent."

- "Do not work for the food that perishes." The crowd who gathered to Jesus had mixed motives. They hoped for a free meal, and they were curious. What can I learn about myself if I list the things which attract me when I have time to spare?

- Lord, there is the same mixture of motives in me—not pure love, but selfishness, weariness, and the hope of relief from anxiety and guilt. You lead me gently.

Tuesday 2nd May · John 6:35

Jesus said to the people: "I am the bread of life. Whoever comes to me will never be hungry, and whoever believes in me will never be thirsty."

- Alfred Noyes wrote: "I am full-fed and yet I hunger. What means this deeper hunger in my heart?" When we have eaten to fullness, food becomes distasteful.
- Love is different; the appetite is not sated by the one we love. If God gives us a taste for prayer, it means a delight in his company. We gravitate towards prayer and seek time for it.

Wednesday 3rd May, Sts. Philip & James · John 14:6–14

Jesus said to Thomas, "I am the way, and the truth, and the life. No one comes to the Father except through me. If you know me, you will know my Father also. From now on you do know him and have seen him." Philip said to him, "Lord, show us the Father, and we will be satisfied." Jesus said to him, "Have I been with you all this time, Philip, and you still do not know me? Whoever has seen me has seen the Father. How can you say, 'Show us the Father'? Do you not believe that I am in the Father and the Father is in me? The words that I say to you I do not speak on my own; but the Father who dwells in me does his works. Believe me that I am in the Father and the Father is in me; but if you do not, then believe me because of the works themselves. Very truly, I tell you, the one who believes in me will also do the works that I do and, in fact, will do greater works than these, because I am going to the Father. I will do whatever you ask in my name, so that the Father may be glorified in the Son. If in my name you ask me for anything, I will do it.

- Can I allow these words, addressed to Philip, to be spoken to me?
- Do these mysterious concepts about Jesus and his heavenly Father intrigue me, delight me, confuse me?
- The "one who believes in me" can, it seems, take part in the mystery too. Does this mean me? Am I open to that?

Thursday 4th May   John 6:45

Jesus said to the people: "It is written in the prophets, 'And they shall all be taught by God.' Everyone who has heard and learned from the Father comes to me."

- "And they shall all be taught by God." When St. Francis of Assisi sent his friars out to preach, he told them: "You will spread the good news wherever you go. Sometimes you will use words." When God teaches us, it is usually without words, touching us by the encounters, pleasures, and pains of everyday living.
- Lord, as I pray, show me, in the movements of my heart, what you want me to learn from you.

Friday 5th May   Acts 9:1–9

Meanwhile Saul, still breathing threats and murder against the disciples of the Lord, went to the high priest and asked him for letters to the synagogues at Damascus, so that if he found any who belonged to the Way, men or women, he might bring them bound to Jerusalem. Now as he was going along and approaching Damascus, suddenly a light from heaven flashed around him. He fell to the ground and heard a voice saying to him, "Saul, Saul, why do you persecute me?" He asked, "Who are you, Lord?" The reply came, "I am Jesus, whom you are persecuting. But get up and enter the city, and you will be told what you are to do." The men who were traveling with him stood speechless because they heard the voice but saw no one. Saul got up from the ground, and though his eyes were open, he could see nothing; so they led him by the hand and brought him into Damascus. For three days he was without sight, and neither ate nor drank.

- It took a thunder-bolt, an unsaddling, and sudden blindness to bring a change of heart in Saul. What about my conversion, my turning? Am I gradually turning more towards God, or in some other direction?

Saturday 6th May   **John 6:60, 66–69**
                                                      (New Jerusalem Bible)

After hearing Jesus [promise his flesh to eat], many of his followers said, "This is intolerable language. How could anyone accept it?" After this, many of his disciples went away and accompanied him no more. Then Jesus said to the Twelve, "What about you, do you want to go away too?" Simon Peter answered, "Lord, to whom shall we go? You have the message of eternal life, and we believe; we have come to know that you are the Holy One of God."

- I hear many attractive voices saying: "Listen to me. Come my way." But you, Lord, are my star, the north to which my compass points. Without your words I have no direction.

Something to think and pray about each day this week:

Seeking out the Shepherd

Jesus calls himself the Good Shepherd and says, "My sheep hear my voice. I know them, and they follow me." Those words of Jesus echo Nathan's story, in the Second Book of Samuel, about the poor man who fostered a ewe lamb that grew up with him and his children. It ate and drank with them. It even slept in his arms and was like a daughter to him. When Jesus says that he knows his sheep, this is the sort of thing he means. Following a shepherd like that would be a joy and a delight, not a duty or an obligation.

In prayer, we are invited into this kind of joyful intimacy with Jesus, the Good Shepherd. We won't always feel secure in his presence. Our doubts, fears, misgivings about being worthy of such love might get in the way. But if we stick at it, Jesus will lead us into a place of deep trust. The little steps proposed by *Sacred Space* take us by the hand and bring us gently into that deeper place where the voice of the Master is heard. Let's go there. Let's find there our peace.

The Presence of God

As I sit here, the beating of my heart,
the ebb and flow of my breathing, the movements of my mind
are all signs of God's ongoing creation of me.
I pause for a moment, and become aware
of this presence of God within me.

Freedom

I will ask God's help,
to be free from my own preoccupations,
to be open to God in this time of prayer,
to come to love and serve him more.

Consciousness

Knowing that God loves me unconditionally,
I look honestly over the last day, its events and my feelings.
Do I have something to be grateful for? Then I give thanks.
Is there something I am sorry for? Then I ask forgiveness.

The Word

I take my time to read the Word of God, slowly, a few times,
allowing myself to dwell on anything that strikes me. (Please
turn to your scripture on the following pages. Inspiration points
are there should you need them. When you are ready, return
here to continue.)

Conversation

Remembering that I am still in God's presence,
I imagine Jesus himself standing or sitting beside me,
and say whatever is on my mind, whatever is in my heart,
speaking as one friend to another.

Conclusion

Glory be to the Father, and to the Son, and to the Holy Spirit,
As it was in the beginning, is now and ever shall be,
World without end. Amen

186

Sunday 7th May, Fourth Sunday of Easter   John 10:14–15

Jesus said to the Pharisees, "I am the good shepherd. I know my own and my own know me, just as the Father knows me and I know the Father. And I lay down my life for the sheep."

- The infinitely deep relationship of Jesus with his Father is the measure for the relationship he wants with me! This merits much consideration.
- The shepherd calls each of his sheep by name. We are each one of his sheep.

Monday 8th May   John 10:14–16

Jesus said to the Pharisees: "I am the good shepherd. I know my own and my own know me, just as the Father knows me and I know the Father. And I lay down my life for my sheep. I have other sheep that do not belong to this fold. I must bring them also, and they will listen to my voice. So there will be one flock, one shepherd."

- "There will be one flock, one shepherd." You are the good shepherd, Lord. Grant that I may live to see the day when those who love and follow you may find companionship and unity with one another.
- May I do everything I can to forge unity among the millions of my fellow Christians, and strengthen the fellow-feeling of all who follow you.

Tuesday 9th May   Acts 11:26

The disciples went to Antioch. So it was that for an entire year they met with the church and taught a great many people, and it was in Antioch that the disciples were first called "Christians."

- Do I call myself a Christian?

- In Antioch the name Christian was given to the disciples. A disciple is one who learns from the master. Am I still learning? Am I perhaps able to teach others?

Wednesday 10th May   John 12:44–45

Then Jesus cried aloud: "Whoever believes in me believes not in me but in him who sent me. And whoever sees me sees him who sent me."

- "Whoever sees me sees him who sent me." The God we believe in is not visible, nor even imaginable, since he is outside our categories of time and space. Yet Jesus says: See me and you see God.
- Lord, I look for you, I try to imagine your features and listen to the story of your dealings as a man. You are my way to the Father, and the knowledge of you is precious to me.

Thursday 11th May   John 13:16–17

When Jesus had washed the disciples' feet, he said to them, "Very truly, I tell you, servants are not greater than their master, nor are messengers greater than the one who sent them. If you know these things, you are blessed if you do them."

- Jesus was totally immersed in what he was doing, reaching for dirt between the toes, washing away the mud and the smell, in the position of a slave. For him, service is a sign of love, not of slavery. He has given significance to all sorts of service.
- After this, I can never say that any work is beneath me.

Friday 12th May   John 14:1–3

Jesus said to his disciples, "Do not let your hearts be troubled. Believe in God, believe also in me. In my Father's house there are many dwelling places. If it were not so, would I have told you that I go to prepare a place for you? And if I go and prepare a place for you, I will come again and will take you to myself, so that where I am, there you may be also."

- That matters a lot to me, Lord. So many of my friends would not feel at ease in heaven's guest bedroom. They just hope they can fit in somewhere. The suicides, the thieves, the sexually deviant, the publicly pilloried count on your mercy to find a place for them, no matter how dirty they feel.
- So do I count on your mercy. Any room will do as long as you are there.

Saturday 13th May   **John 14:8**

Philip said to Jesus, "Lord, show us the Father, and we will be satisfied."

- Our hearts are not easily satisfied, Lord. They have huge desires. We run quickly through the pleasures that lift us for a moment, then leave us empty.
- I remember how St. Augustine prayed: "You have made us for yourself, Lord, and our hearts are restless till they rest in you."

Something to think and pray about each day this week:

Staying the distance

When we take the time to enter into a quiet, sacred space, we should not be surprised to find conflicting sentiments rising up within us. We often enter prayer longing for the love, joy, and peace the Lord speaks of and offers to us, but in reality we can meet with our own spiritual aridity or see only the murky waters of our own sinfulness. Negative thoughts and feelings about others and ourselves may seem to have the upper hand. We are tempted to despair. We feel like giving up.

Although painful, these can be special moments of growth. It is important not to run, but to stay with the ambivalences of my own heart, to "let the wheat and cockle grow together." I bring myself as I am before Jesus who is ready to be my Divine Healer, who knows exactly what remedy I need. He says in John's Gospel: "You will have pain, but your pain will turn into joy." If I can sit still with my pain and be patient with myself, this promise of joy can be mine.

The Presence of God

I pause for a moment
and reflect on God's life-giving presence
in every part of my body, in everything around me,
in the whole of my life.

Freedom

God is not foreign to my freedom.
Instead the Spirit breathes life into my most intimate desires,
gently nudging me towards all that is good.
I ask for the grace to let myself be enfolded by the Spirit.

Consciousness

How do I find myself today?
Where am I with God? With others?
Do I have something to be grateful for? Then I give thanks.
Is there something I am sorry for? Then I ask forgiveness.

The Word

God speaks to each one of us individually. I need to listen to
what he is saying to me. (Please turn to your scripture on the
following pages. Inspiration points are there should you need
them. When you are ready, return here to continue.)

Conversation

How has God's Word moved me? Has it left me cold?
Has it consoled me or moved me to act in a new way?
I imagine Jesus standing or sitting beside me,
I turn and share my feelings with him.

Conclusion

Glory be to the Father, and to the Son, and to the Holy Spirit,
As it was in the beginning, is now and ever shall be,
World without end. Amen

Sunday 14th May, Fifth Sunday of Easter   John 15:1–2, 5

Jesus said, "I am the true vine, and my Father is the vine-grower. He removes every branch in me that bears no fruit. Every branch that bears fruit he prunes to make it bear more fruit. I am the vine, you are the branches. Those who abide in me and I in them bear much fruit, because apart from me you can do nothing."

- Grapes grow on a gnarled and craggy branch because the vine has deep roots. In what am I rooted? What is my heart's desire?
- Being a branch on Christ's vine means that I am in solidarity with many others, including the marginalized, people who are different from me, and some people whom I just don't like.
- Can I take "pruning"? How will I bear fruit?

Monday 15th May   John 14:23–26

Jesus answered him, "Those who love me will keep my word, and my Father will love them, and we will come to them and make our home with them. Whoever does not love me does not keep my words; and the word that you hear is not mine, but is from the Father who sent me. I have said these things to you while I am still with you. But the Advocate, the Holy Spirit, whom the Father will send in my name, will teach you every-thing, and remind you of all that I have said to you."

- What will it be like when I fully allow the Trinity to make their home in me? Remember, they are a very dynamic and lively bunch.
- How will I then relate to others, especially to the poor and needy?
- How do I begin to make the Trinity feel at home?

Tuesday 16th May   **John 14:27**

Jesus said to his disciples, "Peace I leave with you; my peace I
give to you. I do not give to you as the world gives. Do not
let your hearts be troubled, and do not let them be afraid."

- Lord, this is not sitting-back-in-an-armchair peace, but something
  active and creative. As Gerard Manley Hopkins wrote:
    O surely, reaving Peace, my Lord should leave in lieu
    Some good! And so he does leave Patience exquisite,
    That plumes to Peace thereafter. And when Peace here
    does house, He comes with work to do, he does not
    come to coo, He comes to brood and sit.

Wednesday 17th May   **John 15:7**

Jesus said to his disciples, "If you abide in me, and my words
abide in you, ask for whatever you wish, and it will be done
for you."

- Think of the music of that lovely hymn:
    Abide with me; fast falls the eventide;
    The darkness deepens; Lord, with me abide;
    When other helpers fail, and comforts flee,
    Help of the helpless, O, abide with me.

Thursday 18th May   **Acts 15:7–9 (New Jerusalem Bible)**

Peter stood up and addressed the council at Jerusalem, "You
know perfectly well that in the early days God made his
choice among you: the gentiles were to learn the good news
from me and so become believers. And God, who can read
everyone's heart, showed his approval of the Gentiles by giving
the Holy Spirit to them just as he had to us Jews. God made no
distinction between them and us, since he purified their hearts
by faith."

- This first council of Jerusalem was a moment of truth for the church. The church set itself against distinctions based on race or culture.
- Lord, whenever I find myself making distinctions between "them" and "us," pull me back to this moment. To you, Lord, women and men, slave and free-born of every color and race, all are equally your children.

Friday 19th May   John 15:15

Jesus said to his disciples: "I do not call you servants any longer, because the servant does not know what the master is doing; but I have called you friends, because I have made known to you everything that I have heard from my Father."

- Jesus my friend, in your company I can relax, be silent or talk, grumble or boast, vent and complain, or feel thankful and light-hearted. You know my heart and make allowances. I do not have to pretend.

Saturday 20th May   John 15:19

Jesus said to his disciples: "If you belonged to the world, the world would love you as its own. Because you do not belong to the world, but I have chosen you out of the world—therefore the world hates you."

- Forgive me, Lord; there are times when I try to keep up with the prejudices and fripperies of fashion, or echo the cynicism and materialism around me.
- When the worldly love me, I need to look hard at myself and remember that you, the most lovable of men, suffered hatred and execution. When people are giving me a hard time, it may well be that I am blessed.

may 21–27

Something to think and pray about each day this week:

Growing into the Spirit

It is often at this time of year that young Christians, on the threshold of adolescence, are confirmed. They receive the gift of the Holy Spirit. It could be really good as I pray in these days to remember these young Christians and also to ask myself about my own experience of the Holy Spirit. Do I experience the Spirit as my Helper, my Consoler, or my Advocate—who always pleads my cause? Does the Spirit help me to be a witness to Christ?

In these days I can be in solidarity with young Christians who are opening their lives to the Holy Spirit. They, like us, are growing up in a world that can easily undermine the self-giving love that the Spirit inspires. In my praying these days, I can pray for young Christians—and for myself—to receive whatever gifts of the Spirit we all need.

The Presence of God

The world is charged with the grandeur of God (Gerard Manley Hopkins).
I dwell for a moment on the presence of God
around me, in every part of my body,
and deep within my being.

Freedom

Everything has the potential to draw forth from me a fuller love and life.
Yet my desires are often fixed, caught, on illusions of fulfillment.
I ask that God, through my freedom, may orchestrate
my desires in a vibrant loving melody rich in harmony.

Consciousness

In God's loving presence I unwind the past day,
starting from now and looking back, moment by moment.
I gather in all the goodness and light, in gratitude.
I attend to the shadows and what they say to me,
seeking healing, courage, forgiveness.

The Word

I read the Word of God slowly, a few times over, and I listen to what God is saying to me. (Please turn to your scripture on the following pages. Inspiration points are there should you need them. When you are ready, return here to continue.)

Conversation

What feelings are rising in me
as I pray and reflect on God's Word?
I imagine Jesus himself sitting or standing beside me,
and open my heart to him.

Conclusion

Glory be to the Father, and to the Son, and to the Holy Spirit,
As it was in the beginning, is now and ever shall be,
World without end. Amen

Sunday 21st May, Sixth Sunday of Easter   John 15:16–17

Jesus said to his disciples, "You did not choose me but I chose you. And I appointed you to go and bear fruit, fruit that will last, so that the Father will give you whatever you ask him in my name. I am giving you these commands so that you may love one another."

- It is really worthwhile spending time listening deeply to what Jesus has said. "I chose YOU."
- This is addressed to me in all the particular details of my life.
- If I have difficulty appreciating that, I should ask for light to understand it.

Monday 22nd May   John 15:26–16:4

Jesus said to his disciples, "When the Advocate comes, whom I will send to you from the Father, the Spirit of truth who comes from the Father, he will testify on my behalf. You also are to testify because you have been with me from the beginning. I have said these things to you to keep you from stumbling. They will put you out of the synagogues. Indeed, an hour is coming when those who kill you will think that by doing so they are offering worship to God. And they will do this because they have not known the Father or me. But I have said these things to you so that when their hour comes you may remember that I told you about them. I did not say these things to you from the beginning, because I was with you."

- "When the Advocate comes." The Holy Spirit, the Advocate, the Counselor, does not operate as an alien intruder whispering surprising news into my ear but helps me to be myself, and to learn from my experience.
- Give me the wisdom, Lord, to learn from what I have lived through.

Tuesday 23rd May   **Acts 16:22–28**

The crowd joined in attacking Paul and Silas, and the magistrates had them stripped of their clothing and ordered them to be beaten with rods. After they had given them a severe flogging, they threw them into prison and ordered the jailer to keep them securely. Following these instructions, he put them in the innermost cell and fastened their feet in the stocks. About midnight Paul and Silas were praying and singing hymns to God, and the prisoners were listening to them. Suddenly there was an earthquake, so violent that the foundations of the prison were shaken; and immediately all the doors were opened and everyone's chains were unfastened. When the jailer woke up and saw the prison doors wide open, he drew his sword and was about to kill himself, since he supposed that the prisoners had escaped. But Paul shouted in a loud voice, "Do not harm yourself, for we are all here."

- Paul's fetters were unfastened but he stayed behind bars.
- Lord, it is not the outer constraints that bother me, but the interior bonds that warp my judgment and limit my freedom of choice: my dislikes, jealousies, and uncontrolled appetites.

Wednesday 24th May   **Acts 17:15, 22–25**

Those who conducted Paul brought him as far as Athens; and after receiving instructions to have Silas and Timothy join him as soon as possible, they left him. Then Paul stood in front of the Areopagus and said, "Athenians, I see how extremely religious you are in every way. For as I went through the city and looked carefully at the objects of your worship, I found among them an altar with the inscription, 'To an unknown god.' What therefore you worship as unknown, this I proclaim to you. The God who made the world and everything in it, he who is Lord of heaven and earth, does not live in shrines made by human hands, nor is he served by human hands, as though he needed anything, since he himself gives to all mortals life and breath and all things."

- "To an unknown God." That is you, Lord. I do not know you but I seek you. I have glimpses of you in the face of Christ. I feel close to you in sacred places, in the sacraments and in prayer.
- I know you in dark times too. When I am in utter desolation, my heart tells me there must be something beyond this. These are glimpses—a gift, a grace, a moment, a promise.

Thursday 25th May   Acts 18:1–3

After this Paul left Athens and went to Corinth. There he found a Jew named Aquila, a native of Pontus, who had recently come from Italy with his wife Priscilla, because Claudius had ordered all Jews to leave Rome. Paul went to see them, and, because he was of the same trade, he stayed with them, and they worked together—by trade they were tentmakers.

- "Paul stayed with them, and they worked together." More than once Paul comments that he earned his keep, and did not seek to use preaching or praying as an excuse for idle hands.
- Lord, I do not want to be one of those beautiful souls who never get their hands dirty. Work is part of our human calling. Even when it is drudgery, and I am weary or bored, I know it puts me in touch with the great mass of the human race.

Friday 26th May   John 16:20–23

Very truly, I tell you, you will weep and mourn, but the world will rejoice; you will have pain, but your pain will turn into joy. When a woman is in labor, she has pain, because her hour has come. But when her child is born, she no longer remembers the anguish because of the joy of having brought a human being into the world. So you have pain now; but I will see you again, and your hearts will rejoice, and no one will take your joy from you. On that day you will ask nothing of me. Very truly, I tell you, if you ask anything of the Father in my name, he will give it to you.

- "When a woman is in labor she has pain." Jesus reminds us today of the price that mothers pay for their children: a fruitful line of prayer if we review the life cycle that brought each of us to today.
- My mother faced the acute pain, which males can hardly imagine, of bringing me into the world; and she continued to feed me, and to watch over and care for me. Let me never take for granted the price that has been paid for my existence.

Saturday 27th May   John 16:23–27

Jesus said to his disciples, "On that day you will ask nothing of me. Very truly, I tell you, if you ask anything of the Father in my name, he will give it to you. Until now you have not asked for anything in my name. Ask and you will receive, so that your joy may be complete. I have said these things to you in figures of speech. The hour is coming when I will no longer speak to you in figures, but will tell you plainly of the Father. On that day you will ask in my name. I do not say to you that I will ask the Father on your behalf; for the Father himself loves you, because you have loved me and have believed that I came from God."

- "The Father himself loves you." This is where I fit into the inner dynamic of the Blessed Trinity. As Jesus is joined to the Father through the Holy Spirit, so too are we, because Jesus is our brother.

may 28–june 3

Something to think and pray about each day this week:

Looking from the ground up

One of the wonders of ancient Ireland you can visit today is the magnificent burial site at Newgrange in County Meath. The pagan ancestors of today's Irish people labored and toiled for years to build it in such a way that on the Winter Solstice each year, the light of the sun would flood the pitch-dark inner chamber. This annual "miracle" of the Winter Solstice was an important sign that kept their spirits alight and alive. In our daily grind too, we keep in our sights the miracle of our "ascension," of our rising to new life with the Son of God. This is where it is all going. This is what makes sense of it all.

At this time each year we pause on our way and look up to heaven and remember our high calling, our destiny, our destination. This momentary glimpse at what will be is salutary. It keeps us grounded, focused, and directed.

The Presence of God
As I sit here, God is present,
breathing life into me and into everything around me.
For a few moments, I sit silently,
and become aware of God's loving presence.

Freedom
There are very few people
who realize what God would make of them
if they abandoned themselves into his hands,
and let themselves be formed by his grace (St. Ignatius).
I ask for the grace to trust myself totally to God's love.

Consciousness
I exist in a web of relationships—links to nature, people, God.
I trace out these links, giving thanks for the life that flows
through them.
Some links are twisted or broken: I may feel regret, anger, disappointment.
I pray for the gift of acceptance and forgiveness.

The Word
I take my time to read the Word of God, slowly, a few times,
allowing myself to dwell on anything that strikes me. (Please
turn to your scripture on the following pages. Inspiration points
are there should you need them. When you are ready, return
here to continue.)

Conversation
What is stirring in me as I pray?
Am I consoled, troubled, left cold?
I imagine Jesus himself standing or sitting at my side,
and share my feelings with him.

Conclusion
Glory be to the Father, and to the Son, and to the Holy Spirit,
As it was in the beginning, is now and ever shall be,
World without end. Amen

Sunday 28th May, The Feast of the Ascension   Acts 1:6–11

So when they had come together, they asked him, "Lord, is this the time when you will restore the kingdom to Israel?" He replied, "It is not for you to know the times or periods that the Father has set by his own authority. But you will receive power when the Holy Spirit has come upon you; and you will be my witnesses in Jerusalem, in all Judea and Samaria, and to the ends of the earth." When he had said this, as they were watching, he was lifted up, and a cloud took him out of their sight. While he was going and they were gazing up toward heaven, suddenly two men in white robes stood by them. They said, "Men of Galilee, why do you stand looking up toward heaven? This Jesus, who has been taken up from you into heaven, will come in the same way as you saw him go into heaven."

- These are the men who have walked with Jesus for three years. Yet here on the mountain of revelation, their faith and worship is mixed with questioning and doubt. We know how it feels.
- To the same shaky, ambivalent men, Jesus gave his mandate to preach to all nations. To them, and to us, he says: I am with you. I need you to be with me, Lord.

Monday 29th May   Acts 19:1–2, 6–8

While Apollos was in Corinth, Paul passed through the interior regions and came to Ephesus, where he found some disciples. He said to them, "Did you receive the Holy Spirit when you became believers?" They replied, "No, we have not even heard that there is a Holy Spirit." When Paul had laid his hands on them, the Holy Spirit came upon them, and they spoke in tongues and prophesied—altogether there were about twelve of them. He entered the synagogue and for three months spoke out boldly, and argued persuasively about the kingdom of God.

- "We have not even heard that there is a Holy Spirit." Let me focus on the Paraclete, our Advocate before the Father.
- How intimate is the Holy Spirit to my existence: not as a separate God, but rather that by which we—and Jesus—are wrapped into the Godhead.

Tuesday 30th May   John 17:1–3

After Jesus had spoken these words, he looked up to heaven and said, "Father, the hour has come; glorify your Son so that the Son may glorify you, since you have given him authority over all people, to give eternal life to all whom you have given him. And this is eternal life, that they may know you, the only true God, and Jesus Christ whom you have sent."

- "This is eternal life, that they may know you, the only true God, and Jesus Christ whom you have sent." Islam too knows Allah as the one true God, and recognizes Jesus as sent by God. All our life we struggle to know him, through words and parables, and through the world which he has entrusted to us.
- Lord, I relax my body, quieten my mind, and focus on my breathing. Then I seek you there, in the silence.

Wednesday 31st May, Visitation
of the Virgin Mary to Elizabeth   Luke 1:39–47

In those days Mary set out and went with haste to a Judean town in the hill country, where she entered the house of Zechariah and greeted Elizabeth. When Elizabeth heard Mary's greeting, the child leaped in her womb. And Elizabeth was filled with the Holy Spirit and exclaimed with a loud cry, "Blessed are you among women, and blessed is the fruit of your womb. And why has this happened to me, that the mother of my Lord comes to me? For as soon as I heard the sound of your greeting, the child in my womb leaped for joy. And blessed is she who believed that there would be a fulfillment of what was spoken to

206

her by the Lord." And Mary said, "My soul magnifies the Lord, and my spirit rejoices in God my Savior."

- Stay with the scene. Both of the women are aware that something awesome is at work in them.
- In their meeting there is the ordinariness of friends meeting and also a profound sense of destiny.
- Can I explore how they are responding?

Thursday 1st June   Acts 23:6–8

When Paul noticed that some in the Sanhedrin were Sadducees and others were Pharisees, he called out in the council, "Brothers, I am a Pharisee, a son of Pharisees. I am on trial concerning the hope of the resurrection of the dead." When he said this, a dissension began between the Pharisees and the Sadducees, and the assembly was divided. (The Sadducees say that there is no resurrection, or angel, or spirit; but the Pharisees acknowledge all three.)

- Paul played on the theological divisions between the ruling factions, Pharisees and Sadducees. Jesus had warned us: "When you are dragged before the Sanhedrin, do not think beforehand how you will answer." Paul did not think beforehand. He used his wits, and jumped at an opportunity of diverting anger from himself. To be a Christian does not mean that you are a fool.
- Give me the grace, Lord, to use my head in the here and now.

Friday 2nd June   John 21:15–17

When they had finished breakfast, Jesus said to Simon Peter, "Simon son of John, do you love me more than these?" He said to him, "Yes, Lord; you know that I love you." Jesus said to him, "Feed my lambs." A second time he said to him, "Simon son of John, do you love me?" He said to him, "Yes, Lord; you know that I love you." Jesus said to him, "Tend my sheep." He said to him the third time, "Simon son of John, do you love me?" Peter felt hurt because he said to him the third time, "Do you love me?" And he said to him, "Lord, you know everything; you know that I love you." Jesus said to him, "Feed my sheep."

- "Simon, son of John, do you love me?" Jews do not have to love Moses. Moslems are not asked if they love Mohammed. But Jesus asks Peter, as a condition of his mission: "Do you love me?"
- Lord, I want to answer like Peter: "You know all things. You know that I love you." Maybe my life does not square with that—neither did Peter's when he denied you. But you know my heart and make allowance. May I grow in your love.

Saturday 3rd June   John 21:20–24

Peter turned and saw the disciple whom Jesus loved following them; he was the one who had reclined next to Jesus at the supper and had said, "Lord, who is it that is going to betray you?" When Peter saw him, he said to Jesus, "Lord, what about him?" Jesus said to him, "If it is my will that he remain until I come, what is that to you? Follow me!" So the rumor spread in the community that this disciple would not die. Yet Jesus did not say to him that he would not die, but, "If it is my will that he remain until I come, what is that to you?" This is the disciple who is testifying to these things and has written them, and we know that his testimony is true.

- I listen to the Easter testimony of John, the beloved disciple.
- This witness has been passed down through the centuries and now again is offered to me.
- Can I hear Jesus say to me, "Follow me"?

june 4–10

Something to think and pray about each day this week:

Invaded by the Spirit

When Jesus promised to send his Spirit on his disciples, he added a curious note: "There are many things I have to tell you, but not now. The Spirit will remind you of all things I have said to you."

In prayer we are reminded rather than changed. Prayer helps us to realize what we already know. The Holy Spirit is not an alien invader, but the one who enables us to be ourselves. On Whit Sunday, Peter and the apostles had the same personalities as before Pentecost, but they had the courage to be themselves, to speak out from their hearts about what they had heard from Jesus. The apostles at Pentecost did not get more lectures on Christianity. Instead they had the confidence to use what they already knew. The Irish poet Paddy Kavanagh used to say that we only learn what we already know. We learn by reflecting on our experience.

This means listening to our hearts. When Ignatius Loyola was recovering after breaking his leg in battle, he used to enjoy the romances they gave him to read; but he found that their after-taste was empty and unsatisfying. When he read the gospels or saints' lives, the after-taste was of solid food, something he could live on. He became an expert in discerning the after-taste of experiences. That is the way the Holy Spirit can shape our lives.

The Presence of God

As I sit here with my book, God is here.
Around me, in my sensations, in my thoughts and deep within me.
I pause for a moment, and become aware
of God's life-giving presence.

Freedom

A thick and shapeless tree-trunk would never believe
that it could become a statue, admired as a miracle of sculpture,
and would never submit itself to the chisel of the sculptor,
who sees by her genius what she can make of it (St. Ignatius).
I ask for the grace to let myself be shaped by my loving Creator.

Consciousness

How am I really feeling? Light-hearted? Heavy-hearted?
I may be very much at peace, happy to be here.
Equally, I may be frustrated, worried or angry.
I acknowledge how I really am. It is the real me that the Lord loves.

The Word

God speaks to each one of us individually. I need to listen to what he is saying to me. (Please turn to your scripture on the following pages. Inspiration points are there should you need them. When you are ready, return here to continue.)

Conversation

Do I notice myself reacting as I pray with the Word of God?
Do I feel challenged, comforted, angry?
Imagining Jesus sitting or standing by me,
I speak out my feelings, as one trusted friend to another.

Conclusion

Glory be to the Father, and to the Son, and to the Holy Spirit,
As it was in the beginning, is now and ever shall be,
World without end. Amen

Sunday 4th June, Pentecost   Acts 2:1–4

When the day of Pentecost had come, they were all together in one place. And suddenly from heaven there came a sound like the rush of a violent wind, and it filled the entire house where they were sitting. Divided tongues, as of fire, appeared among them, and a tongue rested on each of them. All of them were filled with the Holy Spirit and began to speak in other languages, as the Spirit gave them ability.

- Imagine the scene: the initial fear, the rush of wind, the shock, the confusion, the amazement, the power, the joy, the communication.
- We pray on behalf of all who come to *Sacred Space*, "Come Holy Spirit."

Monday 5th June   2 Peter 1:2–7

May grace and peace be yours in abundance in the knowledge of God and of Jesus our Lord. His divine power has given us everything needed for life and godliness, through the knowledge of him who called us by his own glory and goodness. Thus he has given us, through these things, his precious and very great promises, so that through them you may escape from the corruption that is in the world because of lust, and may become participants of the divine nature. For this very reason, you must make every effort to support your faith with goodness, and goodness with knowledge, and knowledge with self-control, and self-control with endurance, and endurance with godliness, and godliness with mutual affection, and mutual affection with love.

- Faith, action, love are inextricably linked together in this passage. According to Peter, my faith needs to be in tune with what I do and with the way I behave towards others, and my treatment of others has to be based on love.

- If going to church is "just something I do on Sundays" and my faith and my prayer make no difference to the rest of my life, then I am ignoring Peter's advice. If I claim to be a Christian but don't care about suffering or injustice going on around me, I am a hypocrite.

- Allowing my faith to challenge the way I behave can be difficult, but if I face that challenge and faith, action and love are united in me, I will feel the difference—a certain peace and confidence in the face of difficulties. And others will notice it too.

Tuesday 6th June   Mark 12:13–17

Then they sent to Jesus some Pharisees and some Herodians to trap him in what he said. And they came and said to him, "Teacher, we know that you are sincere, and show deference to no one; for you do not regard people with partiality, but teach the way of God in accordance with truth. Is it lawful to pay taxes to the emperor, or not? Should we pay them, or should we not?" But knowing their hypocrisy, he said to them, "Why are you putting me to the test? Bring me a denarius and let me see it." And they brought one. Then he said to them, "Whose head is this, and whose title?" They answered, "The emperor's." Jesus said to them, "Give to the emperor the things that are the emperor's, and to God the things that are God's." And they were utterly amazed at him.

- The Pharisees and Herodians are not really seeking the truth when they ask this question of Jesus. They are trying to get him to say something that will suit their own ends. When I pray, am I trying to get the Lord to do my bidding, or am I listening to hear what God is asking of me?

- Jesus knew what was in their hearts, and he knows what is in mine too. There is no point in pretending or trying to make a good impression when I approach Jesus. He loves me just as I am, and wants me to speak to him straight from the heart.

- What would it mean for me to "give to God the things that are God's"? Is there something I am keeping back? Can I talk to the Lord about this?

Wednesday 7th June   Mark 12:18–27

Some Sadducees, who say there is no resurrection, came to Jesus and asked him a question, saying, "Teacher, Moses wrote for us that 'if a man's brother dies, leaving a wife but no child, the man shall marry the widow and raise up children for his brother.' There were seven brothers; the first married and, when he died, left no children; and the second married her and died, leaving no children; and the third likewise; none of the seven left children. Last of all the woman herself died. In the resurrection whose wife will she be? For the seven had married her." Jesus said to them, "Is not this the reason you are wrong, that you know neither the scriptures nor the power of God? For when they rise from the dead, they neither marry nor are given in marriage, but are like angels in heaven. And as for the dead being raised, have you not read in the book of Moses, in the story about the bush, how God said to him, 'I am the God of Abraham, the God of Isaac, and the God of Jacob'? He is God not of the dead, but of the living; you are quite wrong."

- Here we see a group of "sophisticates," who thought they knew it all, trying to best the Son of God.
- What do they know about the resurrection? What does Jesus know about it?
- Do I ever play the Sadducee in my dealings with Jesus?

Thursday 8th June   Mark 12:28–34

One of the scribes came near and heard them disputing with one another, and seeing that Jesus answered them well, he asked him, "Which commandment is the first of all?" Jesus answered, "The first is, 'Hear, O Israel: the Lord our God, the

Lord is one; you shall love the Lord your God with all your heart, and with all your soul, and with all your mind, and with all your strength.' The second is this, 'You shall love your neighbor as yourself.' There is no other commandment greater than these." Then the scribe said to him, "You are right, Teacher; you have truly said that 'he is one, and besides him there is no other'; and 'to love him with all the heart, and with all the understanding, and with all the strength,' and 'to love one's neighbor as oneself,'—this is much more important than all whole burnt offerings and sacrifices." When Jesus saw that he answered wisely, he said to him, "You are not far from the kingdom of God." After that no one dared to ask him any question.

- This scribe is an honest searcher. Jesus warms to his integrity.
- Do I sense that Jesus looks on me with similar respect in my search to understand God's Word?

Friday 9th June, St. Colmcille   Psalm 16:1–2, 5, 7–8, 11

Protect me, O God, for in you I take refuge. I say to the Lord, "You are my Lord; I have no good apart from you." The Lord is my chosen portion and my cup; you hold my lot. I bless the Lord who gives me counsel; in the night also my heart instructs me. I keep the Lord always before me; because he is at my right hand, I shall not be moved. You show me the path of life. In your presence there is fullness of joy; in your right hand are pleasures forevermore.

- These are words of complete trust and confidence in the Lord.
- Is there anything I would love to hand over totally to the Lord?
- The "Lord who gives me counsel" is trustworthy.

Saturday 10th June   Mark 12:38–44

As Jesus taught, he said, "Beware of the scribes, who like to walk around in long robes, and to be greeted with respect in the marketplaces, and to have the best seats in the synagogues and places of honor at banquets! They devour widows' houses and for the sake of appearance say long prayers. They will receive the greater condemnation." He sat down opposite the treasury, and watched the crowd putting money into the treasury. Many rich people put in large sums. A poor widow came and put in two small copper coins, which are worth a penny. Then he called his disciples and said to them, "Truly I tell you, this poor widow has put in more than all those who are contributing to the treasury. For all of them have contributed out of their abundance; but she out of her poverty has put in everything she had, all she had to live on."

- If I was collecting money for charity, which donation would make me happier: twenty thousand from a wealthy friend or five from a poor one?
- What is Jesus telling us about God's view of things?
- How does Jesus look at me?

june 11–17

Something to think and pray about each day this week:

Tuning in to the Spirit of God

Around the feast of the Holy Trinity, we contemplate our role in a mystery: one God in three persons. Holy Spirit has an exact meaning, though hard to grasp. The Spirit personifies the bond of communication and love that links Jesus to his Father. As sisters and brothers of Jesus we share that bond. We are temples of the Spirit, who speaks on our behalf to the Father.

"The Spirit too comes to help us in our weakness. For when we cannot choose words in order to pray properly, the Spirit expresses our plea in a way that could never be put into words" (Romans 8:26). That is St. Paul's guide to prayer: it is mainly the job of the Holy Spirit, who links us to the Father even when we cannot manage our own thoughts. What are we doing in prayer but attempting to tune in to this unbroken dialogue between the Holy Spirit speaking on our behalf and the Father who loves us as his children?

To tune in, I need to reduce internal noise and static. If I quiet the body, breathe deeply and regularly and cut out stimulation from outside, I can focus on being aware of my own body and my own heart.

The Presence of God
I pause for a moment, aware that God is here.
I think of how everything around me,
the air I breathe, my whole body,
is tingling with the presence of God.

Freedom
I ask for the grace
to let go of my own concerns
and be open to what God is asking of me,
to let myself be guided and formed by my loving Creator.

Consciousness
Knowing that God loves me unconditionally,
I can afford to be honest about how I am.
How has the last day been, and how do I feel now?
I share my feelings openly with the Lord.

The Word
I read the Word of God slowly, a few times over, and I listen to
what God is saying to me. (Please turn to your scripture on the
following pages. Inspiration points are there should you need
them. When you are ready, return here to continue.)

Conversation
Remembering that I am still in God's presence,
I imagine Jesus himself standing or sitting beside me,
and say whatever is on my mind, whatever is in my heart,
speaking as one friend to another.

Conclusion
Glory be to the Father, and to the Son, and to the Holy Spirit,
As it was in the beginning, is now and ever shall be,
World without end. Amen

Sunday 11th June, Trinity Sunday   Matthew 28:16–20

Now the eleven disciples went to Galilee, to the mountain to which Jesus had directed them. When they saw him, they worshiped him; but some doubted. And Jesus came and said to them, "All authority in heaven and on earth has been given to me. Go therefore and make disciples of all nations, baptizing them in the name of the Father and of the Son and of the Holy Spirit, and teaching them to obey everything that I have commanded you. And remember, I am with you always, to the end of the age."

- In my imagination I can stand among the disciples on the mountain.
- Am I moved to worship or do I doubt?
- I listen to the parting words of Jesus as if for the first time.
- I can talk to Jesus about my reactions.

Monday 12th June   Matthew 5:1–6

When Jesus saw the crowds, he went up the mountain; and after he sat down, his disciples came to him. Then he began to speak, and taught them, saying: "Blessed are the poor in spirit, for theirs is the kingdom of heaven. Blessed are those who mourn, for they will be comforted. Blessed are the meek, for they will inherit the earth. Blessed are those who hunger and thirst for righteousness, for they will be filled."

- These are the opening words of Jesus' first great sermon, where he introduces us to a new world order.
- Whether these new ideas sit easily with me or not, it is good to play them over in my mind and chew on them.
- What message or challenge do these words hold for me?

Tuesday 13th June, St. Anthony of Padua   Isaiah 61:1–3a

The spirit of the Lord God is upon me, because the Lord has anointed me; he has sent me to bring good news to the oppressed, to bind up the brokenhearted, to proclaim liberty to the captives, and release to the prisoners; to proclaim the year of the Lord's favor, and the day of vengeance of our God; to comfort all who mourn; to provide for those who mourn in Zion—to give them a garland instead of ashes, the oil of gladness instead of mourning, the mantle of praise instead of a faint spirit.

- If I could say with the same verve, "The Spirit of the Lord is upon ME . . . and has sent ME . . ." I would have powerful focus and energy in my life.
- Can I stop and get in touch with the Spirit in my life?
- How am I being sent?

Wednesday 14th June   Matthew 5:17–19

Jesus said to the crowds, "Do not think that I have come to abolish the law or the prophets; I have come not to abolish but to fulfill. For truly I tell you, until heaven and earth pass away, not one letter, not one stroke of a letter, will pass from the law until all is accomplished. Therefore, whoever breaks one of the least of these commandments, and teaches others to do the same, will be called least in the kingdom of heaven; but whoever does them and teaches them will be called great in the kingdom of heaven."

- These are strong words from Jesus about the law. He didn't come to make life softer but deeper.
- What is my own relationship with law and tradition? Am I naturally submissive or automatically rebellious?
- How is Jesus calling me to go deeper?

Thursday 15th June   Matthew 5:21–24

Jesus said to the crowds, "You have heard that it was said to those of ancient times, 'You shall not murder'; and 'whoever murders shall be liable to judgment.' But I say to you that if you are angry with a brother or sister, you will be liable to judgment; and if you insult a brother or sister, you will be liable to the council; and if you say, 'You fool,' you will be liable to the hell of fire. So when you are offering your gift at the altar, if you remember that your brother or sister has something against you, leave your gift there before the altar and go; first be reconciled to your brother or sister, and then come and offer your gift."

- Jesus is using fiery language probably because he wants our full attention.
- What is he saying to me about my relationships?
- Is there some action I need to take right now?

Friday 16th June   Matthew 5:27–30

Jesus said to the crowds, "You have heard that it was said, 'You shall not commit adultery.' But I say to you that everyone who looks at a woman with lust has already committed adultery with her in his heart. If your right eye causes you to sin, tear it out and throw it away; it is better for you to lose one of your members than for your whole body to be thrown into hell. And if your right hand causes you to sin, cut it off and throw it away; it is better for you to lose one of your members than for your whole body to go into hell."

- Jesus is saying that the truly godly person is not only authentic in action but pure in heart as well.
- How does the vehemence—violence even—of his words affect me? Does it frighten me? Threaten me? Challenge me? Or simply upset me?
- Can I be in God's presence, with my reactions, whatever they are, and allow myself to be confident that God is leading me and building me up?

Saturday 17th June   **Matthew 5:33–37**

J esus said to the crowds, "Again, you have heard that it was said to those of ancient times, 'You shall not swear falsely, but carry out the vows you have made to the Lord.' But I say to you, Do not swear at all, either by heaven, for it is the throne of God, or by the earth, for it is his footstool, or by Jerusalem, for it is the city of the great King. And do not swear by your head, for you cannot make one hair white or black. Let your word be 'Yes, Yes' or 'No, No'; anything more than this comes from the evil one."

- God's view of things seems to cut away all excess. It goes to the core of the matter.
- What learning is here for me? What is Jesus trying to teach me?

june 18–24

Something to think and pray about each day this week:

The intimate presence
In these days many of us are celebrating the extraordinary gift of the eucharist with the feast that used to be called *Corpus Christi*. God enters into the material world by his presence in bread and wine, which has become the body and blood of his son, a memorial of his passion, and nourishment for each of us.

We do it in memory of him: slake our hunger and thirst on the sacramental bread and wine, and through this come closest to meeting our deepest desire for union with God. What we receive at the eucharistic table becomes part of our body; we speak with the Lord who has become part of us. Now we are not looking up to a Father in heaven, but speaking to the God within us, who has become our strength and sustenance. Not just speaking but listening, enjoying his presence without words.

The Presence of God
For a few moments, I think of God's veiled presence in things:
in the elements, giving them existence;
in plants, giving them life; in animals, giving them sensation;
and finally, in me, giving me all this and more,
making me a temple, a dwelling-place of the Spirit.

Freedom
I ask for the grace to believe
in what I could be and do
if I only allowed God, my loving Creator,
to continue to create me, guide me and shape me.

Consciousness
In the presence of my loving Creator,
I look honestly at my feelings over the last day,
the highs, the lows and the level ground.
Can I see where the Lord has been present?

The Word
I take my time to read the Word of God, slowly, a few times, allowing myself to dwell on anything that strikes me. (Please turn to your scripture on the following pages. Inspiration points are there should you need them. When you are ready, return here to continue.)

Conversation
How has God's Word moved me? Has it left me cold?
Has it consoled me or moved me to act in a new way?
I imagine Jesus standing or sitting beside me,
I turn and share my feelings with him.

Conclusion
Glory be to the Father, and to the Son, and to the Holy Spirit,
As it was in the beginning, is now and ever shall be,
World without end. Amen

Sunday 18th June, The Body and Blood of Christ
Mark 14:22–26a

While they were eating, Jesus took a loaf of bread, and after blessing it he broke it, gave it to them, and said, "Take; this is my body." Then he took a cup, and after giving thanks he gave it to them, and all of them drank from it. He said to them, "This is my blood of the covenant, which is poured out for many. Truly I tell you, I will never again drink of the fruit of the vine until that day when I drink it new in the kingdom of God."

- In this moment of institution of the eucharist, what is Jesus doing for us? (His actions are not meant only for those present on that night.)
- Can I reflect humbly on the love behind his pouring out of himself for me?

Monday 19th June
Matthew 5:38–42

Jesus said to the crowds, "You have heard that it was said, 'An eye for an eye and a tooth for a tooth.' But I say to you, Do not resist an evildoer. But if anyone strikes you on the right cheek, turn the other also; and if anyone wants to sue you and take your coat, give your cloak as well; and if anyone forces you to go one mile, go also the second mile. Give to everyone who begs from you, and do not refuse anyone who wants to borrow from you."

- We hear Jesus calling us, his followers, to a way of life that is truly super human.
- How do I experience this call? Can I speak honestly with Jesus about this? It is the real me who is called to this love.

Tuesday 20th June
Matthew 5:43–47

Jesus said to the crowds, "You have heard that it was said, 'You shall love your neighbor and hate your enemy.' But I say to you, Love your enemies and pray for those who persecute you, so that you may be children of your Father in heaven; for he makes his sun rise on the evil and on the good, and sends rain on the righteous and on the unrighteous. For if you love those who love you, what reward do you have? Do not even the tax collectors do the same? And if you greet only your brothers and sisters, what more are you doing than others? Do not even the Gentiles do the same?"

- Jesus is calling us to attitudes which come from the heart and mind of God. If they are beyond our human capabilities right now, then it is obviously meant to be part of a process under God's grace.
- Where am I in this process?

Wednesday 21st June, St. Aloysius Gonzaga
Mark 10:23–27

Then Jesus looked around and said to his disciples, "How hard it will be for those who have wealth to enter the kingdom of God!" And the disciples were perplexed at these words. But Jesus said to them again, "Children, how hard it is to enter the kingdom of God! It is easier for a camel to go through the eye of a needle than for someone who is rich to enter the kingdom of God." They were greatly astounded and said to one another, "Then who can be saved?" Jesus looked at them and said, "For mortals it is impossible, but not for God; for God all things are possible."

- Why is it so hard for wealthy people?
- To whom is Jesus referring?
- Am I included?
- Do I find this challenging or confusing? Do I need to speak to Jesus about it?

Thursday 22nd June   Matthew 6:9–13

Jesus said to the crowds, "Pray then in this way: Our Father in heaven, hallowed be your name. Your kingdom come. Your will be done, on earth as it is in heaven. Give us this day our daily bread. And forgive us our debts, as we also have forgiven our debtors. And do not bring us to the time of trial, but rescue us from the evil one."

- Can I set aside the familiarity of the Lord's prayer and hear Jesus present it to me afresh? I linger on each of the seven petitions. They express perfectly our true stance before God.

Friday 23rd June, Feast of the Sacred Heart of Jesus
Luke 15:3–7

Jesus told them this parable: "Which one of you, having a hundred sheep and losing one of them, does not leave the ninety-nine in the wilderness and go after the one that is lost until he finds it? When he has found it, he lays it on his shoulders and rejoices. And when he comes home, he calls together his friends and neighbors, saying to them, 'Rejoice with me, for I have found my sheep that was lost.' Just so, I tell you, there will be more joy in heaven over one sinner who repents than over ninety-nine righteous persons who need no repentance."

- "More joy in heaven …." Can I let myself be surprised by this idea of God's delight when someone comes home?
- Do I imagine myself as the cause of this delighting?
- Do I think of myself as one of the ninety-nine? How does all of this move me?

Saturday 24th June, The Birth of John the Baptist
Luke 1:57–64

Now the time came for Elizabeth to give birth, and she bore a son. Her neighbors and relatives heard that the Lord had shown his great mercy to her, and they rejoiced with her. On the eighth day they came to circumcise the child, and they were going to name him Zechariah after his father. But his mother said, "No; he is to be called John." They said to her, "None of your relatives has this name." Then they began motioning to his father to find out what name he wanted to give him. He asked for a writing tablet and wrote, "His name is John." And all of them were amazed. Immediately his mouth was opened and his tongue freed, and he began to speak, praising God.

- Watch this remarkable little scene.
- God has intervened in the affairs of this family in an unexpected way.
- How do the different parties react? Elizabeth? The relatives? Zechariah?
- What can I learn from this?

june 25–july 1

Something to think and pray about each day this week:

Calming the inner storm

In the Middle East today, split between Jews and Arabs, you must be careful what stamp you allow on your passport. At some frontiers you are in trouble if you are seen as being friendly with the enemy. Jesus met that attitude in his own time. On one occasion the Samaritans rejected his party because they saw them as pilgrims going to the Temple, which they hated. The disciples were furious and wanted divine revenge. Jesus said no.

When we calm down in prayer, similar furies and indignations can rock us. As we stop moving, and quiet our bodies, resentments can bubble to the surface of our mind. Let them bubble—and burst. It will not take us long to see that anger, if we indulge it, becomes a burden on us, not on those who offended us. As long as we want revenge and withhold forgiveness, we are wasting adrenalin, and in one part of our mind we are holding God at bay.

Jesus portrayed his Father as a farmer who sees that an enemy has sown cockle in his wheat. Instead of dashing out and pulling up cockle and wheat together, he waits till the plants have grown, then separates them. When we arrive at that sort of patience, it leaves our hearts free to turn fully to the Lord.

The Presence of God

In the silence of my innermost being,
in the fragments of my yearned-for wholeness,
can I hear the whispers of God's presence?
Can I remember when I felt God's nearness?
When we walked together and I let myself be embraced by God's love.

Freedom

I need to close out the noise, to rise above the noise;
The noise that interrupts, that separates,
The noise that isolates.
I need to listen to God again.

Consciousness

In God's loving presence I unwind the past day,
starting from now and looking back, moment by moment.
I gather in all the goodness and light, in gratitude.
I attend to the shadows and what they say to me,
seeking healing, courage, forgiveness.

The Word

I take my time to read the Word of God, slowly, a few times, allowing myself to dwell on anything that strikes me. (Please turn to your scripture on the following pages. Inspiration points are there should you need them. When you are ready, return here to continue.)

Conversation

Do I notice myself reacting as I pray with the Word of God?
Do I feel challenged, comforted, angry?
Imagining Jesus sitting or standing by me,
I speak out my feelings, as one trusted friend to another.

Conclusion

Glory be to the Father, and to the Son, and to the Holy Spirit,
As it was in the beginning, is now and ever shall be,
World without end. Amen

Sunday 25th June, Twelfth Sunday in Ordinary Time
Mark 4:35–41

On that day, when evening had come, Jesus said to the disciples, "Let us go across to the other side." And leaving the crowd behind, they took him with them in the boat, just as he was. Other boats were with him. A great windstorm arose, and the waves beat into the boat, so that the boat was already being swamped. But he was in the stern, asleep on the cushion; and they woke him up and said to him, "Teacher, do you not care that we are perishing?" He woke up and rebuked the wind, and said to the sea, "Peace! Be still!" Then the wind ceased, and there was a dead calm. He said to them, "Why are you afraid? Have you still no faith?" And they were filled with great awe and said to one another, "Who then is this, that even the wind and the sea obey him?"

- I should really let my powers of imagination get me a place in this boat. Jesus' invitation to his disciples is also addressed to me.
- What happens? Do I feel the force of it all? What feelings arise in me?
- Where is God? What is he up to? What happens next?

Monday 26th June
Matthew 7:1–5

Jesus said to the crowds, "Do not judge, so that you may not be judged. For with the judgment you make you will be judged, and the measure you give will be the measure you get. Why do you see the speck in your neighbor's eye, but do not notice the log in your own eye? Or how can you say to your neighbor, 'Let me take the speck out of your eye,' while the log is in your own eye? You hypocrite, first take the log out of your own eye, and then you will see clearly to take the speck out of your neighbor's eye."

- This challenge is practical, relevant, and concrete.
- If Jesus is calling me to a change of heart in relation to specific individuals, then he will give me the necessary grace. It is good to talk to him about this.

Tuesday 27th June   Matthew 7:6, 12–14

Jesus said to the crowds, "Do not give what is holy to dogs; and do not throw your pearls before swine, or they will trample them under foot and turn and maul you.
In everything do to others as you would have them do to you; for this is the law and the prophets. Enter through the narrow gate; for the gate is wide and the road is easy that leads to destruction, and there are many who take it. For the gate is narrow and the road is hard that leads to life, and there are few who find it."

- All of these sayings are so profound that they have become part of everyday language and thereby their power to challenge is perhaps weakened.
- I need to stop and hear some of this as for the first time.
- How do these sayings challenge me?

Wednesday 28th June   Matthew 7:15–20

Jesus told the crowds, "Beware of false prophets, who come to you in sheep's clothing but inwardly are ravenous wolves. You will know them by their fruits. Are grapes gathered from thorns, or figs from thistles? In the same way, every good tree bears good fruit, but the bad tree bears bad fruit. A good tree cannot bear bad fruit, nor can a bad tree bear good fruit. Every tree that does not bear good fruit is cut down and thrown into the fire. Thus you will know them by their fruits."

- These sayings in the Sermon on the Mount are not just wise proverbs. Spoken by Jesus they come from the mouth of God.
- Can I open my heart to hear what God wants me to hear?

Thursday 29th June, Sts. Peter & Paul   Matthew 16:13–19

Now when Jesus came into the district of Caesarea Philippi, he asked his disciples, "Who do people say that the Son of Man is?" And they said, "Some say John the Baptist, but others Elijah, and still others Jeremiah or one of the prophets." He said to them, "But who do you say that I am?" Simon Peter answered, "You are the Messiah, the Son of the living God." And Jesus answered him, "Blessed are you, Simon son of Jonah! For flesh and blood has not revealed this to you, but my Father in heaven. And I tell you, you are Peter, and on this rock I will build my church, and the gates of Hades will not prevail against it. I will give you the keys of the kingdom of heaven, and whatever you bind on earth will be bound in heaven, and whatever you loose on earth will be loosed in heaven."

- This is the big question that every follower is asked, again and again, "Who do you say I am?" What is my answer?
- Does my answer depend mainly on me, or on my Father in heaven?
- As I watch this scene between Jesus and the disciples, I might ponder where I am in relation to knowing and appreciating who Jesus really is.

Friday 30th June   Matthew 8:1–4

When Jesus had come down from the mountain, great crowds followed him; and there was a leper who came to him and knelt before him, saying, "Lord, if you choose, you can make me clean." He stretched out his hand and touched him, saying, "I do choose. Be made clean!" Immediately his leprosy was cleansed. Then Jesus said to him, "See that you say nothing to anyone; but go, show yourself to the priest, and offer the gift that Moses commanded, as a testimony to them."

- Can you sincerely pray with the leper in your own words? Lord, I experience within myself an uncleanness. I know you can make me clean. I come humbly before you and beg to be cleansed. If it is your will, if you consider it is what is best for me, I trust that you will grant me this grace.

Saturday 1st July   **Matthew 8:5–13**

When he entered Capernaum, a centurion came to him, appealing to him and saying, "Lord, my servant is lying at home paralyzed, in terrible distress." And he said to him, "I will come and cure him." The centurion answered, "Lord, I am not worthy to have you come under my roof; but only speak the word, and my servant will be healed. For I also am a man under authority, with soldiers under me; and I say to one, 'Go,' and he goes, and to another, 'Come,' and he comes, and to my slave, 'Do this,' and the slave does it." When Jesus heard him, he was amazed and said to those who followed him, "Truly I tell you, in no one in Israel have I found such faith. I tell you, many will come from east and west and will eat with Abraham and Isaac and Jacob in the kingdom of heaven, while the heirs of the kingdom will be thrown into the outer darkness, where there will be weeping and gnashing of teeth." And to the centurion Jesus said, "Go; let it be done for you according to your faith." And the servant was healed in that hour.

- Imagine this scene. A band of Jews with their traveling rabbi are entering the town. Up comes a Roman centurion.
- What do these two men look like? How do they compare with each other? Do I hear what is said?
- What is my attitude to Jesus?

Something to think and pray about each day this week:

Choosing the new

"It does not matter if a person is circumcised or not. What matters is to become an altogether new creature" (Galatians 6:15). Paul warns the Jews against the complacency they found in circumcision, as a sign of their being chosen. Paul says he will boast only about the cross. He is always moving us from the outside (circumcision as a sign of holiness) to the interior, which is less comforting.

When we settle in to prayer, our hearts gravitate to warm, comforting thoughts. We need to outgrow that. Jesus pictured the Pharisee coming before God in a self-congratulatory mode, listing the good works that set him apart from the rest of men. That is religion as a form of self-centeredness.

When St. Paul points towards the cross, he does not mean the penances I may choose for myself. Rather it is what the Holy Spirit does to me. The Holy Spirit is the sanctifier; that is his *métier*. I become an altogether new creature by going along with God, allowing him to shape me. In prayer I reflect on my experience, especially on the pricks and points of unease at what has happened to me; and I say "Yes, Amen" to the Holy Spirit who through them is forming me into a new creature.

The Presence of God

I remind myself that, as I sit here now,
God is gazing on me with love and holding me in being.
I pause for a moment and think of this.

Freedom

I will ask God's help,
to be free from my own preoccupations,
to be open to God in this time of prayer,
to come to love and serve him more.

Consciousness

I exist in a web of relationships—links to nature, people, God.
I trace out these links, giving thanks for the life that flows
through them.
Some links are twisted or broken: I may feel regret, anger, disappointment.
I pray for the gift of acceptance and forgiveness.

The Word

God speaks to each one of us individually. I need to listen to
what he is saying to me. (Please turn to your scripture on the
following pages. Inspiration points are there should you need
them. When you are ready, return here to continue.)

Conversation

Remembering that I am still in God's presence,
I imagine Jesus himself standing or sitting beside me,
and say whatever is on my mind, whatever is in my heart,
speaking as one friend to another.

Conclusion

Glory be to the Father, and to the Son, and to the Holy Spirit,
As it was in the beginning, is now and ever shall be,
World without end. Amen

Sunday 2nd July, Thirteenth Sunday in Ordinary Time
Mark 5:25–30, 33–34

Now there was a woman who had been suffering from hemorrhages for twelve years. She had endured much under many physicians, and had spent all that she had; and she was no better, but rather grew worse. She had heard about Jesus, and came up behind him in the crowd and touched his cloak, for she said, "If I but touch his clothes, I will be made well." Immediately her hemorrhage stopped; and she felt in her body that she was healed of her disease. Immediately aware that power had gone forth from him, Jesus turned about in the crowd and said, "Who touched my clothes?" … But the woman, knowing what had happened to her, came in fear and trembling, fell down before him, and told him the whole truth. He said to her, "Daughter, your faith has made you well; go in peace, and be healed of your disease."

- In my imagination I can see this scene as if I were present.
- I imagine the feelings that this woman carries with her: frustration born of much disappointment, fear, uncertainty, a timid hope, etc.
- Watch Jesus. How does he respond? Who is he? What is he like?

Monday 3rd July, St. Thomas
John 20:24–29

But Thomas (who was called the Twin), one of the twelve, was not with them when Jesus came. So the other disciples told him, "We have seen the Lord." But he said to them, "Unless I see the mark of the nails in his hands, and put my finger in the mark of the nails and my hand in his side, I will not believe." A week later his disciples were again in the house, and Thomas was with them. Although the doors were shut, Jesus came and stood among them and said, "Peace be with you." Then he said to Thomas, "Put your finger here and see my hands. Reach out your hand and put it in my side. Do not doubt but believe."

Thomas answered him, "My Lord and my God!" Jesus said to him, "Have you believed because you have seen me? Blessed are those who have not seen and yet have come to believe."

- When Thomas says "Unless … I will not believe," what do I hear in that voice? A hard man? A skeptic? "I've been hurt once and won't let it happen again"?
- Whatever was going on in Thomas' heart was made right in the meeting with Jesus. How does this speak to me?

Tuesday 4th July   Matthew 8:23–27

And when Jesus got into the boat, his disciples followed him. A windstorm arose on the sea, so great that the boat was being swamped by the waves; but he was asleep. And they went and woke him up, saying, "Lord, save us! We are perishing!" And he said to them, "Why are you afraid, you of little faith?" Then he got up and rebuked the winds and the sea; and there was a dead calm. They were amazed, saying, "What sort of man is this, that even the winds and the sea obey him?"

- Can I see myself in the boat with the others as the storm blows up? (What "storms" in my own life come to mind?)
- How does it all feel, especially as Jesus is asleep?
- Do I end up with the same final question as the others?

Wednesday 5th July   Amos 5:21–24

I hate, I despise your festivals, and I take no delight in your solemn assemblies. Even though you offer me your burnt offerings and grain offerings, I will not accept them; and the offerings of well-being of your fatted animals I will not look upon. Take away from me the noise of your songs; I will not listen to the melody of your harps. But let justice roll down like waters, and righteousness like an everflowing stream.

- In Amos' time there was much outward religious observance especially by rich and powerful people who cared nothing for the poor. Here the Lord chastises them for hypocrisy and calls for a change of heart.

- Can I hear the Lord's chastisement for hypocrisy in my life? How does the call to justice and righteousness impinge on me?

Thursday 6th July　　　　　　　　　　　　**Matthew 9:1–8**

And after getting into a boat Jesus crossed the sea and came to his own town. And just then some people were carrying a paralyzed man lying on a bed. When Jesus saw their faith, he said to the paralytic, "Take heart, son; your sins are forgiven." Then some of the scribes said to themselves, "This man is blaspheming." But Jesus, perceiving their thoughts, said, "Why do you think evil in your hearts? For which is easier, to say, 'Your sins are forgiven,' or to say, 'Stand up and walk'? But so that you may know that the Son of Man has authority on earth to forgive sins"—he then said to the paralytic—"Stand up, take your bed and go to your home." And he stood up and went to his home. When the crowds saw it, they were filled with awe, and they glorified God, who had given such authority to human beings.

- There is so much in this section: the faith and care of friends; the dire need of the paralytic; the compassion and mercy of Jesus; the dysfunction and distortion of the authorities; the forgiveness of sins; steadfast strength; the awesome power of God.

- What speaks to me?

Friday 7th July　　　　　　　　　　　　**Matthew 9:9–13**

As Jesus was walking along, he saw a man called Matthew sitting at the tax booth; and he said to him, "Follow me." And he got up and followed him. And as he sat at dinner in the house, many tax collectors and sinners came and were sitting with him and his disciples. When the Pharisees saw this, they said to his disciples, "Why does your teacher eat with tax collectors and sinners?" But when he heard this, he said, "Those who are well have no need of a physician, but those who are sick. Go and learn what this means, 'I desire mercy, not sacrifice.' For I have come to call not the righteous but sinners."

- Jesus calls whomever he wants and he is not at all choosy.
- What feelings does the call of Matthew and the reaction of the others stir up in me?
- What does all this say about my call?

Saturday 8th July   Matthew 9:14–17

Then the disciples of John came to him, saying, "Why do we and the Pharisees fast often, but your disciples do not fast?" And Jesus said to them, "The wedding guests cannot mourn as long as the bridegroom is with them, can they? The days will come when the bridegroom is taken away from them, and then they will fast. No one sews a piece of unshrunk cloth on an old cloak, for the patch pulls away from the cloak, and a worse tear is made. Neither is new wine put into old wineskins; otherwise, the skins burst, and the wine is spilled, and the skins are destroyed; but new wine is put into fresh wineskins, and so both are preserved."

- Jesus is the start of a new era in humankind's relationship with God. He is raising all that went before to a new plane.
- We are listening in on a conversation by people who are confused at big changes taking place.
- As Jesus' coming shook up the world of those he met, how can I let him shake up my world?

july 9–15

Something to think and pray about each day this week:

Meeting my Samaritan
More than any other occupation, prayer draws us back to the now. The present moment is like a sacrament, an outward channel of grace. God reaches me in the present moment. To become aware of him, we first calm down our body, feel the breath passing through our nostrils, cooler air coming in, warmer as we breathe out. We grow aware of what we feel, see, hear, smell. We recognize in our hearts the deep delights, or anxieties, or resentments that are masked by the activities of the day. In all of these God, is speaking to us.

From this presence in our bodies, we move towards recognizing God in those we meet. Jesus' commandment was "Love your neighbor." To the question: "Who is my neighbor?" he told the parable of the Good Samaritan. My neighbor is the one close to me, who makes demands on me, the one I stumble across unwittingly and reluctantly, wishing I was on the other side of the road. Those I meet on my side of the road are part of the sacrament of the present moment.

Slow me down, Lord. Bring me back to the here and now.

The Presence of God
God is with me, but more,
God is within me, giving me existence.
Let me dwell for a moment on God's life-giving presence
in my body, my mind, my heart
and in the whole of my life.

Freedom
God is not foreign to my freedom.
Instead the Spirit breathes life into my most intimate desires,
gently nudging me towards all that is good.
I ask for the grace to let myself be enfolded by the Spirit.

Consciousness
How am I really feeling? Light-hearted? Heavy-hearted?
I may be very much at peace, happy to be here.
Equally, I may be frustrated, worried or angry.
I acknowledge how I really am. It is the real me that the Lord
loves.

The Word
I read the Word of God slowly, a few times over, and I listen to
what God is saying to me. (Please turn to your scripture on the
following pages. Inspiration points are there should you need
them. When you are ready, return here to continue.)

Conversation
How has God's Word moved me? Has it left me cold?
Has it consoled me or moved me to act in a new way?
I imagine Jesus standing or sitting beside me,
I turn and share my feelings with him.

Conclusion
Glory be to the Father, and to the Son, and to the Holy Spirit,
As it was in the beginning, is now and ever shall be,
World without end. Amen

Sunday 9th July, Fourteenth Sunday in Ordinary Time
Mark 6:1–6

Jesus left that place and came to his hometown, and his disciples followed him. On the sabbath he began to teach in the synagogue, and many who heard him were astounded. They said, "Where did this man get all this? What is this wisdom that has been given to him? What deeds of power are being done by his hands! Is not this the carpenter, the son of Mary and brother of James and Joses and Judas and Simon, and are not his sisters here with us?" And they took offense at him. Then Jesus said to them, "Prophets are not without honor, except in their hometown, and among their own kin, and in their own house." And he could do no deed of power there, except that he laid his hands on a few sick people and cured them. And he was amazed at their unbelief. Then he went about among the villages teaching.

- It might be good to stand among the crowds around Jesus and see the different reactions. Some people are astonished and full of admiration. Nearby, others are blinded by familiarity and take offense.
- In the depths of my heart, how do some of these same reactions— positive and negative—arise in me?
- Do I allow Jesus to be who he really is for me?

Monday 10th July   Matthew 9:18–19, 23–26

While he was saying these things to them, suddenly a leader of the synagogue came in and knelt before him, saying, "My daughter has just died; but come and lay your hand on her, and she will live." And Jesus got up and followed him, with his disciples. When Jesus came to the leader's house and saw the flute players and the crowd making a commotion, he said, "Go away; for the girl is not dead but sleeping." And they laughed at him. But when the crowd had been put outside, he went in and took her by the hand, and the girl got up. And the report of this spread throughout that district.

- What is my reaction to the faith of the father whose daughter has just died?
- What about the response to the noisy crowd who laughed at Jesus?
- How do I respond to Jesus in this situation?

Tuesday 11th July, St. Benedict   Matthew 19:27–29

Then Peter said in reply, "Look, we have left everything and followed you. What then will we have?" Jesus said to them, "Truly I tell you, at the renewal of all things, when the Son of Man is seated on the throne of his glory, you who have followed me will also sit on twelve thrones, judging the twelve tribes of Israel. And everyone who has left houses or brothers or sisters or father or mother or children or fields, for my name's sake, will receive a hundredfold, and will inherit eternal life."

- Jesus had just been saying how difficult it is for the "rich," the people who cling to things, to enter the Kingdom of Heaven. Peter asks, what about us?
- Does this talk of leaving things—and even people—behind strike a chord with me?
- Have I been asked to let go of things? Are there things I need to let go of but find it hard?
- Can I talk to Jesus about these things?
- What does Jesus' invitation to leave everything mean in the context of my life?
- What are my hopes for the promised eternal life?

Wednesday 12th July   Matthew 10:1–7

Then Jesus summoned his twelve disciples and gave them authority over unclean spirits, to cast them out, and to cure every disease and every sickness. These are the names of the twelve apostles: first, Simon, also known as Peter, and his brother Andrew; James son of Zebedee, and his brother John; Philip and Bartholomew; Thomas and Matthew the tax collector; James son of Alphaeus, and Thaddaeus; Simon the Cananaean, and Judas Iscariot, the one who betrayed him. These twelve Jesus sent out with the following instructions: "Go nowhere among the Gentiles, and enter no town of the Samaritans, but go rather to the lost sheep of the house of Israel. As you go, proclaim the good news, 'The kingdom of heaven has come near.'"

- The Twelve were called by name. Do I feel called by name?
- They were sent out to play their part in God's plan. Do I need to ask for an understanding of my part in it?
- The message is always the same: "the kingdom of heaven has come near." Can I proclaim that with conviction?

Thursday 13th July   Hosea 11:1–4

When Israel was a child, I loved him, and out of Egypt I called my son. The more I called them, the more they went from me; they kept sacrificing to the Baals, and offering incense to idols. Yet it was I who taught Ephraim to walk, I took them up in my arms; but they did not know that I healed them. I led them with cords of human kindness, with bands of love. I was to them like those who lift infants to their cheeks. I bent down to them and fed them.

- The Lord is speaking here, full of tenderness for his children—no matter what.
- Can I put myself into the picture here?

Friday 14th July   Matthew 10:16–20

Jesus said to his disciples, "See, I am sending you out like sheep into the midst of wolves; so be wise as serpents and innocent as doves. Beware of them, for they will hand you over to councils and flog you in their synagogues; and you will be dragged before governors and kings because of me, as a testimony to them and the Gentiles. When they hand you over, do not worry about how you are to speak or what you are to say; for what you are to say will be given to you at that time; for it is not you who speak, but the Spirit of your Father speaking through you."

- Jesus is preparing his followers for dangers and trials ahead.
- How does this relate to my life? Can I hear Jesus speaking to me about my experience?
- Can I truly hear his great promise of protection and support?

Saturday 15th July   Matthew 10:28–31

Jesus said to his disciples, "Do not fear those who kill the body but cannot kill the soul; rather fear him who can destroy both soul and body in hell. Are not two sparrows sold for a penny? Yet not one of them will fall to the ground apart from your Father. And even the hairs of your head are all counted. So do not be afraid; you are of more value than many sparrows."

- In the space of four verses, Jesus tells us that there is a great deal to fear in our lives and also that we have no reason to be afraid!
- Do I need to acknowledge the danger, moral and physical, around me?
- But then, can I accept just how special I am to God and live in complete trust?

Something to think and pray about each day this week:

Taking our time

Jesus loved parties, loved eating with his friends. It is no accident that many of his parables center on banquets, and many of his moving encounters were at parties. Remember his dinner with Martha, who was distracted with all the serving, and Mary, who sat down at his feet and listened to him speaking. When Martha complained, Jesus told her affectionately: "Martha, Martha, you worry and fret about so many things, and yet few are needed, indeed only one. Mary has chosen the better part."

We need to be reminded of that. It is easy to feel lazy, self-indulgent, guilty, when all we are doing is sitting at Jesus' feet. There are clothes to be washed, cars to be cleaned, meals to be readied. We will reach those jobs in due time. What we do in prayer is the better part. We see ourselves at the feet of Jesus and fill our imagination with his presence. Then we listen to him speaking, take a phrase or two, and savor it slowly, hear what he is saying to me here and now.

The Presence of God
To be present is to arrive as one is and open up to the other.
At this instant, as I arrive here, God is present waiting for me.
God always arrives before me, desiring to connect with me
even more than my most intimate friend.
I take a moment and greet my loving God.

Freedom
Everything has the potential to draw forth from me a fuller love
and life.
Yet my desires are often fixed, caught, on illusions of fulfillment.
I ask that God, through my freedom, may orchestrate
my desires in a vibrant loving melody rich in harmony.

Consciousness
Knowing that God loves me unconditionally,
I can afford to be honest about how I am.
How has the last day been, and how do I feel now?
I share my feelings openly with the Lord.

The Word
I take my time to read the Word of God, slowly, a few times,
allowing myself to dwell on anything that strikes me. (Please
turn to your scripture on the following pages. Inspiration points
are there should you need them. When you are ready, return
here to continue.)

Conversation
What feelings are rising in me
as I pray and reflect on God's Word?
I imagine Jesus himself sitting or standing beside me,
and open my heart to him.

Conclusion
Glory be to the Father, and to the Son, and to the Holy Spirit,
As it was in the beginning, is now and ever shall be,
World without end. Amen

Sunday 16th July, Fifteenth Sunday in Ordinary Time
Mark 6:7–13

Jesus called the twelve and began to send them out two by two, and gave them authority over the unclean spirits. He ordered them to take nothing for their journey except a staff; no bread, no bag, no money in their belts; but to wear sandals and not to put on two tunics. He said to them, "Wherever you enter a house, stay there until you leave the place. If any place will not welcome you and they refuse to hear you, as you leave, shake off the dust that is on your feet as a testimony against them." So they went out and proclaimed that all should repent. They cast out many demons, and anointed with oil many who were sick and cured them.

- The ones who were called are now sent out on a mission. Do I make the transition from being called and loved to being sent out?
- Like all pilgrims, the Christian missionary travels light. Is there anything here for me?

Monday 17th July
Matthew 10:37–39

Jesus said to his disciples, "Whoever loves father or mother more than me is not worthy of me; and whoever loves son or daughter more than me is not worthy of me; and whoever does not take up the cross and follow me is not worthy of me. Those who find their life will lose it, and those who lose their life for my sake will find it."

- These hard words are in fact an offer of life.
- What might the call to "take up the cross" or "lose my life" mean in my context?
- Do I believe that this kind of losing will lead to true life?

Tuesday 18th July
Matthew 11:20–24

Then Jesus began to reproach the cities in which most of his deeds of power had been done, because they did not repent.

"Woe to you, Chorazin! Woe to you, Bethsaida! For if the deeds of power done in you had been done in Tyre and Sidon, they would have repented long ago in sackcloth and ashes. But I tell you, on the day of judgment it will be more tolerable for Tyre and Sidon than for you. And you, Capernaum, will you be exalted to heaven? No, you will be brought down to Hades. For if the deeds of power done in you had been done in Sodom, it would have remained until this day. But I tell you that on the day of judgment it will be more tolerable for the land of Sodom than for you."

- If sin is a turning away from God, then repentance is a turning back. Can I recognize my need to turn back?
- What "deeds of power" is Jesus doing around me? Can I ask for the grace to see them, recognize them, respond to them?
- If I think repentance is for other, really sinful people, Jesus is telling me, "Wake up and smell the coffee."

Wednesday 19th July   Matthew 11:25–27

At that time Jesus said, "I thank you, Father, Lord of heaven and earth, because you have hidden these things from the wise and the intelligent and have revealed them to infants; yes, Father, for such was your gracious will. All things have been handed over to me by my Father; and no one knows the Son except the Father, and no one knows the Father except the Son and anyone to whom the Son chooses to reveal him."

- Jesus chooses those to whom he reveals "these things." It may not always be those considered by society to be wise or in the know.
- The disciples were a pretty motley crew, and yet they were open to hearing about the kingdom.
- Wherever I may be in the process of knowing the Son, can I be like a child and open my heart?

Thursday 20th July   Matthew 11:28–30

Jesus said, "Come to me, all you that are weary and are carrying heavy burdens, and I will give you rest. Take my yoke upon you, and learn from me; for I am gentle and humble in heart, and you will find rest for your souls. For my yoke is easy, and my burden is light."

- I imagine Jesus beside me, speaking these words to me as if for the first time.
- I look at my journey. Am I carrying heavy burdens or am I sailing along? I can talk to Jesus about this.
- Are there certain steps I need to take if I am burdened? I rest assured that Jesus is happy to help.

Friday 21st July   Matthew 12:1–8

At that time Jesus went through the grainfields on the sabbath; his disciples were hungry, and they began to pluck heads of grain and to eat. When the Pharisees saw it, they said to him, "Look, your disciples are doing what is not lawful to do on the sabbath." He said to them, "Have you not read what David did when he and his companions were hungry? He entered the house of God and ate the bread of the Presence, which it was not lawful for him or his companions to eat, but only for the priests. Or have you not read in the law that on the sabbath the priests in the temple break the sabbath and yet are guiltless? I tell you, something greater than the temple is here. But if you had known what this means, 'I desire mercy and not sacrifice,' you would not have condemned the guiltless. For the Son of Man is lord of the sabbath."

- What is the top priority for the Pharisees in this scene? What is the be-all and end-all for them?
- What is the priority for Jesus?
- What is the priority for me?

Saturday 22nd July, Feast of Mary Magdalene
John 20:11–18

But Mary stood weeping outside the tomb. As she wept, she bent over to look into the tomb; and she saw two angels in white, sitting where the body of Jesus had been lying, one at the head and the other at the feet. They said to her, "Woman, why are you weeping?" She said to them, "They have taken away my Lord, and I do not know where they have laid him." When she had said this, she turned around and saw Jesus standing there, but she did not know that it was Jesus. Jesus said to her, "Woman, why are you weeping? Whom are you looking for?" Supposing him to be the gardener, she said to him, "Sir, if you have carried him away, tell me where you have laid him, and I will take him away." Jesus said to her, "Mary!" She turned and said to him in Hebrew, "Rabbouni!" (which means Teacher). Jesus said to her, "Do not hold on to me, because I have not yet ascended to the Father. But go to my brothers and say to them, 'I am ascending to my Father and your Father, to my God and your God.'" Mary Magdalene went and announced to the disciples, "I have seen the Lord"; and she told them that he had said these things to her.

- Allow yourself to see Mary in great distress. The one she longs to see is there and she can't recognize him.
- The sound of her own name breaks through the cloud of her unknowing.
- Can I imagine Jesus calling me by my name? How does it sound?

july 23–29

Something to think and pray about each day this week:

Being at home

In one of the gospel parables, the rich man is mulling over his treasures and plans to build even bigger barns to store all his crops. He relishes his security: "My soul, you have plenty of good things laid by for many years to come." Jesus reflects: "A person's life is not made secure by what he owns."

As we grow quiet in prayer, our hearts can be invaded in the same way by false securities. By measuring my heart in past treasures, I am fossilized and dead, for life is only in the present. So to each of these past treasures, I say goodbye, explaining that, grateful though I am that it came into my life, it must move out, or my heart will never learn to love the present.

We draw energy from prayer to the extent that it draws us into the here and now. The only place I can meet God is in this body, with this heart and mind, in this room. It is not an exercise of fantasy, or placing myself above the clouds in some imaginary heaven. I find God, or rather God finds me, when I am home to myself.

The Presence of God

What is present to me is what has a hold on my becoming.
I reflect on the presence of God always there in love,
amidst the many things that have a hold on me.
I pause and pray that I may let God
affect my becoming in this precise moment.

Freedom

There are very few people
who realize what God would make of them
if they abandoned themselves into his hands,
and let themselves be formed by his grace (St. Ignatius).
I ask for the grace to trust myself totally to God's love.

Consciousness

In the presence of my loving Creator,
I look honestly at my feelings over the last day,
the highs, the lows and the level ground.
Can I see where the Lord has been present?

The Word

God speaks to each one of us individually. I need to listen to
what he is saying to me. (Please turn to your scripture on the
following pages. Inspiration points are there should you need
them. When you are ready, return here to continue.)

Conversation

What is stirring in me as I pray?
Am I consoled, troubled, left cold?
I imagine Jesus himself standing or sitting at my side,
and share my feelings with him.

Conclusion

Glory be to the Father, and to the Son, and to the Holy Spirit,
As it was in the beginning, is now and ever shall be,
World without end. Amen

Sunday 23rd July, Sixteenth Sunday in Ordinary Time
Mark 6:30–34

The apostles gathered around Jesus, and told him all that they had done and taught. He said to them, "Come away to a deserted place all by yourselves and rest a while." For many were coming and going, and they had no leisure even to eat. And they went away in the boat to a deserted place by themselves. Now many saw them going and recognized them, and they hurried there on foot from all the towns and arrived ahead of them. As he went ashore, he saw a great crowd; and he had compassion for them, because they were like sheep without a shepherd; and he began to teach them many things.

- I imagine myself in the scene for a few moments. Who am I? How do I feel?
- Jesus has time for the disciples and for the crowds. Can I see the chances I have to spend time with him in my day?
- These can be times of just being, of listening, of challenge. What can I hear from the one who wants to be with me today?

Monday 24th July
Matthew 12:38–42

Then some of the scribes and Pharisees said to him, "Teacher, we wish to see a sign from you." But he answered them, "An evil and adulterous generation asks for a sign, but no sign will be given to it except the sign of the prophet Jonah. For just as Jonah was three days and three nights in the belly of the sea monster, so for three days and three nights the Son of Man will be in the heart of the earth. The people of Nineveh will rise up at the judgment with this generation and condemn it, because they repented at the proclamation of Jonah, and see, something greater than Jonah is here! The queen of the South will rise up at the judgment with this generation and condemn it, because she came from the ends of the earth to listen to the wisdom of Solomon, and see, something greater than Solomon is here!"

- Perhaps if I was a Pharisee and I met this wandering healer—prophet, I would ask for a sign too.
- But Jesus is having none of it. Something greater is here, standing in front of me. What is my reaction? Doubt, trust, fear, confusion, love? Or something else?
- The people of Nineveh listened and responded. Can I do the same? Can I hear the words Jesus speaks to me now?

Tuesday 25th July, St. James, Apostle   Matthew 20:20–28

Then the mother of the sons of Zebedee came to him with her sons, and kneeling before him, she asked a favor of him. And he said to her, "What do you want?" She said to him, "Declare that these two sons of mine will sit, one at your right hand and one at your left, in your kingdom." But Jesus answered, "You do not know what you are asking. Are you able to drink the cup that I am about to drink?" They said to him, "We are able." He said to them, "You will indeed drink my cup, but to sit at my right hand and at my left, this is not mine to grant, but it is for those for whom it has been prepared by my Father." When the ten heard it, they were angry with the two brothers. But Jesus called them to him and said, "You know that the rulers of the Gentiles lord it over them, and their great ones are tyrants over them. It will not be so among you; but whoever wishes to be great among you must be your servant, and whoever wishes to be first among you must be your slave; just as the Son of Man came not to be served but to serve, and to give his life a ransom for many."

- Jesus had just finished speaking in detail about the awful suffering that awaited him when this scene transpired.
- It seems the disciples and their mother wanted to avoid any suffering on the road to glory.
- What does Jesus say?

Wednesday 26th July, Sts. Joachim and Anne
Matthew 13:4–9

Jesus told the crowds many things in parables, saying, "Listen! A sower went out to sow. And as he sowed, some seeds fell on the path, and the birds came and ate them up. Other seeds fell on rocky ground, where they did not have much soil, and they sprang up quickly, since they had no depth of soil. But when the sun rose, they were scorched; and since they had no root, they withered away. Other seeds fell among thorns, and the thorns grew up and choked them. Other seeds fell on good soil and brought forth grain, some a hundredfold, some sixty, some thirty. Let anyone with ears listen!"

- What kind of soil am I? Do I quickly become enthusiastic but cannot maintain the enthusiasm? Do I let bad influences that surround me thwart my good intentions? Or do I bear fruit abundantly?
- Jesus starts by commanding the crowd to listen, and ends by enjoining "Let anyone with ears listen!" Is being a good listener essential to being good soil?
- Am I careful about who I listen to? Do I listen to Christ, as he commands, or am I more influenced by everything else around me?

Thursday 27th July
Matthew 13:16–17

Jesus said to the disciples, "But blessed are your eyes, for they see, and your ears, for they hear. Truly I tell you, many prophets and righteous people longed to see what you see, but did not see it, and to hear what you hear, but did not hear it."

- What was it that the disciples saw and heard?
- What are the things that I long to see and hear?
- What are my deepest longings? Can I talk to the Lord about them?

Friday 28th July   **Jeremiah 3:14–17**

Return, O faithless children, says the Lord, for I am your master; I will take you, one from a city and two from a family, and I will bring you to Zion. I will give you shepherds after my own heart, who will feed you with knowledge and understanding. And when you have multiplied and increased in the land, in those days, says the Lord, they shall no longer say, "The ark of the covenant of the Lord." It shall not come to mind, or be remembered, or missed; nor shall another one be made. At that time Jerusalem shall be called the throne of the Lord, and all nations shall gather to it, to the presence of the Lord in Jerusalem, and they shall no longer stubbornly follow their own evil will.

- Do I think that God would stop giving us shepherds after his own heart?
- Who are the shepherds in my own life? If I stop to think about it, I may realize that someone is hugely important in ways I rarely appreciate.
- Am I a shepherd for other people? Are there ways in which I could be?
- Do those words, "stubbornly follow their own will," ring any bells for me?

Saturday 29th July, Feast of Martha   **John 11:19–27**

Many of the Jews had come to Martha and Mary to console them about their brother. When Martha heard that Jesus was coming, she went and met him, while Mary stayed at home. Martha said to Jesus, "Lord, if you had been here, my brother would not have died. But even now I know that God will give you whatever you ask of him." Jesus said to her, "Your brother will rise again." Martha said to him, "I know that he will rise again in the resurrection on the last day." Jesus said to her, "I am the resurrection and the life. Those who believe in me, even though they die, will live, and everyone who lives and believes in me will never die. Do you believe this?" She said to him, "Yes, Lord, I believe that you are the Messiah, the Son of God, the one coming into the world."

- In her moment of grief Martha, the woman of faith, still believes in Jesus' power to do something for her dead brother. But Jesus is going to lead her to an even deeper knowledge of himself.
- "I am the resurrection and the life," he says. This is an awesome claim. What can it mean?
- When Jesus asks "Do you believe this?" Martha makes her response. What is my response? Remember, I don't have to compare myself with Martha or anyone else.

july 30–august 5

Something to think and pray about each day this week:

Teaching us to pray

When Jesus was asked for a lesson in prayer, he spoke the *Our Father*. Ignatius Loyola, whose feast is on 31st July, suggested a way of using the Lord's Prayer. Take the words one by one, and linger on each word "as long as you find meanings, comparisons, relish and consolation in the consideration of it."

For instance, the first word, "Our," sets me in the company of all God's children. I have no corner on God. He is not just my father. I share him with the human race, and because they are his children, they are my brothers and sisters. This prayer lifts me out of self-centeredness. I am God's child, but not his only child. As he has room in his heart for others, I also need to have room.

That is just one person's approach. Each of us has distinctive angles on words like Father, heaven, forgive, daily bread, temptation, deliverance. We do not exhaust the meaning in one half-hour. As we grow older, words and language matter less in our prayer than silent contemplation. But as a lead-in to that, Ignatius's way of praying the *Our Father* is precious.

The Presence of God

God is with me, but more, God is within me.
Let me dwell for a moment on God's life-giving presence
in my body, in my mind, in my heart,
as I sit here, right now.

Freedom

A thick and shapeless tree-trunk would never believe
that it could become a statue, admired as a miracle of sculpture,
and would never submit itself to the chisel of the sculptor,
who sees by her genius what she can make of it (St. Ignatius).
I ask for the grace to let myself be shaped by my loving Creator.

Consciousness

Knowing that God loves me unconditionally,
I look honestly over the last day, its events and my feelings.
Do I have something to be grateful for? Then I give thanks.
Is there something I am sorry for? Then I ask forgiveness.

The Word

I read the Word of God slowly, a few times over, and I listen to
what God is saying to me. (Please turn to your scripture on the
following pages. Inspiration points are there should you need
them. When you are ready, return here to continue.)

Conversation

Do I notice myself reacting as I pray with the Word of God?
Do I feel challenged, comforted, angry?
Imagining Jesus sitting or standing by me,
I speak out my feelings, as one trusted friend to another.

Conclusion

Glory be to the Father, and to the Son, and to the Holy Spirit,
As it was in the beginning, is now and ever shall be,
World without end. Amen

Sunday 30th July, Seventeenth Sunday in Ordinary Time
John 6:5–13

When Jesus looked up and saw a large crowd coming toward him, he said to Philip, "Where are we to buy bread for these people to eat?" He said this to test him, for he himself knew what he was going to do. Philip answered him, "Six months' wages would not buy enough bread for each of them to get a little." One of his disciples, Andrew, Simon Peter's brother, said to him, "There is a boy here who has five barley loaves and two fish. But what are they among so many people?" Jesus said, "Make the people sit down." Now there was a great deal of grass in the place; so they sat down, about five thousand in all. Then Jesus took the loaves, and when he had given thanks, he distributed them to those who were seated; so also the fish, as much as they wanted. When they were satisfied, he told his disciples, "Gather up the fragments left over, so that nothing may be lost." So they gathered them up, and from the fragments of the five barley loaves, left by those who had eaten, they filled twelve baskets.

- Jesus shows how much God's generous power can do with just a little cooperation from us.
- Could the little boy have imagined how much good his five loaves and two fish would do in Jesus' hands?
- What is my "five loaves and two fish"? Is there a really personal message here for me?

Monday 31st July, St. Ignatius Loyola   Luke 9:23–26

Then Jesus said to the disciples, "If any want to become my followers, let them deny themselves and take up their cross daily and follow me. For those who want to save their life will lose it, and those who lose their life for my sake will save it. What does it profit them if they gain the whole world, but lose or forfeit themselves? Those who are ashamed of me and of my words, of them the Son of Man will be ashamed when he comes in his glory and the glory of the Father and of the holy angels."

- In these hard words, Jesus reminds us that following him will involve struggle and some painful choices.
- Worldly success, of itself, doesn't impress Jesus; he wants us to be impressed with other things entirely.
- Am I carrying my cross? If so, can I let Jesus encourage and strengthen me? If I am dodging the cross, can I trust him to lead me into true life?

Tuesday 1st August   Jeremiah 14:20–22

We acknowledge our wickedness, O Lord, the iniquity of our ancestors, for we have sinned against you. Do not spurn us, for your name's sake; do not dishonor your glorious throne; remember and do not break your covenant with us. Can any idols of the nations bring rain? Or can the heavens give showers? Is it not you, O Lord our God? We set our hope on you, for it is you who do all this.

- Time and again Israel had to turn back to the Lord because they had wandered off and worshipped idols, followed false gods.
- Each time, when they came to their senses they realized that false gods can do them no good like the Lord can.
- Have I been seduced by false gods, perhaps without even knowing it? I could pray for light.

Wednesday 2nd August   Matthew 13:44–46

Jesus said to the disciples, "The kingdom of heaven is like treasure hidden in a field, which someone found and hid; then in his joy he goes and sells all that he has and buys that field. Again, the kingdom of heaven is like a merchant in search of fine pearls; on finding one pearl of great value, he went and sold all that he had and bought it."

- What is my treasure? For what would I sell everything?

264

- Pearls can be deceptive. We cannot always tell fine pearls from false ones.
- How does the Kingdom of Heaven challenge my treasure or my notion of fine pearls?

Thursday 3rd August   Jeremiah 18:1–6

The word that came to Jeremiah from the Lord: "Come, go down to the potter's house, and there I will let you hear my words." So I went down to the potter's house, and there he was working at his wheel. The vessel he was making of clay was spoiled in the potter's hand, and he reworked it into another vessel, as seemed good to him. Then the word of the Lord came to me: Can I not do with you, O house of Israel, just as this potter has done? says the Lord. Just like the clay in the potter's hand, so are you in my hand, O house of Israel.

- It might be good to imagine the potter at the wheel shaping the clay in their hands, as they see best.
- How does the idea of my being clay in God's hands move me? Is it consoling? Is it threatening?
- After reading the passage again, I might want to discuss this with the Lord.

Friday 4th August   Matthew 13:54–58

Jesus came to his hometown and began to teach the people in their synagogue, so that they were astounded and said, "Where did this man get this wisdom and these deeds of power? Is not this the carpenter's son? Is not his mother called Mary? And are not his brothers James and Joseph and Simon and Judas? And are not all his sisters with us? Where then did this man get all this?" And they took offense at him. But Jesus said to them, "Prophets are not without honor except in their own country and in their own house." And he did not do many deeds of power there, because of their unbelief.

- They knew his name, his family, where he came from. They think they know all about him, but they don't know who he is.
- Their failure or refusal to acknowledge and accept him limits what Jesus can do among them.
- Do I pigeonhole Jesus in a way that restricts him, or do I label others in a way that limits them and me? Perhaps I could pray for light and help ...

Saturday 5th August   Psalm 69:15–16, 29–30

Do not let the flood sweep over me, or the deep swallow me up, or the Pit close its mouth over me. Answer me, O Lord, for your steadfast love is good; according to your abundant mercy, turn to me. But I am lowly and in pain; let your salvation, O God, protect me. I will praise the name of God with a song; I will magnify him with thanksgiving.

- This is an anguished prayer from somebody at the point of desperation.
- Can I identify with these images and feelings, either for myself or someone else?
- Even at the edge of the abyss, the psalmist seems to know that God is steadfast. Can I remember feeling that way?

Something to think and pray about each day this week:

Everyday Jesus
There is a special intimacy when we are with our closest friends. And a special responsibility.

Peter and the brothers James and John were Jesus' close friends, and they were together on a holy mountain when they saw Jesus transformed. How dazzled they must have been to see Jesus with Moses and Elijah, the two men who represented the whole of Jewish tradition!

But there was even more, almost beyond imagining: the very presence of God in the cloud, and the voice saying, "This is my beloved Son. Listen to him!"

Do we listen to and accept everything that Jesus says and does—about rejection, suffering, dying, and rising again? Or do we resist and seek out only the good news we want to hear? Or like Peter, do we prefer to put down roots, to build, and stay where we are comfortable?

When the vision disappeared and they walked off the holy mountain, they were left with "only" Jesus, the ordinary Jesus who is with each of us, each day.

The Presence of God
As I sit here, the beating of my heart,
the ebb and flow of my breathing, the movements of my mind
are all signs of God's ongoing creation of me.
I pause for a moment, and become aware
of this presence of God within me.

Freedom
I ask for the grace
to let go of my own concerns
and be open to what God is asking of me,
to let myself be guided and formed by my loving Creator.

Consciousness
How do I find myself today?
Where am I with God? With others?
Do I have something to be grateful for? Then I give thanks.
Is there something I am sorry for? Then I ask forgiveness.

The Word
I take my time to read the Word of God, slowly, a few times,
allowing myself to dwell on anything that strikes me. (Please
turn to your scripture on the following pages. Inspiration points
are there should you need them. When you are ready, return
here to continue.)

Conversation
Remembering that I am still in God's presence,
I imagine Jesus himself standing or sitting beside me,
and say whatever is on my mind, whatever is in my heart,
speaking as one friend to another.

Conclusion
Glory be to the Father, and to the Son, and to the Holy Spirit,
As it was in the beginning, is now and ever shall be,
World without end. Amen

Sunday 6th August, The Transfiguration of the Lord
Luke 9:28b–36

Jesus took with him Peter and John and James, and went up on the mountain to pray. And while he was praying, the appearance of his face changed, and his clothes became dazzling white. Suddenly they saw two men, Moses and Elijah, talking to him. They appeared in glory and were speaking of his departure, which he was about to accomplish at Jerusalem. Now Peter and his companions were weighed down with sleep; but since they had stayed awake, they saw his glory and the two men who stood with him. Just as they were leaving him, Peter said to Jesus, "Master, it is good for us to be here; let us make three dwellings, one for you, one for Moses, and one for Elijah"—not knowing what he said. While he was saying this, a cloud came and overshadowed them; and they were terrified as they entered the cloud. Then from the cloud came a voice that said, "This is my Son, my Chosen; listen to him!" When the voice had spoken, Jesus was found alone. And they kept silent and in those days told no one any of the things they had seen.

- This scene invites me to "be there" and see and hear what is happening.
- In the presence of Jesus' glory how do I respond? Peter seems to ramble on with excitement. What about me?
- The Father's words are a remarkable affirmation. How do they touch me?

Monday 7th August
Matthew 14:15–21

When it was evening, the disciples came to Jesus and said, "This is a deserted place, and the hour is now late; send the crowds away so that they may go into the villages and buy food for themselves." Jesus said to them, "They need not go away; you give them something to eat." They replied, "We have nothing here but five loaves and two fish." And he said, "Bring them here to me." Then he ordered the crowds to sit down on the grass. Taking the five loaves and the two fish, he looked up to heaven, and blessed and broke the loaves, and gave them to the disciples, and the disciples gave them to the crowds. And all ate and were filled; and they took up what was left over of the broken pieces, twelve baskets full. And those who ate were about five thousand men, besides women and children.

- This story shows the enormity of human need for sustenance and, even more, the desire of God to be lavish in response.
- Can I identify with the hunger of the crowd?
- I consider the ways that God responds through the details of the story.

Tuesday 8th August   Matthew 14:22–33

Jesus made the disciples get into the boat and go on ahead to the other side, while he dismissed the crowds. And after he had dismissed the crowds, he went up the mountain by himself to pray. When evening came, he was there alone, but by this time the boat, battered by the waves, was far from the land, for the wind was against them. And early in the morning he came walking toward them on the sea. But when the disciples saw him walking on the sea, they were terrified, saying, "It is a ghost!" And they cried out in fear. But immediately Jesus spoke to them and said, "Take heart, it is I; do not be afraid." Peter answered him, "Lord, if it is you, command me to come to you on the water." He said, "Come." So Peter got out of the boat, started walking on the water, and came toward Jesus. But when he noticed the strong wind, he became frightened, and beginning to sink, he cried out, "Lord, save me!" Jesus immediately reached out his hand and caught him, saying to him, "You of little faith, why did you doubt?" When they got into the boat, the wind ceased. And those in the boat worshiped him, saying, "Truly you are the Son of God."

- Can I imagine myself in the boat going through all of this? I might even be Peter.
- What happens? What do I see and hear? What emotions do I have as the scene unfolds?
- Who is this Jesus?

Wednesday 9th August   Matthew 15:21–28

Jesus left that place and went away to the district of Tyre and Sidon. Just then a Canaanite woman from that region came out and started shouting, "Have mercy on me, Lord, Son of David; my daughter is tormented by a demon." But he did not answer her at all. And his disciples came and urged him, saying, "Send her away, for she keeps shouting after us." He answered, "I was sent only to the lost sheep of the house of Israel." But she came and knelt before him, saying, "Lord, help me." He answered, "It is not fair to take the children's food and throw it to the dogs." She said, "Yes, Lord, yet even the dogs eat the crumbs that fall from their masters' table." Then Jesus answered her, "Woman, great is your faith! Let it be done for you as you wish." And her daughter was healed instantly.

- What motivates this strong and tenacious woman? What deep desires and hopes keep her going in the face of rejection?
- God seems to be incapable of refusing this woman's determined faith.
- What does this say to me about my own life, about different forms of rejection and discouragement?

Thursday 10th August, St. Lawrence   John 12:24–26

Jesus said, "Very truly, I tell you, unless a grain of wheat falls into the earth and dies, it remains just a single grain; but if it dies, it bears much fruit. Those who love their life lose it, and those who hate their life in this world will keep it for eternal life.

Whoever serves me must follow me, and where I am, there will my servant be also. Whoever serves me, the Father will honor."

- Is this business of the grain of wheat just a cliché for me?
- Can I think of any experience of suffering and loss that has borne fruit because of God's grace? How did it happen?
- Does the idea of losing my life simply frighten or confuse me? Can I talk about this to the Lord?

Friday 11th August   Matthew 16:24–28

Then Jesus told his disciples, "If any want to become my followers, let them deny themselves and take up their cross and follow me. For those who want to save their life will lose it, and those who lose their life for my sake will find it. For what will it profit them if they gain the whole world but forfeit their life? Or what will they give in return for their life? For the Son of Man is to come with his angels in the glory of his Father, and then he will repay everyone for what has been done. Truly I tell you, there are some standing here who will not taste death before they see the Son of Man coming in his kingdom."

- Following Jesus means taking up my cross daily. How do I react to this? Do I rebel at the thought? Do I nod in acceptance but in reality ignore it? Does it frighten me?
- Am I carrying a cross right now? Can it really be the way to deeper life?
- I ask God to help me understand these things.

Saturday 12th August   Matthew 17:14–20

When they came to the crowd, a man came to Jesus, knelt before him, and said, "Lord, have mercy on my son, for he is an epileptic and he suffers terribly; he often falls into the fire and often into the water. And I brought him to your disciples, but they could not cure him." Jesus answered, "You faithless and perverse generation, how much longer must I be with you? How much longer must I put up with you? Bring him here to me." And Jesus rebuked the demon, and it came out of him, and the boy was cured instantly. Then the disciples came to Jesus privately and said, "Why could we not cast it out?" He said to them, "Because of your little faith. For truly I tell you, if you have faith the size of a mustard seed, you will say to this mountain, 'Move from here to there,' and it will move; and nothing will be impossible for you."

- Here is a short story with many elements: a boy in great distress; his father on his knees at his wit's end; Jesus' disciples doing the best they could; Jesus frustrated with their failure to understand and believe.
- Where do I fit in to these elements?
- Jesus is very challenging in his words to the disciples. Can I hear the challenge in a way that leads me forward?

Something to think and pray about each day this week:

The changed community

The sixth chapter of John's gospel is rich in spiritual nourishment. The feeding of the 5,000 with five loaves of bread and two fish is linked to the Last Supper and to the eucharist. It was at the Last Supper that Jesus linked his flesh with the bread that he broke and shared with his disciples, and also linked his blood with the cup that was passed around, the blood that was the pledge of an unbreakable bond between Jesus and his people.

By sharing the eucharist we are proclaiming our deepest desire to be totally identified with Jesus. And we do this as a united community coming to the table to share the body and the blood of Christ.

The community gathering has great value as a support to those in the community, yet the eucharist is more than a community gathering.

We say that Jesus is present in the gathered community, but do we accept his presence to allow him to bring about a transformation in us? In faith we know that the risen Jesus wants to change us, but his offered gift has to be received, appreciated, used, and shared.

Lord, help us to change, to grow as human beings, to be a part of a community that is being transformed into the family of God.

The Presence of God
I pause for a moment
and reflect on God's life-giving presence
in every part of my body, in everything around me,
in the whole of my life.

Freedom
I ask for the grace to believe
in what I could be and do
if I only allowed God, my loving Creator,
to continue to create me, guide me and shape me.

Consciousness
In God's loving presence I unwind the past day,
starting from now and looking back, moment by moment.
I gather in all the goodness and light, in gratitude.
I attend to the shadows and what they say to me,
seeking healing, courage, forgiveness.

The Word
God speaks to each one of us individually. I need to listen to
what he is saying to me. (Please turn to your scripture on the
following pages. Inspiration points are there should you need
them. When you are ready, return here to continue.)

Conversation
How has God's Word moved me? Has it left me cold?
Has it consoled me or moved me to act in a new way?
I imagine Jesus standing or sitting beside me,
I turn and share my feelings with him.

Conclusion
Glory be to the Father, and to the Son, and to the Holy Spirit,
As it was in the beginning, is now and ever shall be,
World without end. Amen

Sunday 13th August, Nineteenth Sunday in Ordinary Time
John 6:47–51

Jesus said to the crowd, "Very truly, I tell you, whoever believes has eternal life. I am the bread of life. Your ancestors ate the manna in the wilderness, and they died. This is the bread that comes down from heaven, so that one may eat of it and not die. I am the living bread that came down from heaven. Whoever eats of this bread will live forever; and the bread that I will give for the life of the world is my flesh."

- I might think, firstly, of my relationship with bread (food), the daily essential for life and energy.
- By extension, then, what does it mean to me that Jesus is the Bread of Life or Living Bread?

Monday 14th August, St. Maximilian Kolbe
John 15:16–17

Jesus said to the disciples, "You did not choose me but I chose you. And I appointed you to go and bear fruit, fruit that will last, so that the Father will give you whatever you ask him in my name. I am giving you these commands so that you may love one another."

- How do I respond to the idea that Jesus chose—and continues to choose—me? Can I let that truth sink in? Choose me.
- In my particular circumstances, how does Jesus want me to bear fruit? It is his will that I love concretely in these circumstances of mine. I might ask him to show me where and how.

Tuesday 15th August, The Assumption of the Blessed Virgin Mary
Luke 1:39–47

In those days Mary set out and went with haste to a Judean town in the hill country, where she entered the house of Zechariah and greeted Elizabeth. When Elizabeth heard Mary's greeting, the child leaped in her womb. And Elizabeth was filled with the Holy Spirit and exclaimed with a loud cry, "Blessed are you among women, and blessed is the fruit of your womb. And why has this happened to me, that the mother of my Lord comes to me? For as soon as I heard the sound of your greeting, the child in my womb leaped for joy. And blessed is she who believed that there would be a fulfillment of what was spoken to her by the Lord." And Mary said, "My soul magnifies the Lord, and my spirit rejoices in God my Savior."

- Here is a meeting between two extraordinary women, each of whom is expecting a baby. They both show a tremendous capacity to go beyond themselves.
- As I look at the scene what details catch my attention? How does it move me?

Wednesday 16th August   Matthew 18:18–20

Jesus said to the disciples, "Truly I tell you, whatever you bind on earth will be bound in heaven, and whatever you loose on earth will be loosed in heaven. Again, truly I tell you, if two of you agree on earth about anything you ask, it will be done for you by my Father in heaven. For where two or three are gathered in my name, I am there among them."

- This is a wonderful promise that Jesus is among us when we are united in his name.
- What quality of presence is evident when we are in his name? Am I present to others in a way that allows Jesus to be among us?
- What does the Lord want to teach me about this?

Thursday 17th August   **Matthew 18:21–22**

Then Peter came and said to Jesus, "Lord, if another member of the church sins against me, how often should I forgive? As many as seven times?" Jesus said to him, "Not seven times, but, I tell you, seventy-seven times."

- Jesus' answer is short and sweet. Perhaps I should take some time to try and see how the call to forgiveness affects me.

Friday 18th August   **Matthew 19:3–6**

Some Pharisees came to Jesus, and to test him they asked, "Is it lawful for a man to divorce his wife for any cause?" He answered, "Have you not read that the one who made them at the beginning 'made them male and female,' and said, 'For this reason a man shall leave his father and mother and be joined to his wife, and the two shall become one flesh'? So they are no longer two, but one flesh. Therefore what God has joined together, let no one separate."

- As with everything in Jesus' life and ministry, this strong and demanding teaching comes from his desire to love and support men and women in their lives.
- In my own life—or close to me—I will know of both the joy and the pain of people's struggles to respond to Jesus' teaching.
- Can I simply be in God's loving presence, wherever I am?

Saturday 19th August   **Matthew 19:13–15**

Then little children were being brought to Jesus in order that he might lay his hands on them and pray. The disciples spoke sternly to those who brought them; but Jesus said, "Let the little children come to me, and do not stop them; for it is to such as these that the kingdom of heaven belongs." And he laid his hands on them and went on his way.

- Imagine the scene: Jesus is calling for the children to be let through. What attitudes do I see in him? Can I learn from him?
- What does Jesus see in children that he wants to see grow in me?

Something to think and pray about each day this week:

The strong hand
Walking in Jerusalem many years ago, I passed a Jewish family walking to the Western Wall. The tall bearded father was holding his four-year-old son with one hand, his wife with the other while she held onto her daughter. A few minutes later in a thickening crowd, I heard wailing. The little boy had come loose from his father's hand and felt lost. He was crying desperately for his Daddy: "Abba! Abba!"

Abba, Father, in prayer I reach for you. You are my secure base. Let me feel your strong hand holding mine, your fingers sensing my weakness, guiding me with a sense of purpose and direction. I do not take it for granted that I can call you "Abba, Daddy." I treasure it. That is precious to me. To know that you love me as a father fuels me on my way.

The Presence of God
The world is charged with the grandeur of God (Gerard Manley Hopkins).
I dwell for a moment on the presence of God
around me, in every part of my body,
and deep within my being.

Freedom
"In these days, God taught me
as a schoolteacher teaches a pupil" (St. Ignatius).
I remind myself that there are things God has to teach me yet,
and ask for the grace to hear them and let them change me.

Consciousness
I exist in a web of relationships—links to nature, people, God.
I trace out these links, giving thanks for the life that flows
through them.
Some links are twisted or broken: I may feel regret, anger,
disappointment.
I pray for the gift of acceptance and forgiveness.

The Word
I read the Word of God slowly, a few times over, and I listen to
what God is saying to me. (Please turn to your scripture on the
following pages. Inspirations points are there should you need
them. When you are ready, return here to continue.)

Conversation
What feelings are rising in me
as I pray and reflect on God's Word?
I imagine Jesus himself sitting or standing beside me,
and open my heart to him.

Conclusion
Glory be to the Father, and to the Son, and to the Holy Spirit,
As it was in the beginning, is now and ever shall be,
World without end. Amen

Sunday 20th August, Twentieth Sunday in Ordinary Time
Ephesians 5:15–20

Be careful then how you live, not as unwise people but as wise, making the most of the time, because the days are evil. So do not be foolish, but understand what the will of the Lord is. Do not get drunk with wine, for that is debauchery; but be filled with the Spirit, as you sing psalms and hymns and spiritual songs among yourselves, singing and making melody to the Lord in your hearts, giving thanks to God the Father at all times and for everything in the name of our Lord Jesus Christ.

- Here Paul is exhorting the Christians in Ephesus to remember the fabulous vocation they each have and not to be misled. He is highlighting the negative influences that can undermine our best intentions.
- What's my reaction to this exhortation? Do I dismiss it as too negative? Do I turn too quickly to guilt that paralyzes me?
- Can I sit in the presence of the Lord who is calling me forward to a new and deeper life?

Monday 21st August   Matthew 19:16–22

Then someone came to Jesus and said, "Teacher, what good deed must I do to have eternal life?" And he said to him, "Why do you ask me about what is good? There is only one who is good. If you wish to enter into life, keep the commandments." He said to him, "Which ones?" And Jesus said, "You shall not murder; You shall not commit adultery; You shall not steal; You shall not bear false witness; Honor your father and mother; also, You shall love your neighbor as yourself." The young man said to him, "I have kept all these; what do I still lack?" Jesus said to him, "If you wish to be perfect, go, sell your possessions, and give the money to the poor, and you will have treasure in heaven; then come, follow me." When the young man heard this word, he went away grieving, for he had many possessions.

- The young man very much wanted to be united with God and to gain eternal life. However, there were other things that he wanted more.
- His attachment to possessions was not obvious to him before he met Jesus.
- Are there any attachments in my life that stand between me and God, especially any that are not obvious?

Tuesday 22nd August   **Matthew 19:23–26**

Then Jesus said to his disciples, "Truly I tell you, it will be hard for a rich person to enter the kingdom of heaven. Again I tell you, it is easier for a camel to go through the eye of a needle than for someone who is rich to enter the kingdom of God." When the disciples heard this, they were greatly astounded and said, "Then who can be saved?" But Jesus looked at them and said, "For mortals it is impossible, but for God all things are possible."

- It is hard for a "rich" person to enter the kingdom of God.
- What are my riches? It may be money. My riches may be something else entirely.
- In what way is God, for whom all things are possible, trying to move my heart away from riches?

Wednesday 23rd August   **Psalm 23:1–4**

The Lord is my shepherd, I shall not want. He makes me lie down in green pastures; he leads me beside still waters; he restores my soul. He leads me in right paths for his name's sake. Even though I walk through the darkest valley, I fear no evil; for you are with me; your rod and your staff—they comfort me.

- These holy words have been made even holier by their constant repetition over thousands of years.
- Can I sit with them, mull over them, and allow their freshness to touch me?

Thursday 24th August, St. Bartholomew   John 1:45–51

Philip found Nathanael and said to him, "We have found him about whom Moses in the law and also the prophets wrote, Jesus son of Joseph from Nazareth." Nathanael said to him, "Can anything good come out of Nazareth?" Philip said to him, "Come and see." When Jesus saw Nathanael coming toward him, he said of him, "Here is truly an Israelite in whom there is no deceit!" Nathanael asked him, "Where did you get to know me?" Jesus answered, "I saw you under the fig tree before Philip called you." Nathanael replied, "Rabbi, you are the Son of God! You are the King of Israel!" Jesus answered, "Do you believe because I told you that I saw you under the fig tree? You will see greater things than these." And he said to him, "Very truly, I tell you, you will see heaven opened and the angels of God ascending and descending upon the Son of Man."

- Can I put myself in Nathanael's shoes?
- When I hear great news, is my reaction like his? How do I react?
- Do I hear the words "come and see" addressed to me?
- How do I respond?

Friday 25th August   Matthew 22:34–40

When the Pharisees heard that Jesus had silenced the Sadducees, they gathered together, and one of them, a lawyer, asked him a question to test him. "Teacher, which commandment in the law is the greatest?" He said to him, "'You shall love the Lord your God with all your heart, and with all your soul, and with all your mind.' This is the greatest and first commandment. And a second is like it: 'You shall love your neighbor as yourself.' On these two commandments hang all the law and the prophets."

- The Pharisees' question was probably guided by their narrow assumptions of what is really important. Jesus' answer shows that what's really important is utterly simple.

- Can I let myself be moved by the great command? In what way does the "Pharisee" in me make me lose sight of what's really important?

Saturday 26th August   Matthew 23:1–7

Then Jesus said to the crowds and to his disciples, "The scribes and the Pharisees sit on Moses' seat; therefore, do whatever they teach you and follow it; but do not do as they do, for they do not practice what they teach. They tie up heavy burdens, hard to bear, and lay them on the shoulders of others; but they themselves are unwilling to lift a finger to move them. They do all their deeds to be seen by others; for they make their phylacteries broad and their fringes long. They love to have the place of honor at banquets and the best seats in the synagogues, and to be greeted with respect in the marketplaces, and to have people call them rabbi."

- When we hear Jesus' words about the scribes and Pharisees, it is often quite easy to apply them today. We can often think of other people to whom the various images and scenarios apply.
- What about me?

Something to think and pray about each day this week:

Coming home

We start prayer by coming into the presence of God, meaning what? "Nothing known to the senses," we read in the Letter to the Hebrews. The imagination boggles: "not a blazing fire, or trumpeting thunder, or a great voice speaking. . . . What you have come to is Mount Zion and the city of the living God, the heavenly Jerusalem, with the whole church in which everyone is a first-born child and a citizen of heaven."

A "first-born child," he says. We belong here, not as strangers creeping into an awesome temple, but as children taking our places at the family table. Those who have come close to death remember an overwhelming sense of happiness within reach; they know they are coming home. We are not there on sufferance, but because it is our place.

When I seek you, Lord, I find you waiting for me, responding to all the movements of my heart. Let me live more and more in your presence.

The Presence of God
As I sit here, God is present,
breathing life into me and into everything around me.
For a few moments, I sit silently,
and become aware of God's loving presence.

Freedom
If God were trying to tell me something, would I know?
If God were reassuring me or challenging me, would I notice?
I ask for the grace to be free of my own preoccupations
and open to what God may be saying to me.

Consciousness
How am I really feeling? Light-hearted? Heavy-hearted?
I may be very much at peace, happy to be here.
Equally, I may be frustrated, worried or angry.
I acknowledge how I really am. It is the real me that the Lord
loves.

The Word
I take my time to read the Word of God, slowly, a few times,
allowing myself to dwell on anything that strikes me. (Please
turn to your scripture on the following pages. Inspiration points
are there should you need them. When you are ready, return
here to continue.)

Conversation
What is stirring in me as I pray?
Am I consoled, troubled, left cold?
I imagine Jesus himself standing or sitting at my side,
and share my feelings with him.

Conclusion
Glory be to the Father, and to the Son, and to the Holy Spirit,
As it was in the beginning, is now and ever shall be,
World without end. Amen

Sunday 27th August, Twenty-first Sunday in Ordinary Time
John 6:64–69

Jesus said to the disciples, "But among you there are some who do not believe." For he knew from the first who were the ones that did not believe, and who was the one that would betray him. And he said, "For this reason I have told you that no one can come to me unless it is granted by the Father." Because of this many of his disciples turned back and no longer went about with him. So Jesus asked the twelve, "Do you also wish to go away?" Simon Peter answered him, "Lord, to whom can we go? You have the words of eternal life. We have come to believe and know that you are the Holy One of God."

- When Jesus spoke strongly about his oneness with the Father and his role in salvation, some people felt it was more than they could take and turned away. How do I respond to that: with shock, sadness, resentment, sympathy?
- Jesus' challenge, "Do you also wish to go away?" is addressed to me too.

Monday 28th August, St. Augustine   Matthew 23:8–12

Jesus said to the crowds and to his disciples, "But you are not to be called rabbi, for you have one teacher, and you are all students. And call no one your father on earth, for you have one Father—the one in heaven. Nor are you to be called instructors, for you have one instructor, the Messiah. The greatest among you will be your servant. All who exalt themselves will be humbled, and all who humble themselves will be exalted."

- Jesus is unmasking the perennial tendency of leaders to exalt themselves over others. Among his followers the authentic leadership would be exercised by servants.
- What does this say to me? Do I need to change my attitude, whether as a leader or as a follower?

Tuesday 29th August Matthew 23:23–26

Jesus said, "Woe to you, scribes and Pharisees, hypocrites! For you tithe mint, dill, and cummin, and have neglected the weightier matters of the law: justice and mercy and faith. It is these you ought to have practiced without neglecting the others. You blind guides! You strain out a gnat but swallow a camel! Woe to you, scribes and Pharisees, hypocrites! For you clean the outside of the cup and of the plate, but inside they are full of greed and self-indulgence. You blind Pharisee! First clean the inside of the cup, so that the outside also may become clean."

- Here Jesus is really raising his voice. The human tendency to concentrate on superficial details to the exclusion of what really matters is deeply engrained and needs to be challenged.
- Can I let him challenge me?
- Do I need to be challenged about justice, mercy, and faith?

Wednesday 30th August Matthew 23:27–28

Jesus said, "Woe to you, scribes and Pharisees, hypocrites! For you are like whitewashed tombs, which on the outside look beautiful, but inside they are full of the bones of the dead and of all kinds of filth. So you also on the outside look righteous to others, but inside you are full of hypocrisy and lawlessness."

- "What really matters is to look good!" Does this ring a bell with me?
- Can I allow my preoccupation with appearances to be examined?
- Any challenge must be seen in the context of the infinite love of the Father who wants me to be with him.

Thursday 31st August Matthew 24:42–44

Jesus said to the disciples, "Keep awake therefore, for you do not know on what day your Lord is coming. But understand this: if the owner of the house had known in what part of the night the thief was coming, he would have stayed awake and would not have let his house be broken into. Therefore you also must be ready, for the Son of Man is coming at an unexpected hour."

- How do I respond to the idea of the Son of Man arriving unexpectedly?
- Am I threatened or do I welcome the prospect?
- What does it mean to "keep awake"?

Friday 1st September   Matthew 25:1–13

Jesus said to his disciples, "Then the kingdom of heaven will be like this. Ten bridesmaids took their lamps and went to meet the bridegroom. Five of them were foolish, and five were wise. When the foolish took their lamps, they took no oil with them; but the wise took flasks of oil with their lamps. As the bridegroom was delayed, all of them became drowsy and slept. But at midnight there was a shout, 'Look! Here is the bridegroom! Come out to meet him.' Then all those bridesmaids got up and trimmed their lamps. The foolish said to the wise, 'Give us some of your oil, for our lamps are going out.' But the wise replied, 'No! there will not be enough for you and for us; you had better go to the dealers and buy some for yourselves.' And while they went to buy it, the bridegroom came, and those who were ready went with him into the wedding banquet; and the door was shut. Later the other bridesmaids came also, saying, 'Lord, lord, open to us.' But he replied, 'Truly I tell you, I do not know you.' Keep awake therefore, for you know neither the day nor the hour."

- The Kingdom of Heaven is like a banquet that could start any minute. We could miss it.
- In my life, how am I missing out on it right now?
- What do I need to change?

Saturday 2nd September   **1 Corinthians 1:26–31**

Consider your own call, brothers and sisters: not many of you were wise by human standards, not many were powerful, not many were of noble birth. But God chose what is foolish in the world to shame the wise; God chose what is weak in the world to shame the strong; God chose what is low and despised in the world, things that are not, to reduce to nothing things that are, so that no one might boast in the presence of God. He is the source of your life in Christ Jesus, who became for us wisdom from God, and righteousness and sanctification and redemption, in order that, as it is written, "Let the one who boasts, boast in the Lord."

- Paul does not pull any punches in telling the Corinthians—and us—that of ourselves, we have little to boast about.
- But, we have been chosen by God. . .

september 3–9

Something to think and pray about each day this week:

Accepting my cross

You tell me to "carry my cross," Lord. You are not telling me to go out looking for the cross in practices or penances. Rather I can find it under my nose. If I seek it.

Every encounter that costs me, that rubs off my ego, is part of your plan for me. I start with my own body and heart. The aches and limitations of my limbs, my awkwardness and shyness, are part of my cross. I often wish I was different, but this is me, and I will learn to love me as you do. When I can't think of anything to say in company, or when I think of the wrong things, I'm carrying my cross.

What consoles me is that you like my company. You can put up with my silences. You accept the grumpy mutterings that at times are the closest I come to conversation. I don't always feel good about myself. There are moments when, like Groucho Marx, I would not want to belong to any club that was ready to accept me as a member. You not only accept me, but you make me feel I belong, a first-born child in whom you delight.

The Presence of God
As I sit here with my book, God is here.
Around me, in my sensations, in my thoughts and deep within me.
I pause for a moment, and become aware
of God's life-giving presence.

Freedom
I need to close out the noise, to rise above the noise;
The noise that interrupts, that separates,
The noise that isolates.
I need to listen to God again.

Consciousness
Knowing that God loves me unconditionally,
I can afford to be honest about how I am.
How has the last day been, and how do I feel now?
I share my feelings openly with the Lord.

The Word
God speaks to each one of us individually. I need to listen to what he is saying to me. (Please turn to your scripture on the following pages. Inspiration points are there should you need them. When you are ready, return here to continue.)

Conversation
Do I notice myself reacting as I pray with the Word of God?
Do I feel challenged, comforted, angry?
Imagining Jesus sitting or standing by me,
I speak out my feelings, as one trusted friend to another.

Conclusion
Glory be to the Father, and to the Son, and to the Holy Spirit,
As it was in the beginning, is now and ever shall be,
World without end. Amen

Sunday 3rd September, Twenty-second
Sunday in Ordinary Time   **Mark 7:14–15**

Then Jesus called the crowd again and said to them, "Listen to me, all of you, and understand: there is nothing outside a person that by going in can defile, but the things that come out are what defile."

- What is really important for Jesus is the integrity of our hearts.
- I may not be obsessed with strict dietary laws like Jesus' listeners, but what superficial concerns preoccupy me? It is good to acknowledge them because they may be holding my heart back.
- Jesus wants to challenge me but he also is there to support me.

Monday 4th September   **Luke 4:16–21**

When Jesus came to Nazareth, where he had been brought up, he went to the synagogue on the sabbath day, as was his custom. He stood up to read, and the scroll of the prophet Isaiah was given to him. He unrolled the scroll and found the place where it was written: "The Spirit of the Lord is upon me, because he has anointed me to bring good news to the poor. He has sent me to proclaim release to the captives and recovery of sight to the blind, to let the oppressed go free, to proclaim the year of the Lord's favor." And he rolled up the scroll, gave it back to the attendant, and sat down. The eyes of all in the synagogue were fixed on him. Then he began to say to them, "Today this scripture has been fulfilled in your hearing."

- At Jesus' first opportunity to say publicly what he was about, this is what he said.
- It would be good to mull over his words a few times and ask, "How is this to be fulfilled in my hearing?"

Tuesday 5th September   **Luke 4:31–37**

Jesus went down to Capernaum, a city in Galilee, and was teaching them on the sabbath. They were astounded at his teaching, because he spoke with authority. In the synagogue there was a man who had the spirit of an unclean demon, and he cried out with a loud voice, "Let us alone! What have you to do with us, Jesus of Nazareth? Have you come to destroy us? I know who you are, the Holy One of God." But Jesus rebuked him, saying, "Be silent, and come out of him!" When the demon had thrown him down before them, he came out of him without having done him any harm. They were all amazed and kept saying to one another, "What kind of utterance is this? For with authority and power he commands the unclean spirits, and out they come!" And a report about him began to reach every place in the region.

- Because of his authority as the "Holy One of God," all evil is ultimately powerless before Jesus.
- Can I bring the evil that I confront in my life—and in our world—before him?
- How do I feel when I consider these things? Confidence in God? Doubt and fear? Perhaps I should talk this over with Jesus.

Wednesday 6th September   Luke 4:38–39

After leaving the synagogue Jesus entered Simon's house. Now Simon's mother-in-law was suffering from a high fever, and they asked him about her. Then he stood over her and rebuked the fever, and it left her. Immediately she got up and began to serve them.

- In my imagination I picture the scene: a woman in pain, Jesus— presumably unexpected—comes into the room and heals her.
- What is her response?
- How is God's power to heal and make new evident in my world, in our world? What response does it call forth?

Thursday 7th September   **Luke 5:4–11**

When Jesus had finished speaking, he said to Simon, "Put out into the deep water and let down your nets for a catch." Simon answered, "Master, we have worked all night long but have caught nothing. Yet if you say so, I will let down the nets." When they had done this, they caught so many fish that their nets were beginning to break. So they signaled their partners in the other boat to come and help them. And they came and filled both boats, so that they began to sink. But when Simon Peter saw it, he fell down at Jesus' knees, saying, "Go away from me, Lord, for I am a sinful man!" For he and all who were with him were amazed at the catch of fish that they had taken; and so also were James and John, sons of Zebedee, who were partners with Simon. Then Jesus said to Simon, "Do not be afraid; from now on you will be catching people." When they had brought their boats to shore, they left everything and followed him.

- When Peter lets Jesus direct him, things turn out in a way that leave him awestruck and humbled.
- Maybe I can imagine myself in one of these boats and watch this extraordinary scene unfold.
- How can I allow Jesus to direct things in my life in a way that allows the greatness of God to unfold?

Friday 8th September, Nativity of the Blessed Virgin Mary
                                              Matthew 1:18–23

Now the birth of Jesus the Messiah took place in this way. When his mother Mary had been engaged to Joseph, but before they lived together, she was found to be with child from the Holy Spirit. Her husband Joseph, being a righteous man and unwilling to expose her to public disgrace, planned to dismiss her quietly. But just when he had resolved to do this, an angel of the Lord appeared to him in a dream and said, "Joseph, son of David, do not be afraid to take Mary as your wife, for the child conceived in her is from the Holy Spirit. She will bear a son, and you are to name him Jesus, for he will save his people from their sins." All this took place to fulfill what had been spoken by the Lord through the prophet: "Look, the virgin shall conceive and bear a son, and they shall name him Emmanuel," which means, "God is with us."

- Ponder the mystery of Mary's motherhood.
- Mary's life is changed utterly, then Joseph's, and then . . .
- Emmanuel—God is with us.

Saturday 9th September   Luke 6:1–5

One sabbath while Jesus was going through the grainfields, his disciples plucked some heads of grain, rubbed them in their hands, and ate them. But some of the Pharisees said, "Why are you doing what is not lawful on the sabbath?" Jesus answered, "Have you not read what David did when he and his companions were hungry? He entered the house of God and took and ate the bread of the Presence, which it is not lawful for any but the priests to eat, and gave some to his companions?" Then he said to them, "The Son of Man is lord of the sabbath."

- Here the Pharisees' clinging to the law degenerates to the point of being utterly ridiculous in relation to Jesus and his disciples.
- I might wonder what sort of fears and insecurities have driven them to become at once so petty and so vicious?
- How does Jesus respond?
- How does Jesus respond to the "Pharisee" in me?

Something to think and pray about each day this week:

Searching in the shadow

Jesus spoke tenderly of looking for the lost sheep, the only one in a flock of a hundred that could not stay with the shepherd. That lost sheep is the bit of myself that does not belong with the rest, the behavior or qualities that I really dislike in myself, and that I would hate to see in the public gaze. There are ugly little bits of myself that I wish were not there, and that I prefer to forget, part of what has been called the shadow side of me.

It is hard to believe that God wants me to go looking for these unseemly bits. He wants me to acknowledge and accept them as part of me. If they are denied or buried they will give trouble. Lord, what will I do about that dirty, mean, destructive bit of me? I'll bring it back to the main body; not merely that, but cherish it, haul it home on my shoulders. I'll put a name on it and know where it is. Once I've done that, I am more at home in my own skin, more integrated and realistic.

This is a hard lesson, Lord, not the one I wanted from you. Open my heart to it.

The Presence of God

I pause for a moment, aware that God is here.
I think of how everything around me,
the air I breathe, my whole body,
is tingling with the presence of God.

Freedom

I will ask God's help,
to be free from my own preoccupations,
to be open to God in this time of prayer,
to come to love and serve him more.

Consciousness

In the presence of my loving Creator,
I look honestly at my feelings over the last day,
the highs, the lows and the level ground.
Can I see where the Lord has been present?

The Word

I read the Word of God slowly, a few times over, and I listen to
what God is saying to me. (Please turn to your scripture on the
following pages. Inspiration points are there should you need
them. When you are ready, return here to continue.)

Conversation

Remembering that I am still in God's presence,
I imagine Jesus himself standing or sitting beside me,
and say whatever is on my mind, whatever is in my heart,
speaking as one friend to another.

Conclusion

Glory be to the Father, and to the Son, and to the Holy Spirit,
As it was in the beginning, is now and ever shall be,
World without end. Amen

Sunday 10th September, Twenty-third Sunday
in Ordinary Time Mark 7:31–37

Then Jesus returned from the region of Tyre, and went by way of Sidon towards the Sea of Galilee, in the region of the Decapolis. They brought to him a deaf man who had an impediment in his speech; and they begged him to lay his hand on him. He took him aside in private, away from the crowd, and put his fingers into his ears, and he spat and touched his tongue. Then looking up to heaven, he sighed and said to him, "Ephphatha," that is, "Be opened." And immediately his ears were opened, his tongue was released, and he spoke plainly. Then Jesus ordered them to tell no one; but the more he ordered them, the more zealously they proclaimed it. They were astounded beyond measure, saying, "He has done everything well; he even makes the deaf to hear and the mute to speak."

- The man couldn't hear and couldn't talk; he was "cut off."
- The touch of Jesus opened him up again to the world and to the people around him.
- How am I cut off? Are there others who are cut off? How can the touch of Jesus heal us?

Monday 11th September Luke 6:6–11

On another sabbath Jesus entered the synagogue and taught, and there was a man there whose right hand was withered. The scribes and the Pharisees watched him to see whether he would cure on the sabbath, so that they might find an accusation against him. Even though he knew what they were thinking, he said to the man who had the withered hand, "Come and stand here." He got up and stood there. Then Jesus said to them, "I ask you, is it lawful to do good or to do harm on the sabbath, to save life or to destroy it?" After looking around at all of them, he said to him, "Stretch out your hand." He did so, and his hand was restored. But they were filled with fury and discussed with one another what they might do to Jesus.

- When I see Jesus in the synagogue surrounded by his listeners, the man with a withered hand, his friends, the scribes, and the Pharisees, where does my gaze rest?
- The man, withered and deformed, stands with confidence because Jesus wants to heal him, no matter the opposition.
- Perhaps I can look into my own heart and soul. Do I feel that some parts of me are withered? And what about those around me?
- I can bring this reality before Jesus, knowing that he wants to heal me, no matter what.

Tuesday 12th September   **Luke 6:12–16**

Now during those days Jesus went out to the mountain to pray; and he spent the night in prayer to God. And when day came, he called his disciples and chose twelve of them, whom he also named apostles: Simon, whom he named Peter, and his brother Andrew, and James, and John, and Philip, and Bartholomew, and Matthew, and Thomas, and James son of Alphaeus, and Simon, who was called the Zealot, and Judas son of James, and Judas Iscariot, who became a traitor.

- I see the man Jesus spending the whole night in prayer. Can I allow myself to begin to imagine the depth of the relationship between him and his Father?
- These closest followers are being called, by their names, by the very Son of God.
- Can I appreciate—accept, even—that God wants and calls me by name?

Wednesday 13th September   **Luke 6:20–23a**

Then Jesus looked up at his disciples and said: "Blessed are you who are poor, for yours is the kingdom of God. Blessed are you who are hungry now, for you will be filled. Blessed are you who weep now, for you will laugh. Blessed are you when people hate you, and when they exclude you, revile you, and defame you on account of the Son of Man. Rejoice in that day and leap for joy, for surely your reward is great in heaven."

- These words are not addressed to people who are gliding through life without a care. Jesus is speaking to those who know rejection and sorrow.
- His words seem to turn our understanding of "the good life" on its head.
- What is Jesus saying about the misery and pain of so many lives? What right does he have to speak like this?

Thursday 14th September, Exaltation of the Holy Cross
John 3:14–17

Jesus said, "And just as Moses lifted up the serpent in the wilderness, so must the Son of Man be lifted up, that whoever believes in him may have eternal life. For God so loved the world that he gave his only Son, so that everyone who believes in him may not perish but may have eternal life. Indeed, God did not send the Son into the world to condemn the world, but in order that the world might be saved through him."

- Jesus says these words to Nicodemus, a Pharisee who came to him at night, searching for answers.
- His answer is not condemnation, but God's love and a promise of eternal life.
- What does all of this mean to me?

Friday 15th September, Feast of Our Lady of Sorrows
Luke 2:33–35

And the child Jesus's father and mother were amazed at what was being said about him. Then Simeon blessed them and said to his mother Mary, "This child is destined for the falling and the rising of many in Israel, and to be a sign that will be

opposed so that the inner thoughts of many will be revealed—
and a sword will pierce your own soul too."

- Simeon recognized this apparently helpless child for who he really
  was. Can we?
- Jesus is "a sign that will be opposed." Are there parts of me that
  oppose Jesus?
- If I take a stand with Jesus, I too will have to face opposition.

Saturday 16th September   Luke 6:46–49

Jesus said to the disciples, "Why do you call me 'Lord, Lord,'
and do not do what I tell you? I will show you what someone
is like who comes to me, hears my words, and acts on them.
That one is like a man building a house, who dug deeply and
laid the foundation on rock; when a flood arose, the river burst
against that house but could not shake it, because it had been
well built. But the one who hears and does not act is like a man
who built a house on the ground without a foundation. When
the river burst against it, immediately it fell, and great was the
ruin of that house."

- These are strong and challenging words about friendship with
  Jesus. I may need to read them a few times.
- What foundations can I lay down? What new way of acting is
  Jesus calling me to?

september 17–23

Something to think and pray about each day this week:

Seeking my Master

"You cannot be the slave of two masters," says Jesus. God and money are pulling in opposite directions. It does not get easier as you age; Hilaire Belloc, as a devout old man, still felt the tug:

> I'm tired of love and still more tired of rhyme,
> But money gives me pleasure all the time.

We cannot do without it; but it is for use, not enjoyment. God gave us passing things, like money, to use, but gave us himself to enjoy. Our hearts do not find rest in money—we never feel we have enough. God fashioned our hearts for himself; they are restless till they rest in him.

In the parable of the crafty steward, Jesus suggests the complicated relationship we have with money; use it, but never let it be your master. As I move into prayer, I wonder: Where is my heart in this tug of war between God and Mammon?

The Presence of God

For a few moments, I think of God's veiled presence in things:
in the elements, giving them existence;
in plants, giving them life; in animals, giving them sensation;
and finally, in me, giving me all this and more,
making me a temple, a dwelling-place of the Spirit.

Freedom

God is not foreign to my freedom.
Instead the Spirit breathes life into my most intimate desires,
gently nudging me towards all that is good.
I ask for the grace to let myself be enfolded by the Spirit.

Consciousness

Knowing that God loves me unconditionally,
I look honestly over the last day, its events and my feelings.
Do I have something to be grateful for? Then I give thanks.
Is there something I am sorry for? Then I ask forgiveness.

The Word

I take my time to read the Word of God, slowly, a few times,
allowing myself to dwell on anything that strikes me. (Please
turn to your scripture on the following pages. Inspiration points
are there should you need them. When you are ready, return
here to continue.)

Conversation

How has God's Word moved me? Has it left me cold?
Has it consoled me or moved me to act in a new way?
I imagine Jesus standing or sitting beside me,
I turn and share my feelings with him.

Conclusion

Glory be to the Father, and to the Son, and to the Holy Spirit,
As it was in the beginning, is now and ever shall be,
World without end. Amen

Sunday 17th September, Twenty–fourth Sunday
in Ordinary Time   Mark 8:27–30

Jesus went on with his disciples to the villages of Caesarea Philippi; and on the way he asked his disciples, "Who do people say that I am?" And they answered him, "John the Baptist; and others, Elijah; and still others, one of the prophets." He asked them, "But who do you say that I am?" Peter answered him, "You are the Messiah." And he sternly ordered them not to tell anyone about him.

- The same question is always relevant: "Who is Jesus?"
- Peter said, "You are the Messiah." That is, Jesus is the one sent by God to set his people free.
- Do I allow Jesus to be my Messiah and set me free? If not, what is holding me back? Can I talk to him about it?

Monday 18th September   Luke 7:1–10

After Jesus had finished all his sayings in the hearing of the people, he entered Capernaum. A centurion there had a slave whom he valued highly, and who was ill and close to death. When he heard about Jesus, he sent some Jewish elders to him, asking him to come and heal his slave. When they came to Jesus, they appealed to him earnestly, saying, "He is worthy of having you do this for him, for he loves our people, and it is he who built our synagogue for us." And Jesus went with them, but when he was not far from the house, the centurion sent friends to say to him, "Lord, do not trouble yourself, for I am not worthy to have you come under my roof; therefore I did not presume to come to you. But only speak the word, and let my servant be healed. For I also am a man set under authority, with soldiers under me; and I say to one, 'Go,' and he goes, and to another, 'Come,' and he comes, and to my slave, 'Do this,' and the slave does it." When Jesus heard this he was amazed at him, and turning to the crowd that followed him, he said, "I tell you, not even in Israel have I found such faith." When those who had been sent returned to the house, they found the slave in good health.

- It would have been almost impossible for a Roman centurion to put his faith, humbly, in an itinerant Jewish preacher. The culture and politics of supremacy would have ruled out contact, let alone this act of faith and homage.
- His act of faith, so unexpected and against the culture, was a gift. It made a huge impression on Jesus.
- Do I find myself, at times, weak in faith, discouraged by the atmosphere and culture around me? What about the gift that the centurion received? Am I open to receive it?

Tuesday 19th September   **Luke 7:11–17**

Soon afterwards Jesus went to a town called Nain, and his disciples and a large crowd went with him. As he approached the gate of the town, a man who had died was being carried out. He was his mother's only son, and she was a widow; and with her was a large crowd from the town. When the Lord saw her, he had compassion for her and said to her, "Do not weep." Then he came forward and touched the bier, and the bearers stood still. And he said, "Young man, I say to you, rise!" The dead man sat up and began to speak, and Jesus gave him to his mother. Fear seized all of them; and they glorified God, saying, "A great prophet has risen among us!" and "God has looked favorably on his people!" This word about him spread throughout Judea and all the surrounding country.

- Picture this scene. Nain was a walled town and Jesus and his followers were approaching the gate.
- What do they see? How does he react? What happens?
- How do I react to the scene? What do I want to say to Jesus?

Wednesday 20th September 1 Corinthians 13:1–3

If I speak in the tongues of mortals and of angels, but do not have love, I am a noisy gong or a clanging cymbal. And if I have prophetic powers, and understand all mysteries and all knowledge, and if I have all faith, so as to remove mountains, but do not have love, I am nothing. If I give away all my possessions, and if I hand over my body so that I may boast, but do not have love, I gain nothing.

- If familiarity prevents me from appreciating these words, I might need to stop myself for a while.
- It is good to take time to mull over these words, savoring their eloquence.
- Love is a mystery that we can only grow into gradually with God's grace. I may not be perfect in love right now, but that is okay. It would be good to get in touch with my desire to grow in love. Can I express that desire with the One who is love?

Thursday 21st September, St. Matthew Matthew 9:9–13

As Jesus was walking along, he saw a man called Matthew sitting at the tax booth; and he said to him, "Follow me." And he got up and followed him. And as he sat at dinner in the house, many tax collectors and sinners came and were sitting with him and his disciples. When the Pharisees saw this, they said to his disciples, "Why does your teacher eat with tax collectors and sinners?" But when he heard this, he said, "Those who are well have no need of a physician, but those who are sick. Go and learn what this means, 'I desire mercy, not sacrifice.' For I have come to call not the righteous but sinners."

- Tax collectors were shunned and reviled, yet Jesus calls one of them, Matthew, to be his disciple.
- Notice Jesus' attitude to people and compare it to the Pharisees' attitude.

- Do I see myself as a sinner or a "righteous" person? What is my attitude towards other sinners and "righteous" people?

Friday 22nd September   Luke 8:1–3

Soon afterwards Jesus went on through cities and villages, proclaiming and bringing the good news of the kingdom of God. The twelve were with him, as well as some women who had been cured of evil spirits and infirmities: Mary, called Magdalene, from whom seven demons had gone out, and Joanna, the wife of Herod's steward Chuza, and Susanna, and many others, who provided for them out of their resources.

- What sort of a motley crew was this, moving through the towns and villages?
- What motivated Joanna to leave home and join this group? What kind of loyalty moved Mary, after being relieved of her many demons? Who else was there?
- What—or who—explains this particular bunch of travelers? Is there room in the group for new members?

Saturday 23rd September   Luke 8:4–8

When a great crowd gathered and people from town after town came to him, Jesus said in a parable: "A sower went out to sow his seed; and as he sowed, some fell on the path and was trampled on, and the birds of the air ate it up. Some fell on the rock; and as it grew up, it withered for lack of moisture. Some fell among thorns, and the thorns grew with it and choked it. Some fell into good soil, and when it grew, it produced a hundredfold." As he said this, he called out, "Let anyone with ears to hear listen!"

- "Let anyone with ears to hear listen!"

september 24–30

Something to think and pray about each day this week:

Passing into a new light
The last week of September: We have passed the equinox and in northern lands the nights begin to take up daylight's hours; the time of warmth and light is passing. Lord, you made us creatures bound by time, so unlike you in your eternity.

"You dwell in inaccessible light," says St. Paul. But for some of us, the lengthening nights are hard to endure. As the year moves towards its end, we feel our own mortality. The changing seasons affect our mood, and we have to remind ourselves that this mood will not last for ever.

Psalm 90 reflects our human condition and lifts us into God's presence. "Lord, you have been our refuge age after age. . . . To you a thousand years are as a single day, a yesterday now over, an hour of the night. . . . Teach us to count how few days we have, and so gain wisdom of heart. . . . Let us wake in the morning filled with your love. . . . May the sweetness of the Lord be on us! Make all we do succeed!"

The Presence of God
I pause for a moment
and think of the love and the grace that God showers on me,
creating me in his image and likeness, making me his temple.

Freedom
Everything has the potential to draw forth from me a fuller love
and life.
Yet my desires are often fixed, caught, on illusions of fulfillment.
I ask that God, through my freedom, may orchestrate
my desires in a vibrant loving melody rich in harmony.

Consciousness
How do I find myself today?
Where am I with God? With others?
Do I have something to be grateful for? Then I give thanks.
Is there something I am sorry for? Then I ask forgiveness.

The Word
God speaks to each one of us individually. I need to listen to
what he is saying to me. (Please turn to your scripture on the
following pages. Inspiration points are there should you need
them. When you are ready, return here to continue.)

Conversation
What feelings are rising in me
as I pray and reflect on God's Word?
I imagine Jesus himself sitting or standing beside me,
and open my heart to him.

Conclusion
Glory be to the Father, and to the Son, and to the Holy Spirit,
As it was in the beginning, is now and ever shall be,
World without end. Amen

Sunday 24th September, Twenty-fifth Sunday in Ordinary Time   Mark 9:33–37

Then Jesus and the disciples came to Capernaum; and when he was in the house he asked them, "What were you arguing about on the way?" But they were silent, for on the way they had argued with one another who was the greatest. He sat down, called the twelve, and said to them, "Whoever wants to be first must be last of all and servant of all." Then he took a little child and put it among them; and taking it in his arms, he said to them, "Whoever welcomes one such child in my name welcomes me, and whoever welcomes me welcomes not me but the one who sent me."

- This is a call to a life of radical humility and service, following the pattern of Jesus' own life.
- How do I hear his call to be "last of all and servant of all"? Does it challenge me? Does it leave me feeling insecure? Do I feel I'm at the bottom of the heap anyway?
- Can I hear the tender challenge of Jesus calling me to join him in his way of living?

Monday 25th September   Luke 8:16–18

Jesus said to his disciples, "No one after lighting a lamp hides it under a jar, or puts it under a bed, but puts it on a lampstand, so that those who enter may see the light. For nothing is hidden that will not be disclosed, nor is anything secret that will not become known and come to light. Then pay attention to how you listen; for to those who have, more will be given; and from those who do not have, even what they seem to have will be taken away."

- Have I had a share of the "light"? How has God enlightened my life, or how does he continue to do so?
- Do I see my light or my blessings as something private that I keep to myself?
- What is Jesus saying to me about the light that he shares with me?

Tuesday 26th September   **Luke 8:19–21**

Then his mother and his brothers came to Jesus, but they could not reach him because of the crowd. And he was told, "Your mother and your brothers are standing outside, wanting to see you." But he said to them, "My mother and my brothers are those who hear the word of God and do it."

- It would be good to consider how close Jesus was to his mother and those closest to him.
- He wants to affirm, even at the risk of being blunt, that others are welcome in the same intimate relationship.
- Do I share in this closeness? What call do Jesus' words extend to me?

Wednesday 27th September, St. Vincent de Paul
Matthew 9:35–38

Then Jesus went about all the cities and villages, teaching in their synagogues, and proclaiming the good news of the kingdom, and curing every disease and every sickness. When he saw the crowds, he had compassion for them, because they were harassed and helpless, like sheep without a shepherd. Then he said to his disciples, "The harvest is plentiful, but the laborers are few; therefore ask the Lord of the harvest to send out laborers into his harvest."

- Do I know any people who are harassed, who seem helpless, who look around in vain for some purpose and direction? Can I take some moments now to think about them?
- Can I imagine how Jesus would think about them? Can I imagine the look on his face as he gazes at them?
- If I feel helpless, whom do I look to?
- Can I ask for the grace to look at those around me with the compassion of Jesus?

Thursday 28th September   Luke 9:7–9

Now Herod the ruler heard about all that had taken place, and he was perplexed, because it was said by some that John had been raised from the dead, by some that Elijah had appeared, and by others that one of the ancient prophets had arisen. Herod said, "John I beheaded; but who is this about whom I hear such things?" And he tried to see Jesus.

- Lots of stories are circulating about Jesus.
- Everyone wants to have a way of pinning him down, a category to put him in.
- But what Jesus is interested in is, "who am I to you?"

Friday 29th September, Sts. Michael, Gabriel and Raphael
John 1:47–51

When Jesus saw Nathanael coming toward him, he said of him, "Here is truly an Israelite in whom there is no deceit!" Nathanael asked him, "Where did you get to know me?" Jesus answered, "I saw you under the fig tree before Philip called you." Nathanael replied, "Rabbi, you are the Son of God! You are the King of Israel!" Jesus answered, "Do you believe because I told you that I saw you under the fig tree? You will see greater things than these." And he said to him, "Very truly, I tell you, you will see heaven opened and the angels of God ascending and descending upon the Son of Man."

- When did Jesus "get to know me"? What would he say about me?
- What is my reaction to his presence in my life?
- Is it anything like Nathanael's reaction?
- How do I respond to Jesus' invitation?

Saturday 30th September   Luke 9:43b–45

Jesus said to his disciples, "Let these words sink into your ears: The Son of Man is going to be betrayed into human hands." But they did not understand this saying; its meaning was concealed from them, so that they could not perceive it. And they were afraid to ask him about this saying.

- When Jesus starts off saying, "Let these words sink in to your ears," we had better listen carefully to what comes next.
- He knew, it seems, that his disciples had difficulty accepting the painful realities that they had to face. He wanted to prepare them for what was to come.
- I too may find it hard to face some of the truth in my life that is painful. Do I believe that Jesus likewise wants to prepare and support me? Does he stand with me in my painful times? Can I accept my struggle and pain as a sharing in his?

october 1–7

Something to think and pray about each day this week:

The Christian scandal

The words of James confront us. Are we the rich whose wealth is rotting, the people who cheat others, who live in comfort and luxury, who go on eating while ignoring slaughter around us (James 5:1–6)?

We live in a world where between countries and within countries the gap between the rich and poor continues to grow alarmingly. What is being done by those who regard themselves as good-living, church-going people? What is still to be done?

We Christians can give scandal when we follow a double standard: "Do as I say; don't do as I do." But we can also give scandal when we set standards which are too high, especially when we are unable to maintain those standards ourselves.

What can I do, Lord? Can I solve this problem alone? If we may use the example of Mother Teresa, who was well aware of the millions of destitute people needing help, "Let's begin with this one." Then, perhaps together we can lift up a lot of people. Lord, can we do that together?

The Presence of God
I reflect for a moment on God's presence around me and in me.
Creator of the universe, the sun and the moon, the earth,
every molecule, every atom, everything that is:
God is in every beat of my heart. God is with me, now.

Freedom
There are very few people
who realize what God would make of them
if they abandoned themselves into his hands,
and let themselves be formed by his grace (St. Ignatius).
I ask for the grace to trust myself totally to God's love.

Consciousness
In God's loving presence I unwind the past day,
starting from now and looking back, moment by moment.
I gather in all the goodness and light, in gratitude.
I attend to the shadows and what they say to me,
seeking healing, courage, forgiveness.

The Word
I read the Word of God slowly, a few times over, and I listen to
what God is saying to me. (Please turn to your scripture on the
following pages. Inspiration points are there should you need
them. When you are ready, return here to continue.)

Conversation
What is stirring in me as I pray?
Am I consoled, troubled, left cold?
I imagine Jesus himself standing or sitting at my side,
and share my feelings with him.

Conclusion
Glory be to the Father, and to the Son, and to the Holy Spirit,
As it was in the beginning, is now and ever shall be,
World without end. Amen

Sunday 1st October, Twenty-sixth Sunday in Ordinary Time
Mark 9:38–41

John said to Jesus, "Teacher, we saw someone casting out demons in your name, and we tried to stop him, because he was not following us." But Jesus said, "Do not stop him; for no one who does a deed of power in my name will be able soon afterward to speak evil of me. Whoever is not against us is for us. For truly I tell you, whoever gives you a cup of water to drink because you bear the name of Christ will by no means lose the reward."

- We hear two voices here, those of John and Jesus. John speaks out of fear and suspicion which leads to discouragement. Jesus speaks with absolute confidence: Anybody who comes into his sphere, even slightly, can't help but be drawn even further.
- As I listen to my own heart, which voice resonates more strongly: the voice of discouragement or Jesus' voice of encouragement?
- I can talk to Jesus about this.

Monday 2nd October
Luke 9:46–48

An argument arose among the disciples as to which one of them was the greatest. But Jesus, aware of their inner thoughts, took a little child and put it by his side, and said to them, "Whoever welcomes this child in my name welcomes me, and whoever welcomes me welcomes the one who sent me; for the least among all of you is the greatest."

- Imagine the little child in this scene, the expression on the child's face. What is he or she like? Wide-eyed? Innocent? Trusting?
- I come with all my baggage, my skepticism, competitiveness, self-regard. Can I put this aside and be like the little child?
- Jesus welcomes this child with open arms.

Tuesday 3rd October   Luke 9:51–56

When the days drew near for him to be taken up, Jesus set his face to go to Jerusalem. And he sent messengers ahead of him. On their way they entered a village of the Samaritans to make ready for him; but they did not receive him, because his face was set toward Jerusalem. When his disciples James and John saw it, they said, "Lord, do you want us to command fire to come down from heaven and consume them?" But he turned and rebuked them. Then they went on to another village.

- Here was a bit of standard hostility between a local Samaritan community and some Jewish pilgrims passing by. This may well have been a flash point, where tension broke out, on the route to Jerusalem.
- In this case, Jesus' disciples reacted to the prejudice with spontaneous rage and perhaps some prejudice of their own.
- Does this ring any bells with me?
- What is Jesus' reaction here?

Wednesday 4th October, St. Francis of Assisi
Matthew 11:28–30

Jesus said, "Come to me, all you that are weary and are carrying heavy burdens, and I will give you rest. Take my yoke upon you, and learn from me; for I am gentle and humble in heart, and you will find rest for your souls. For my yoke is easy, and my burden is light."

- Jesus is saying these words to me, now; offering to relieve my weariness.
- Can I share the burdens I carry with Jesus?
- Do I trust him when he says "my burden is light"?

Thursday 5th October   Job 19:21–27

Then Job said to his friends, "Have pity on me, have pity on me, O you my friends, for the hand of God has touched me! Why do you, like God, pursue me, never satisfied with my flesh? O that my words were written down! O that they were inscribed in a book! O that with an iron pen and with lead they were engraved on a rock forever! For I know that my Redeemer lives, and that at the last he will stand upon the earth; and after my skin has been thus destroyed, then in my flesh I shall see God, whom I shall see on my side, and my eyes shall behold, and not another. My heart faints within me!"

- Job speaks for every believer who has ever been beaten down by evil and adversity, in great ways or small.
- As I pray over his words, can I get in touch with the negative realities in my own life which weigh me down and dry up the sources of my faith?
- Am I moved, as Job was, to reach up and out in hope? I need to remember that Job's sublime words of trust in God go hand in hand with his plea for pity.

Friday 6th October   Psalm 139:1–3, 7–10

O Lord, you have searched me and known me. You know when I sit down and when I rise up; you discern my thoughts from far away. You search out my path and my lying down, and are acquainted with all my ways. Where can I go from your spirit? Or where can I flee from your presence? If I ascend to heaven, you are there; if I make my bed in Sheol, you are there.

- Can I mull over these words and make them my own?
- When I really think about it, how does God's intimate knowledge of me move me? Is it consoling or, perhaps, unnerving? Or something else?
- What am I prompted to say to the Lord?

Saturday 7th October   **Luke 10:23–24**

Then turning to the disciples, Jesus said to them privately, "Blessed are the eyes that see what you see! For I tell you that many prophets and kings desired to see what you see, but did not see it, and to hear what you hear, but did not hear it."

- The disciples of Jesus have a privileged experience, and so do we.
- Many people long to have a real, living relationship with God. Jesus is offering it to me on a plate, now.

Something to think and pray about each day this week:

The child's path

When Jesus speaks about children, he says "Let them come to me." Parents, relatives, priests, and teachers should guide them along the way; no one should stand in the way of these children finding God.

But do our actions prevent children approaching Jesus: parents not giving them any Christian formation (telling them about Jesus, teaching them how to pray, etc.) or not inviting others (parish, school, etc.) to form them; parents or teachers giving them a Christian education but having no Christian environment in the home or classroom (what signs of Christianity are there in your home or parish school?); community leaders and politicians following double standards (telling children to behave in one way while acting quite differently, or where what is learnt through education programs is contradicted by what happens elsewhere in government)?

As parents, may we express our love for each other; as adults, may our Christian witness to the simple truth and integrity be cherished by the young.

The Presence of God
I remind myself that, as I sit here now,
God is gazing on me with love and holding me in being.
I pause for a moment and think of this.

Freedom
A thick and shapeless tree-trunk would never believe
that it could become a statue, admired as a miracle of sculpture,
and would never submit itself to the chisel of the sculptor,
who sees by her genius what she can make of it (St. Ignatius).
I ask for the grace to let myself be shaped by my loving Creator.

Consciousness
I exist in a web of relationships—links to nature, people, God.
I trace out these links, giving thanks for the life that flows through them.
Some links are twisted or broken: I may feel regret, anger, disappointment.
I pray for the gift of acceptance and forgiveness.

The Word
I take my time to read the Word of God, slowly, a few times, allowing myself to dwell on anything that strikes me. (Please turn to your scripture on the following pages. Inspiration points are there should you need them. When you are ready, return here to continue.)

Conversation
Do I notice myself reacting as I pray with the Word of God?
Do I feel challenged, comforted, angry?
Imagining Jesus sitting or standing by me,
I speak out my feelings, as one trusted friend to another.

Conclusion
Glory be to the Father, and to the Son, and to the Holy Spirit,
As it was in the beginning, is now and ever shall be,
World without end. Amen

Sunday 8th October, Twenty-seventh Sunday
in Ordinary Time   Mark 10:13–16

People were bringing little children to Jesus in order that he might touch them; and the disciples spoke sternly to them. But when Jesus saw this, he was indignant and said to them, "Let the little children come to me; do not stop them; for it is to such as these that the kingdom of God belongs. Truly I tell you, whoever does not receive the kingdom of God as a little child will never enter it." And he took them up in his arms, laid his hands on them, and blessed them.

- When people bring along their little children, we see two contrasting reactions: the disciples get annoyed, Jesus delights in seeing them.
- What does Jesus see that the disciples miss?
- What is this childlike quality prized so highly by Jesus?
- What reactions does this scene evoke in me? Whatever it is, I can speak to Jesus about it.

Monday 9th October   Luke 10:30–37

Jesus replied, "A man was going down from Jerusalem to Jericho, and fell into the hands of robbers, who stripped him, beat him, and went away, leaving him half dead. Now by chance a priest was going down that road; and when he saw him, he passed by on the other side. So likewise a Levite, when he came to the place and saw him, passed by on the other side. But a Samaritan while traveling came near him; and when he saw him, he was moved with pity. He went to him and bandaged his wounds, having poured oil and wine on them. Then he put him on his own animal, brought him to an inn, and took care of him. The next day he took out two denarii, gave them to the innkeeper, and said, 'Take care of him; and when I come back, I will repay you whatever more you spend.' Which of these three, do you think, was a neighbor to the man who fell into the hands of the robbers?" The lawyer said, "The one who showed him mercy." Jesus said to him, "Go and do likewise."

- A lawyer who was anxious to justify himself asked Jesus, "Who is my neighbor?" Jesus replied with this story.
- Who is my neighbor? Jesus seems to suggest that it is the person whom I view with suspicion and don't like, or who views me with suspicion and doesn't like me.
- Do I have any neighbors in this challenging sense of the word? What is Jesus trying to say to me?

Tuesday 10th October   Luke 10:38–42

Now as they went on their way, Jesus entered a certain village, where a woman named Martha welcomed him into her home. She had a sister named Mary, who sat at the Lord's feet and listened to what he was saying. But Martha was distracted by her many tasks; so she came to him and asked, "Lord, do you not care that my sister has left me to do all the work by myself? Tell her then to help me." But the Lord answered her, "Martha, Martha, you are worried and distracted by many things; there is need of only one thing. Mary has chosen the better part, which will not be taken away from her."

- When I read the story of Martha and Mary, do I spontaneously take sides, or at least, identify with one rather than the other?
- If so, can I now ask for the grace to see the beauty and value of the other one? If I find myself resisting and wanting to stick with my own preference, I might have to try a little harder. The Lord is often trying to tell us things at the point where we resist.

Wednesday 11th October   Luke 11:1–4

Jesus was praying in a certain place, and after he had finished, one of his disciples said to him, "Lord, teach us to pray, as John taught his disciples." He said to them, "When you pray, say: Father, hallowed be your name. Your kingdom come. Give us each day our daily bread. And forgive us our sins, for we ourselves forgive everyone indebted to us. And do not bring us to the time of trial."

- When the incarnate Son of God, the one closest to the Father, is asked to put into words the elements of true prayer, this is what he says …

Thursday 12th October   Luke 11:5–10

And Jesus said to them, "Suppose one of you has a friend, and you go to him at midnight and say to him, 'Friend, lend me three loaves of bread; for a friend of mine has arrived, and I have nothing to set before him.' And he answers from within, 'Do not bother me; the door has already been locked, and my children are with me in bed; I cannot get up and give you anything.' I tell you, even though he will not get up and give him anything because he is his friend, at least because of his persistence he will get up and give him whatever he needs. So I say to you, Ask, and it will be given you; search, and you will find; knock, and the door will be opened for you. For everyone who asks receives, and everyone who searches finds, and for everyone who knocks, the door will be opened."

- This guarantee that God will answer persistent prayer may move me in any one of a number of ways. It might excite and encourage me. It could, however, leave me feeling frustrated and dejected, depending on my past experience.
- So, no matter how I'm feeling right now, I might ask the Lord for a deeper understanding of his call to perseverance in prayer.
- What is he trying to teach me about myself and my relationship with him?

Friday 13th October   Psalm 111:1–6

Praise the Lord! I will give thanks to the Lord with my whole heart, in the company of the upright, in the congregation.

Great are the works of the Lord, studied by all who delight in them. Full of honor and majesty is his work, and his righteousness endures forever. He has gained renown by his wonderful deeds; the Lord is gracious and merciful. He provides food for those who fear him; he is ever mindful of his covenant. He has shown his people the power of his works, in giving them the heritage of the nations

- Who is this remarkable God who has evoked such wonder and love in the people throughout the ages?
- Majestic and glorious.
- Tender and compassionate.

Saturday 14th October, St. John Ogilvie   Romans 5:2b–5
We boast in our hope of sharing the glory of God. And not only that, but we also boast in our sufferings, knowing that suffering produces endurance, and endurance produces character, and character produces hope, and hope does not disappoint us, because God's love has been poured into our hearts through the Holy Spirit that has been given to us.

- Suffering isn't something to be desired, and shouldn't be romanticized.
- But when we share our difficulties with God, bearing them together strengthens our relationship.
- What suffering am I going through right now, and can I share it with the Lord?

october 15–21

Something to think and pray about each day this week:

Stopping to give thanks

I have done it myself, Lord. I go looking for something, advertising my need, seeking sympathy. And when somebody helps me, part of me is muttering. "He was only doing his job, or what you'd expect of a neighbor." I take kindness for granted and do not bother to say "Thank you." It was the stranger, the Samaritan, who took the trouble to go back to Jesus and became an icon of gratitude. The other nine went for a drink, feeling "Sure that's only what the priests/doctors/healers are there for."

Thank you, Lord, that I am alive and able to speak to you, that I have access to your word in *Sacred Space*. May I always count my blessings.

The Presence of God
In the silence of my innermost being,
in the fragments of my yearned-for wholeness,
can I hear the whispers of God's presence?
Can I remember when I felt God's nearness?
When we walked together and I let myself be embraced by God's love.

Freedom
I ask for the grace
to let go of my own concerns
and be open to what God is asking of me,
to let myself be guided and formed by my loving Creator.

Consciousness
How am I really feeling? Light-hearted? Heavy-hearted?
I may be very much at peace, happy to be here.
Equally, I may be frustrated, worried or angry.
I acknowledge how I really am. It is the real me that the Lord loves.

The Word
God speaks to each one of us individually. I need to listen to what he is saying to me. (Please turn to your scripture on the following pages. Inspiration points are there should you need them. When you are ready, return here to continue.)

Conversation
Remembering that I am still in God's presence,
I imagine Jesus himself standing or sitting beside me,
and say whatever is on my mind, whatever is in my heart,
speaking as one friend to another.

Conclusion
Glory be to the Father, and to the Son, and to the Holy Spirit,
As it was in the beginning, is now and ever shall be,
World without end. Amen

Sunday 15th October, Twenty-eighth Sunday
in Ordinary Time   Mark 10:17–22

As Jesus was setting out on a journey, a man ran up and knelt before him, and asked him, "Good Teacher, what must I do to inherit eternal life?" Jesus said to him, "Why do you call me good? No one is good but God alone. You know the commandments: 'You shall not murder; You shall not commit adultery; You shall not steal; You shall not bear false witness; You shall not defraud; Honor your father and mother.'" He said to him, "Teacher, I have kept all these since my youth." Jesus, looking at him, loved him and said, "You lack one thing; go, sell what you own, and give the money to the poor, and you will have treasure in heaven; then come, follow me." When he heard this, he was shocked and went away grieving, for he had many possessions.

- This is unusual: A young man runs up to Jesus full of enthusiasm. After his meeting we see him walk away, sad and dejected.
- What happened here? Did he get a raw deal? Was he really unrealistic about his desire for eternal life? Does God simply ask for a lot?
- Can I see anything of myself in this man?

Monday 16th October   Luke 11:29–32

When the crowds were increasing, Jesus began to say, "This generation is an evil generation; it asks for a sign, but no sign will be given to it except the sign of Jonah. For just as Jonah became a sign to the people of Nineveh, so the Son of Man will be to this generation. The queen of the South will rise at the judgment with the people of this generation and condemn them, because she came from the ends of the earth to listen to the wisdom of Solomon, and see, something greater than Solomon is here! The people of Nineveh will rise up at the judgment with this generation and condemn it, because they repented at the proclamation of Jonah, and see, something greater than Jonah is here!"

- Jonah's work was to call a whole people to recognize their sin and need for God's forgiveness.
- Jesus is saying, pretty strongly, that something similar is called for now.
- Do I hear this? How do I react?

Tuesday 17th October   **Luke 11:37–41**

While Jesus was speaking, a Pharisee invited him to dine with him; so he went in and took his place at the table. The Pharisee was amazed to see that he did not first wash before dinner. Then the Lord said to him, "Now you Pharisees clean the outside of the cup and of the dish, but inside you are full of greed and wickedness. You fools! Did not the one who made the outside make the inside also? So give for alms those things that are within; and see, everything will be clean for you."

- When I read Jesus' statement to the Pharisees again, perhaps I could insert my own name instead of the word "Pharisees."
- How does that feel? Remember that Jesus never scolds without the desire for change and growth.
- What do those words "give for alms those things that are within" mean? Can I allow myself to be moved forward by them?

Wednesday 18th October, St. Luke   **Luke 10:1–7a**

After this the Lord appointed seventy others and sent them on ahead of him in pairs to every town and place where he himself intended to go. He said to them, "The harvest is plentiful, but the labourers are few; therefore ask the Lord of the harvest to send out labourers into his harvest. Go on your way. See, I am sending you out like lambs into the midst of wolves. Carry no purse, no bag, no sandals; and greet no one on the road. Whatever house you enter, first say, 'Peace to this house!'

And if anyone is there who shares in peace, your peace will rest on that person; but if not, it will return to you. Remain in the same house, eating and drinking whatever they provide, for the labourer deserves to be paid."

- Jesus does not send them out alone, but in pairs. Do I have a companion on my Christian journey? Am I part of a Christian community or do I feel as though I am on my own?
- Imagine what you might take if someone sent you out on a journey today—food, money, personal transport, clothes for all seasons. But what does Jesus say about this?
- Have I asked Jesus where he wants me to go? Have I avoided that question?

Thursday 19th October   Luke 11:47–54

Jesus said to the lawyers, "Woe to you! For you build the tombs of the prophets whom your ancestors killed. So you are witnesses and approve of the deeds of your ancestors; for they killed them, and you build their tombs. Therefore also the Wisdom of God said, 'I will send them prophets and apostles, some of whom they will kill and persecute,' so that this generation may be charged with the blood of all the prophets shed since the foundation of the world, from the blood of Abel to the blood of Zechariah, who perished between the altar and the sanctuary. Yes, I tell you, it will be charged against this generation. Woe to you lawyers! For you have taken away the key of knowledge; you did not enter yourselves, and you hindered those who were entering." When he went outside, the scribes and the Pharisees began to be very hostile toward him and to cross-examine him about many things, lying in wait for him, to catch him in something he might say.

- Here Jesus is confronting people who, for reasons of vested interest, are resisting the challenge of the truth that Jesus brings.

- How does a righteous and angry Jesus make me feel? Do I want to run away? Do I start getting righteous myself?
- Can I get in touch with the parts of myself that resist the call and action of Jesus? I might humbly ask for help to change.

Friday 20th October   Luke 12:1–3, 6–7

Meanwhile, when the crowd gathered by the thousands, so that they trampled on one another, Jesus began to speak first to his disciples, "Beware of the yeast of the Pharisees, that is, their hypocrisy. Nothing is covered up that will not be uncovered, and nothing secret that will not become known. Therefore whatever you have said in the dark will be heard in the light, and what you have whispered behind closed doors will be proclaimed from the housetops. Are not five sparrows sold for two pennies? Yet not one of them is forgotten in God's sight. But even the hairs of your head are all counted. Do not be afraid; you are of more value than many sparrows."

- "Nothing secret that will not become known. . . ." Do I consider this prospect with calm and equanimity, or does it leave me in the grip of fear?
- Here, there is a challenge from Jesus to live in the truth no matter the cost. Can I face the challenge?
- If the challenge seems too great, can I hear the words "Do not be afraid; you are of more value than . . ."?

Saturday 21st October   Luke 12:8–12

Jesus said to the disciples, "And I tell you, everyone who acknowledges me before others, the Son of Man also will acknowledge before the angels of God; but whoever denies me before others will be denied before the angels of God. And everyone who speaks a word against the Son of Man will be forgiven; but whoever blasphemes against the Holy Spirit will not be forgiven. When they bring you before the synagogues, the rulers, and the authorities, do not worry about how you are to defend yourselves or what you are to say; for the Holy Spirit will teach you at that very hour what you ought to say."

- Jesus' words to his disciples are spoken in anticipation of conflict and persecution ahead.
- When I read them, is my spontaneous response one of being encouraged and challenged or am I frightened and unnerved? Why do I react in this way?
- What words of comfort are here for me?

Something to think and pray about each day this week:

Persistence

Lord, you puzzle me. I hear you telling me to persist in prayer, to entreat God until he is weary of me. You say, "he will quickly grant justice." Then I think of good people suffering famine, Aids, sickness, death, even the death of children, though they pray to God. I think of the Jews in Auschwitz, still singing the psalms as they walked into the gas chambers. Surely there are times when you delay in helping us?

At times like this I turn to the memory of your passion, and your agonized prayer in the garden. You have faced a dark and apparently empty heaven, yet stayed faithful. Keep me with you.

The Presence of God
God is with me, but more,
God is within me, giving me existence.
Let me dwell for a moment on God's life-giving presence
in my body, my mind, my heart
and in the whole of my life.

Freedom
I ask for the grace to believe
in what I could be and do
if I only allowed God, my loving Creator,
to continue to create me, guide me and shape me.

Consciousness
Knowing that God loves me unconditionally,
I can afford to be honest about how I am.
How has the last day been, and how do I feel now?
I share my feelings openly with the Lord.

The Word
I read the Word of God slowly, a few times over, and I listen to
what God is saying to me. (Please turn to your scripture on the
following pages. Inspiration points are there should you need
them. When you are ready, return here to continue.)

Conversation
How has God's Word moved me? Has it left me cold?
Has it consoled me or moved me to act in a new way?
I imagine Jesus standing or sitting beside me,
I turn and share my feelings with him.

Conclusion
Glory be to the Father, and to the Son, and to the Holy Spirit,
As it was in the beginning, is now and ever shall be,
World without end. Amen

Sunday 22nd October, Twenty-ninth Sunday
in Ordinary Time   John 3:16–18

Jesus said to Nicodemus, "For God so loved the world that he gave his only Son, so that everyone who believes in him may not perish but may have eternal life. Indeed, God did not send the Son into the world to condemn the world, but in order that the world might be saved through him. Those who believe in him are not condemned; but those who do not believe are condemned already, because they have not believed in the name of the only Son of God."

- If God had not given his only Son where would I be?
- Can I get in touch with my need to be saved? If not, I might ask for light and guidance.
- If I am in touch with my need for a savior, then I can converse with the One who has given his life for me.

Monday 23rd October   Luke 12:13–21

Someone in the crowd said to Jesus, "Teacher, tell my brother to divide the family inheritance with me." But he said to him, "Friend, who set me to be a judge or arbitrator over you?" And he said to them, "Take care! Be on your guard against all kinds of greed; for one's life does not consist in the abundance of possessions." Then he told them a parable: "The land of a rich man produced abundantly. And he thought to himself, 'What should I do, for I have no place to store my crops?' Then he said, 'I will do this: I will pull down my barns and build larger ones, and there I will store all my grain and my goods. And I will say to my soul, "Soul, you have ample goods laid up for many years; relax, eat, drink, be merry."' But God said to him, 'You fool! This very night your life is being demanded of you. And the things you have prepared, whose will they be?' So it is with those who store up treasures for themselves but are not rich toward God."

- The man in the parable doesn't seem a bad man. He is setting things up nicely for himself, planning an enjoyable life, sitting back and, no doubt, saying "because I'm worth it!"
- Do I hear Jesus sending alarm bells about all kinds of greed? What are those alarms saying to me in my life?
- Do I share in any way in the complacency of the greedy man? Can I let Jesus' sense of urgent excitement move me?

Tuesday 24th October   Luke 12:35–38

Jesus said to his disciples, "Be dressed for action and have your lamps lit; be like those who are waiting for their master to return from the wedding banquet, so that they may open the door for him as soon as he comes and knocks. Blessed are those slaves whom the master finds alert when he comes; truly I tell you, he will fasten his belt and have them sit down to eat, and he will come and serve them. If he comes during the middle of the night, or near dawn, and finds them so, blessed are those slaves."

- When Jesus says to ME, "Be dressed for action and have your lamp lit," what exactly is he referring to?
- Is there any particular distraction, counter-attraction, indulgence that dims or douses my lamp? Is the Lord calling me to be honest and real about myself in some new way?
- I remember that the Lord knows me better than I do myself and loves me as I am. His call to action always respects my reality.

Wednesday 25th October   Luke 12:45–48

Jesus said to his disciples, "But if that slave says to himself, 'My master is delayed in coming,' and if he begins to beat the other slaves, men and women, and to eat and drink and get drunk, the master of that slave will come on a day when he does not expect him and at an hour that he does not know, and will cut him in pieces, and put him with the unfaithful. That slave who knew what his master wanted, but did not prepare himself or do what was wanted, will receive a severe beating. But the one who did not know and did what deserved a beating will receive a light beating. From everyone to whom much has been given, much will be required; and from the one to whom much has been entrusted, even more will be demanded."

- This is a parable about the person to whom the Lord has entrusted certain responsibilities. For what has the Lord made me responsible?
- How do I feel about the responsibility that I carry in life? Do I ever want to "beat the other slaves" or "eat and drink and get drunk"?
- What do I make of Jesus' strong language? Can I hear it as a wake-up call? Deep down, what do I really think God wants from me?

Thursday 26th October   Luke 12:49–53

Jesus said to his disciples, "I came to bring fire to the earth, and how I wish it were already kindled! I have a baptism with which to be baptized, and what stress I am under until it is completed! Do you think that I have come to bring peace to the earth? No, I tell you, but rather division! From now on five in one household will be divided, three against two and two against three; they will be divided: father against son and son against father, mother against daughter and daughter against mother, mother-in-law against her daughter-in-law and daughter-in-law against mother-in-law."

- Jesus says, "What stress I am under until it is completed!" A surprisingly modern sounding idiom in Jesus' mouth.
- What profound contradictions prompted Jesus to speak of this "stress"? The truth that Jesus is evoked a terrible reaction.
- What light do the contradictions faced by Jesus throw on the contradictions of our world and of my own life?

Friday 27th October   **Luke 12:54–59**

Jesus also said to the crowds, "When you see a cloud rising in the west, you immediately say, 'It is going to rain'; and so it happens. And when you see the south wind blowing, you say, 'There will be scorching heat'; and it happens. You hypocrites! You know how to interpret the appearance of earth and sky, but why do you not know how to interpret the present time? And why do you not judge for yourselves what is right? Thus, when you go with your accuser before a magistrate, on the way make an effort to settle the case, or you may be dragged before the judge, and the judge hand you over to the officer, and the officer throw you in prison. I tell you, you will never get out until you have paid the very last penny."

- Jesus clearly feels that many of his listeners are too complacent about the call to conversion and they need to be shaken up.
- In what way am I complacent? How is God calling me to live a new and better life and what are my resistances?
- Can I allow Jesus to challenge my resistance?

Saturday 28th October, Sts. Simon & Jude
                                                   Ephesians 2:19–22

So then you are no longer strangers and aliens, but you are citizens with the saints and also members of the household of God, built upon the foundation of the apostles and prophets, with Christ Jesus himself as the cornerstone. In him the whole structure is joined together and grows into a holy temple in the Lord; in whom you also are built together spiritually into a dwelling place for God.

- These words directed to the Ephesians also have a meaning for us.
- We belong, we are part of God's household, and God dwells in us.
- Can I listen to this message and take reassurance and strength from it?

Something to think and pray about each day this week:

Changing places

The contrast between Pharisee and tax collector has entered so deeply into our culture that it is sometimes reversed, and people are more anxious to hide at the back of the church than to be in the front pews. Pharisee, a term of honor in Jesus' society, is not something we want to be called. To place it in our culture, for tax collector read convicted rapist, pedophile, or those found guilty of wholesale robbery or fraud against the public, or any who become hate-figures in the daily press.

How does the story hit me? I hate to be the object of people's contempt. But Lord, if they knew me as you do, they might be right to feel contempt. I have no right to look down on those whose sins are paraded in the media. Be merciful to me.

The Presence of God
To be present is to arrive as one is and open up to the other.
At this instant, as I arrive here, God is present waiting for me.
God always arrives before me, desiring to connect with me
even more than my most intimate friend.
I take a moment and greet my loving God.

Freedom
"In these days, God taught me
as a schoolteacher teaches a pupil" (St. Ignatius).
I remind myself that there are things God has to teach me yet,
and ask for the grace to hear them and let them change me.

Consciousness
In the presence of my loving Creator,
I look honestly at my feelings over the last day,
the highs, the lows and the level ground.
Can I see where the Lord has been present?

The Word
I take my time to read the Word of God, slowly, a few times,
allowing myself to dwell on anything that strikes me. (Please
turn to your scripture on the following pages. Inspiration points
are there should you need them. When you are ready, return
here to continue.)

Conversation
What feelings are rising in me
as I pray and reflect on God's Word?
I imagine Jesus himself sitting or standing beside me,
and open my heart to him.

Conclusion
Glory be to the Father, and to the Son, and to the Holy Spirit,
As it was in the beginning, is now and ever shall be,
World without end. Amen

Sunday 29th October, Thirtieth Sunday in Ordinary Time
Mark 10:46–52

They came to Jericho. As Jesus and his disciples and a large crowd were leaving Jericho, Bartimaeus son of Timaeus, a blind beggar, was sitting by the roadside. When he heard that it was Jesus of Nazareth, he began to shout out and say, "Jesus, Son of David, have mercy on me!" Many sternly ordered him to be quiet, but he cried out even more loudly, "Son of David, have mercy on me!" Jesus stood still and said, "Call him here." And they called the blind man, saying to him, "Take heart; get up, he is calling you." So throwing off his cloak, he sprang up and came to Jesus. Then Jesus said to him, "What do you want me to do for you?" The blind man said to him, "My teacher, let me see again." Jesus said to him, "Go; your faith has made you well." Immediately he regained his sight and followed him on the way.

- Can I picture this scene on the road leading out of Jericho? What buildings are around? What is the road surface like? Where is Bartimaeus sitting?
- What is going on? Can I imagine myself present and watching the scene unfold? I might even imagine myself as a participant … Bartimaeus, even.
- When I see and hear and am touched by what happens, how does it move me?

Monday 30th October
Luke 13:10–17

Now Jesus was teaching in one of the synagogues on the sabbath. And just then there appeared a woman with a spirit that had crippled her for eighteen years. She was bent over and was quite unable to stand up straight. When Jesus saw her, he called her over and said, "Woman, you are set free from your ailment." When he laid his hands on her, immediately she stood up straight and began praising God. But the leader of the synagogue, indignant because Jesus had cured on the sabbath, kept saying to the crowd, "There are six days on which work ought to be done; come on those days and be cured, and not on the sabbath day." But the Lord answered him and said, "You hypocrites! Does not each of you on the sabbath untie his ox or his donkey from the manger, and lead it away to give it water? And ought not this woman, a daughter of Abraham whom Satan bound for eighteen long years, be set free from this bondage on the sabbath day?" When he said this, all his opponents were put to shame; and the entire crowd was rejoicing at all the wonderful things that he was doing.

- Imagine the synagogue and the congregation listening to Jesus teaching on a sabbath day.
- Can I imagine myself witnessing or taking part in the scene? As I watch it unfold—or experience it—how do I react? With relief? Joy? Skepticism?
- Does the image of the woman bent and crippled speak to me and my experience, whether literally or metaphorically? What do I want to say to Jesus?

Tuesday 31st October   Luke 13:18–21

Jesus said to the crowds, "What is the kingdom of God like? And to what should I compare it? It is like a mustard seed that someone took and sowed in the garden; it grew and became a tree, and the birds of the air made nests in its branches." And again he said, "To what should I compare the kingdom of God? It is like yeast that a woman took and mixed in with three measures of flour until all of it was leavened."

- When Jesus told the parables of the mustard seed and the yeast, what questions was he addressing? Were people frustrated at the lack of signs of the Kingdom of God in the world around them?
- Am I frustrated with the slow speed of the coming of the kingdom in and around me?

- What do the everyday images of kitchen and garden say to me? Can I let Jesus give me some real encouragement?

Wednesday 1st November, Feast of All Saints
Matthew 5:1–6

When Jesus saw the crowds, he went up the mountain; and after he sat down, his disciples came to him. Then he began to speak, and taught them, saying: "Blessed are the poor in spirit, for theirs is the kingdom of heaven. Blessed are those who mourn, for they will be comforted. Blessed are the meek, for they will inherit the earth. Blessed are those who hunger and thirst for righteousness, for they will be filled."

- Society's view of the poor and disadvantaged at this time was that they deserved their suffering and were far from holiness.
- Jesus turns all this upside down. His vision of holiness is revolutionary.
- Whose side am I on?

Thursday 2nd November, Feast of All Souls
Matthew 5:7–12

Jesus said to the crowds, "Blessed are the merciful, for they will receive mercy. Blessed are the pure in heart, for they will see God. Blessed are the peacemakers, for they will be called children of God. Blessed are those who are persecuted for righteousness' sake, for theirs is the kingdom of heaven. Blessed are you when people revile you and persecute you and utter all kinds of evil against you falsely on my account. Rejoice and be glad, for your reward is great in heaven, for in the same way they persecuted the prophets who were before you."

- If it were a criminal offence to be a Christian, would there be enough evidence to convict me?
- Do I do anything that would make people want to persecute me?
- Or is my priority to seek approval and respect?

Friday 3rd November   **Luke 14:1–6**

On one occasion when Jesus was going to the house of a leader of the Pharisees to eat a meal on the sabbath, they were watching him closely. Just then, in front of him, there was a man who had dropsy. And Jesus asked the lawyers and Pharisees, "Is it lawful to cure people on the sabbath, or not?" But they were silent. So Jesus took him and healed him, and sent him away. Then he said to them, "If one of you has a child or an ox that has fallen into a well, will you not immediately pull it out on a sabbath day?" And they could not reply to this.

- It would be good not to rush, but to spend a short time going over this scene in imagination.
- Can I visualize the setting where Jesus meets the man suffering from dropsy and cures him, with a hostile audience of lawyers and Pharisees looking on?
- What feelings and motivations are going on in the various characters? Why do the Pharisees react as they do? What does the man with dropsy make of it?
- How do I see Jesus here?
- Out of my own reactions, what do I want to say to Jesus?

Saturday 4th November, St. Charles Borromeo
                                              John 10:11–16

Jesus said to the Pharisees, "I am the good shepherd. The good shepherd lays down his life for the sheep. The hired hand, who is not the shepherd and does not own the sheep, sees the wolf coming and leaves the sheep and runs away—and the wolf snatches them and scatters them. The hired hand runs away because a hired hand does not care for the sheep. I am the good shepherd. I know my own and my own know me, just as the Father knows me and I know the Father. And I lay down my life for the sheep. I have other sheep that do not belong to this fold.

I must bring them also, and they will listen to my voice. So there will be one flock, one shepherd."

- Not only does Jesus welcome everyone into his flock, but if I'm not there, he invites me in. Where am I?
- Jesus loves me and invites me to love him just like he knows and loves the Father. That is a serious depth of love.
- Do I hear Jesus' voice, or do I sometimes ignore it? If he comes searching, am I going to listen?

november 5–11

Something to think and pray about each day this week:

Simply looking

Lord, you love all that exists, you hold nothing of what you have made in abhorrence. When we are with someone whose love we trust, we do not need to talk. The Curé of Ars described prayer in the words of an old peasant who used to sit for hours in the church: "I look at the good God, and the good God looks at me."

This is the prayer of simple regard, or the prayer of stupidity. No words and no distractions, just a silent presence. If concerns and anxieties bubble up in my mind, let them gently burst on the surface and dissipate.

Presence of God

What is present to me is what has a hold on my becoming.
I reflect on the presence of God always there in love,
amidst the many things that have a hold on me.
I pause and pray that I may let God
affect my becoming in this precise moment.

Freedom

If God were trying to tell me something, would I know?
If God were reassuring me or challenging me, would I notice?
I ask for the grace to be free of my own preoccupations
and open to what God may be saying to me.

Consciousness

Knowing that God loves me unconditionally,
I look honestly over the last day, its events and my feelings.
Do I have something to be grateful for? Then I give thanks.
Is there something I am sorry for? Then I ask forgiveness.

The Word

God speaks to each one of us individually. I need to listen to
what he is saying to me. (Please turn to your scripture on the
following pages. Inspiration points are there should you need
them. When you are ready, return here to continue.)

Conversation

What is stirring in me as I pray?
Am I consoled, troubled, left cold?
I imagine Jesus himself standing or sitting at my side,
and share my feelings with him.

Conclusion

Glory be to the Father, and to the Son, and to the Holy Spirit,
As it was in the beginning, is now and ever shall be,
World without end. Amen

Sunday 5th November, Thirty-first Sunday in Ordinary Time   Mark 12:28–34

One of the scribes came near and heard them disputing with one another, and seeing that Jesus answered them well, he asked him, "Which commandment is the first of all?" Jesus answered, "The first is, 'Hear, O Israel: the Lord our God, the Lord is one; you shall love the Lord your God with all your heart, and with all your soul, and with all your mind, and with all your strength.' The second is this, 'You shall love your neighbor as yourself.' There is no other commandment greater than these." Then the scribe said to him, "You are right, Teacher; you have truly said that 'he is one, and besides him there is no other'; and 'to love him with all the heart, and with all the understanding, and with all the strength,' and 'to love one's neighbor as oneself,'—this is much more important than all whole burnt offerings and sacrifices." When Jesus saw that he answered wisely, he said to him, "You are not far from the kingdom of God." After that no one dared to ask him any question.

- Here we see Jesus in an atmosphere of dispute and discussion and then someone asks a very good question. Jesus' answer to this question seems to bring him and the questioner together. They end up on the same wavelength.
- Do I allow the central question about what's really important to arise in me? Or, am I easily distracted and confused by the "noise" around me?
- Would I like to hear Jesus say to me, "You are not far from the kingdom of God"? Maybe he is already …

Monday 6th November, Feast of All the Saints of Ireland
       Luke 6:17–19

Jesus came down with them and stood on a level place, with a great crowd of his disciples and a great multitude of people from all Judea, Jerusalem, and the coast of Tyre and Sidon. They had come to hear him and to be healed of their diseases; and those who were troubled with unclean spirits were cured. And all in the crowd were trying to touch him, for power came out from him and healed all of them.

- This is a picture of an active Jesus. Imagine yourself in the scene. What would you be there for?
- Do I acknowledge this power that Jesus has? What do I feel about it: disbelief? fear? relief? Something else?
- Healing can happen in many ways, visible and invisible. Are there things in my life that need healing? If so, Jesus is waiting with open arms.

Tuesday 7th November   **Philippians 2:5–11**

Let the same mind be in you that was in Christ Jesus, who, though he was in the form of God, did not regard equality with God as something to be exploited, but emptied himself, taking the form of a slave, being born in human likeness. And being found in human form, he humbled himself and became obedient to the point of death—even death on a cross. Therefore God also highly exalted him and gave him the name that is above every name, so that at the name of Jesus every knee should bend, in heaven and on earth and under the earth, and every tongue should confess that Jesus Christ is Lord, to the glory of God the Father.

- Can I pause for a little while and contemplate the vulnerability, the loss of power and the surrendering of control that Jesus embraced? Why?
- Can I let this speak to my own experience of control and power? What do I find difficult to let go?

Wednesday 8th November   **Luke 14:28–33**

Jesus said to the crowds, "For which of you, intending to build a tower, does not first sit down and estimate the cost, to see whether he has enough to complete it? Otherwise, when he has laid a foundation and is not able to finish, all who see it will begin to ridicule him, saying, 'This fellow began to build and was not able to finish.' Or what king, going out to wage war against another king, will not sit down first and consider whether he is able with ten thousand to oppose the one who comes against him with twenty thousand? If he cannot, then, while the other is still far away, he sends a delegation and asks for the terms of peace. So therefore, none of you can become my disciple if you do not give up all your possessions."

- Jesus is asking his followers, "Are you serious about this Christian project, or not?"
- How do people organize themselves for the things about which they are serious? How do I organize myself for the things about which I am serious?
- What do I want to say to the Lord?

Thursday 9th November, Dedication of the Lateran Basilica
John 2:13–16

The Passover of the Jews was near, and Jesus went up to Jerusalem. In the temple he found people selling cattle, sheep, and doves, and the money changers seated at their tables. Making a whip of cords, he drove all of them out of the temple, both the sheep and the cattle. He also poured out the coins of the money changers and overturned their tables. He told those who were selling the doves, "Take these things out of here! Stop making my Father's house a marketplace!"

- Try to imagine the scene, the place, the sounds, the smells …
- Where and who are you? What does it look like, and feel like?

- How do you feel towards this angry Jesus? Can you talk to him about it?

Friday 10th November   Psalm 122:1–5

I was glad when they said to me, "Let us go to the house of the Lord!"
Our feet are standing within your gates, O Jerusalem.
Jerusalem—built as a city that is bound firmly together.
To it the tribes go up, the tribes of the Lord, as was decreed for Israel, to give thanks to the name of the Lord.
For there the thrones for judgment were set up, the thrones of the house of David.

- Can I simply enjoy this Psalm? It's inviting me to be one of the band of pilgrims on the road to God's house.
- Walking into the Lord's presence, can I hear the words "it is good for us to be here"?

Saturday 11th November   Luke 16:9–13

Jesus said to the disciples, "And I tell you, make friends for yourselves by means of dishonest wealth so that when it is gone, they may welcome you into the eternal homes. Whoever is faithful in a very little is faithful also in much; and whoever is dishonest in a very little is dishonest also in much. If then you have not been faithful with the dishonest wealth, who will entrust to you the true riches? And if you have not been faithful with what belongs to another, who will give you what is your own? No slave can serve two masters; for a slave will either hate the one and love the other, or be devoted to the one and despise the other. You cannot serve God and wealth."

- Again Jesus raises questions for us: "What is your deepest desire? Where does your deepest loyalty lie?"
- What do I make of God's interest and concern about what goes on in my heart? Is this threatening or consoling?

- Am I being led by the quiet prompting of the Holy Spirit? What do I want to do about it?

Something to think and pray about each day this week:

Falling free from fear

"I shall be filled, when I awake, with the sight of your glory, Lord" (Psalm 17:15). What awaits us when we have shuffled off this mortal coil? When I pass beyond that uncharted blank which is the act of dying, will I be waking up at last? Some who have gone to the edge and come back tell a consistent story of moving across a bridge towards a bright, beautiful place on the other side; of feeling happy, buoyed up by a feeling of joy and anticipation; of feeling free of the body and moving at incredible speed towards God, and being bathed in his love like an avalanche of warm light. In that brightness nothing else matters, not sins or misfortunes or words or pains or the body. The soul is filled with the sight of God's glory.

Those who have been surprised by joy in this way, lose their fear of death. They know that there is a lot to look forward to, that the last act of life is beautiful. As the psalmist prays: "I am here and I call, you will hear me, O God. Guard me as the apple of your eye. Hide me in the shadow of your wings" (Psalm 17:6, 8).

The Presence of God
God is with me, but more, God is within me.
Let me dwell for a moment on God's life-giving presence
in my body, in my mind, in my heart,
as I sit here, right now.

Freedom
I need to close out the noise, to rise above the noise;
The noise that interrupts, that separates,
The noise that isolates.
I need to listen to God again.

Consciousness
How do I find myself today?
Where am I with God? With others?
Do I have something to be grateful for? Then I give thanks.
Is there something I am sorry for? Then I ask forgiveness.

The Word
I read the Word of God slowly, a few times over, and I listen to
what God is saying to me. (Please turn to your scripture on the
following pages. Inspiration points are there should you need
them. When you are ready, return here to continue.)

Conversation
Do I notice myself reacting as I pray with the Word of God?
Do I feel challenged, comforted, angry?
Imagining Jesus sitting or standing by me,
I speak out my feelings, as one trusted friend to another.

Conclusion
Glory be to the Father, and to the Son, and to the Holy Spirit,
As it was in the beginning, is now and ever shall be,
World without end. Amen

Sunday 12th November, Thirty-second Sunday in Ordinary Time   Mark 12:38–44

As Jesus taught in the temple, he said, "Beware of the scribes, who like to walk around in long robes, and to be greeted with respect in the marketplaces, and to have the best seats in the synagogues and places of honor at banquets! They devour widows' houses and for the sake of appearance say long prayers. They will receive the greater condemnation." He sat down opposite the treasury, and watched the crowd putting money into the treasury. Many rich people put in large sums. A poor widow came and put in two small copper coins, which are worth a penny. Then he called his disciples and said to them, "Truly I tell you, this poor widow has put in more than all those who are contributing to the treasury. For all of them have contributed out of their abundance; but she out of her poverty has put in everything she had, all she had to live on."

- The Lord watches the widow making her way to the treasury and handing in two coins. This sight fills him with admiration. Why? What attitude of the heart does he discern in her action?
- Where, in my experience, have I seen this kind of lavish sharing? Does it consist in generosity with money, time, personal space, emotional connection, energy? Something else?
- What are my "two small coins"? Do I value them as the Lord does? Do I value the "two small coins" of others around me?
- What is the Lord teaching me here?

Monday 13th November   Luke 17:3–6

Jesus said to his disciples, "Be on your guard! If another disciple sins, you must rebuke the offender, and if there is repentance, you must forgive. And if the same person sins against you seven times a day, and turns back to you seven times and says, 'I repent,' you must forgive." The apostles said to the Lord, "Increase our faith!" The Lord replied, "If you had faith the size of a mustard seed, you could say to this mulberry tree, 'Be uprooted and planted in the sea,' and it would obey you."

- Here are two very strong challenges from the Lord. Is there one that I am meant to hear right now?
- If forgiveness is the issue that I am called to address, can I turn to the Lord and speak frankly about what is involved? If he is calling me to forgive something, then he must give me the means to do it.
- Is faith my issue? If the Lord is really challenging me to make the leap, he will lead me along the way. Can I speak openly to him about this?

Tuesday 14th November   Luke 17:7–10

Jesus said to his disciples, "Who among you would say to your slave who has just come in from plowing or tending sheep in the field, 'Come here at once and take your place at the table'? Would you not rather say to him, 'Prepare supper for me, put on your apron and serve me while I eat and drink; later you may eat and drink'? Do you thank the slave for doing what was commanded? So you also, when you have done all that you were ordered to do, say, 'We are worthless slaves; we have done only what we ought to have done!'"

- How do I feel when I hear Jesus speak like this? How do I like considering myself a "worthless slave"?
- Does it anger or threaten me? Does it confirm old feelings of low self-esteem?
- Does it remind me of where my worth comes from? Does it challenge me to see myself as a creature totally dependent on God?
- Where am I with this?

Wednesday 15th November   Luke 17:11–19

On the way to Jerusalem Jesus was going through the region between Samaria and Galilee. As he entered a village, ten lepers approached him. Keeping their distance, they called out, saying, "Jesus, Master, have mercy on us!" When he saw them, he said to them, "Go and show yourselves to the priests." And as they went, they were made clean. Then one of them, when he saw that he was healed, turned back, praising God with a loud voice. He prostrated himself at Jesus' feet and thanked him. And he was a Samaritan. Then Jesus asked, "Were not ten made clean? But the other nine, where are they? Was none of them found to return and give praise to God except this foreigner?" Then he said to him, "Get up and go on your way; your faith has made you well."

- Have I ever wanted to prostrate myself out of sheer gratitude in front of anyone?
- How did the Samaritan look on Jesus? How do I look on Jesus?
- How did the other nine lepers miss the point?
- Do I feel I have much to give thanks for?

Thursday 16th November **Luke 17:20–25**

Once Jesus was asked by the Pharisees when the kingdom of God was coming, and he answered, "The kingdom of God is not coming with things that can be observed; nor will they say, 'Look, here it is!' or 'There it is!' For, in fact, the kingdom of God is among you." Then he said to the disciples, "The days are coming when you will long to see one of the days of the Son of Man, and you will not see it. They will say to you, 'Look there!' or 'Look here!' Do not go, do not set off in pursuit. For as the lightning flashes and lights up the sky from one side to the other, so will the Son of Man be in his day. But first he must endure much suffering and be rejected by this generation."

- What are the Pharisees waiting for before they are convinced that God is really with them?
- Are there echoes of the same thing in my life? What am I waiting for before I will acknowledge the kingdom of God around me?

- What change in my circumstances, in my heart, in the affairs of those I love would cause me to trust life? Am I waiting for someone to say: "There it is!"?
- What is Jesus saying?

Friday 17th November, St. Elizabeth of Hungary
Luke 6:31–35

Jesus said to the disciples, "Do to others as you would have them do to you. If you love those who love you, what credit is that to you? For even sinners love those who love them. If you do good to those who do good to you, what credit is that to you? For even sinners do the same. If you lend to those from whom you hope to receive, what credit is that to you? Even sinners lend to sinners, to receive as much again. But love your enemies, do good, and lend, expecting nothing in return. Your reward will be great, and you will be children of the Most High; for he is kind to the ungrateful and the wicked."

- How generously have I responded in the last few days to things that were asked of me?
- Are there people in my life that I find difficult to love? Can I ask God for the grace to love them?
- One way to ask for this grace is the following prayer, which you might already know:

  Dearest Jesus, teach me to be generous. Teach me to love as you deserve: to give and not to count the cost, to fight and not to heed the wounds, to toil and not to seek for rest, to labor and to look for no reward, save that of knowing that I do your holy will. Amen.

Saturday 18th November
Luke 18:1–8

Then Jesus told them a parable about their need to pray always and not to lose heart. He said, "In a certain city there was a judge who neither feared God nor had respect for people. In that city there was a widow who kept coming to him and saying, 'Grant me justice against my opponent.' For a while he refused; but later he said to himself, 'Though I have no fear of God and no respect for anyone, yet because this widow keeps bothering me, I will grant her justice, so that she may not wear me out by continually coming.'" And the Lord said, "Listen to what the unjust judge says. And will not God grant justice to his chosen ones who cry to him day and night? Will he delay long in helping them? I tell you, he will quickly grant justice to them. And yet, when the Son of Man comes, will he find faith on earth?"

- How does Jesus' parable about how ready God is to answer our prayers move me? Does it confirm my own experience, or not? Do I sometimes feel like the widow during the long period where she's not getting an answer?

- Can I hold my own experience and listen again to Jesus' sure statement of God's eagerness to be good to me? I might need to ask for more light on this.

- Is there maybe a twinkle in Jesus' eye as he compares God to an unjust and lazy judge?

Something to think and pray about each day this week:

Working your way

"We gave you a rule," says St. Paul, "not to let anyone have any food if he refused to do any work. Now we hear that there are some of you living in idleness, doing no work themselves but interfering with everyone else's. In the Lord Jesus Christ we order and call on people of this kind to go on quietly working and earning the food that they eat."

Lord, save me from the illusions that lead to idleness. Some, like the Thessalonians Paul was addressing, have imagined that the end of the world was close, and that there was no point in planning or working for the future. You have taught us otherwise, Lord: that the world is young, and that we are only beginning to obey your command "to possess the world and make it our own." Being good stewards of your creation takes sweat and intelligence. Work can be a form of prayer—*laborare est orare*—but prayer is never an excuse for idleness.

The Presence of God
As I sit here, the beating of my heart,
the ebb and flow of my breathing, the movements of my mind
are all signs of God's ongoing creation of me.
I pause for a moment, and become aware
of this presence of God within me.

Freedom
I will ask God's help,
to be free from my own preoccupations,
to be open to God in this time of prayer,
to come to love and serve him more.

Consciousness
In God's loving presence I unwind the past day,
starting from now and looking back, moment by moment.
I gather in all the goodness and light, in gratitude.
I attend to the shadows and what they say to me,
seeking healing, courage, forgiveness.

The Word
I take my time to read the Word of God, slowly, a few times,
allowing myself to dwell on anything that strikes me. (Please
turn to your scripture on the following pages. Inspiration points
are there should you need them. When you are ready, return
here to continue.)

Conversation
Remembering that I am still in God's presence,
I imagine Jesus himself standing or sitting beside me,
and say whatever is on my mind, whatever is in my heart,
speaking as one friend to another.

Conclusion
Glory be to the Father, and to the Son, and to the Holy Spirit,
As it was in the beginning, is now and ever shall be,
World without end. Amen

Sunday 19th November, Thirty-third Sunday
in Ordinary Time   Mark 13:28–32

Jesus said to Peter, James, John, and Andrew, "From the fig tree learn its lesson: as soon as its branch becomes tender and puts forth its leaves, you know that summer is near. So also, when you see these things taking place, you know that he is near, at the very gates. Truly I tell you, this generation will not pass away until all these things have taken place. Heaven and earth will pass away, but my words will not pass away. But about that day or hour no one knows, neither the angels in heaven, nor the Son, but only the Father."

- We are coming towards the end of the Church's year. In the scripture today we see Jesus approaching the end of his life in Jerusalem. In that context he asks us to consider the final end.
- What does this talk of the end evoke in me? Does it seem remote and obscure? Does it excite me? Is it frightening? Is it consoling?
- Jesus, who is "near, at the very gates," invites me to trust him and share where I am at.

Monday 20th November   Luke 18:35–43

As he approached Jericho, a blind man was sitting by the roadside begging. When he heard a crowd going by, he asked what was happening. They told him, "Jesus of Nazareth is passing by." Then he shouted, "Jesus, Son of David, have mercy on me!" Those who were in front sternly ordered him to be quiet; but he shouted even more loudly, "Son of David, have mercy on me!" Jesus stood still and ordered the man to be brought to him; and when he came near, he asked him, "What do you want me to do for you?" He said, "Lord, let me see again." Jesus said to him, "Receive your sight; your faith has saved you." Immediately he regained his sight and followed him, glorifying God; and all the people, when they saw it, praised God.

- Can I imagine myself present at this scene—in the scene? Who do I identify with?
- Am I the blind person crying for help? Am I one of the interested bystanders irritated by the cries of the poor man? Am I one of Jesus' followers?
- How does what transpires here move and challenge me?

Tuesday 21st November   Luke 19:1–6

Jesus entered Jericho, and was passing through it. A man was there named Zacchaeus; he was a chief tax collector and was rich. He was trying to see who Jesus was, but on account of the crowd he could not, because he was short in stature. So he ran ahead and climbed a sycamore tree to see him, because he was going to pass that way. When Jesus came to the place, he looked up and said to him, "Zacchaeus, hurry and come down; for I must stay at your house today." So he hurried down and was happy to welcome him.

- Zacchaeus, despite his limitations, was anxious to see who Jesus was.
- Jesus responds with enthusiasm to Zacchaeus' openness, even though tax collectors were shunned by Jewish society, and it was a despised profession.
- Can I overcome blocks in approaching Jesus, knowing that, like Zacchaeus, Jesus will respond and my house will be visited?

Wednesday 22nd November, St. Cecilia
Hosea 2:14–15, 19–20

Therefore, I will now allure her, and bring her into the wilderness, and speak tenderly to her. From there I will give her her vineyards, and make the Valley of Achor a door of hope. There she shall respond as in the days of her youth, as at the time when she came out of the land of Egypt. And I will take you for my wife forever; I will take you for my wife in righteousness and in justice, in steadfast love, and in mercy. I will take you for my wife in faithfulness; and you shall know the Lord.

- For a few brief moments can I turn off all other messages, and allow these lines about the Lord's attitude to his beloved people be addressed to my soul?
- The Lord wants to allure me and speak tenderly to me. Can I allow this to soak in?

Thursday 23rd November, St. Columban   Luke 9:57–62

As they were going along the road, someone said to Jesus, "I will follow you wherever you go." And Jesus said to him, "Foxes have holes, and birds of the air have nests; but the Son of Man has nowhere to lay his head." To another he said, "Follow me." But he said, "Lord, first let me go and bury my father." But Jesus said to him, "Let the dead bury their own dead; but as for you, go and proclaim the kingdom of God." Another said, "I will follow you, Lord; but let me first say farewell to those at my home." Jesus said to him, "No one who puts a hand to the plow and looks back is fit for the kingdom of God."

- Tough words here from Jesus. Following him is no world cruise.
- It is easy to settle down into the comfort of my life and forget the cost of discipleship. The decision to follow Jesus has to be made and re-made.
- Sacrifice is not a fashionable word today, but Jesus doesn't apologize for the fact that it is an essential part of the life of a disciple.

Friday 24th November   Luke 19:45–48

Then Jesus entered the temple and began to drive out those who were selling things there; and he said, "It is written, 'My house shall be a house of prayer'; but you have made it a den of robbers." Every day he was teaching in the temple. The chief priests, the scribes, and the leaders of the people kept looking for a way to kill him; but they did not find anything they could do, for all the people were spellbound by what they heard.

- The Temple, the quintessential place of prayer, seems to have been subverted over time by the preoccupation of little businesses, each necessary in its own way. Jesus needed to challenge the drift and reassert the holiness of the Temple.
- In the same sense my soul, my life, is a Temple where God desires to dwell. It too, perhaps, can be gradually subverted by many little developments, each valuable in its own way.
- The Jesus who cleared the Temple held his listeners spellbound. Can I allow him to speak with clarity to me?

Saturday 25th November　　　　Psalm 144:1–2, 9–10

Blessed be the Lord, my rock, who trains my hands for war, and my fingers for battle; my rock and my fortress, my stronghold and my deliverer, my shield,
in whom I take refuge, who subdues the peoples under me.
I will sing a new song to you, O God; upon a ten-stringed harp I will play to you,
the one who gives victory to kings, who rescues his servant David.

- David delighted in God as his rock and fortress, his stronghold and deliverer, his shield and place of refuge.
- Can I ponder these images and allow my own desires and feelings to surface?
- I may want to sing a new song. I may want to cry out for refuge. I may want to do something else.

Something to think and pray about each day this week:

The King's welcome
We have named the good thief Dismas and bless him for that extraordinary prayer: "Jesus, remember me when you come into your kingdom." In the throes of your final agony, Lord, you answered by welcoming him into paradise. "You will be with me."

I lean on that word, Lord. To call you a king is to use a human metaphor which is tainted by all sorts of associations. It is enough for me that you are my Lord, and that my strongest hope is to be with you when death claims me.

The Presence of God

I pause for a moment
and reflect on God's life-giving presence
in every part of my body, in everything around me,
in the whole of my life.

Freedom

God is not foreign to my freedom.
Instead the Spirit breathes life into my most intimate desires,
gently nudging me towards all that is good.
I ask for the grace to let myself be enfolded by the Spirit.

Consciousness

I exist in a web of relationships—links to nature, people, God.
I trace out these links, giving thanks for the life that flows
through them.
Some links are twisted or broken: I may feel regret, anger,
disappointment.
I pray for the gift of acceptance and forgiveness.

The Word

God speaks to each one of us individually. I need to listen to
what he is saying to me. (Please turn to your scripture on the
following pages. Inspiration points are there should you need
them. When you are ready, return here to continue.)

Conversation

How has God's Word moved me? Has it left me cold?
Has it consoled me or moved me to act in a new way?
I imagine Jesus standing or sitting beside me,
I turn and share my feelings with him.

Conclusion

Glory be to the Father, and to the Son, and to the Holy Spirit,
As it was in the beginning, is now and ever shall be,
World without end. Amen

Sunday 26th November, Feast of Christ the King
John 18:33–37

Then Pilate entered the headquarters again, summoned Jesus, and asked him, "Are you the King of the Jews?" Jesus answered, "Do you ask this on your own, or did others tell you about me?" Pilate replied, "I am not a Jew, am I? Your own nation and the chief priests have handed you over to me. What have you done?" Jesus answered, "My kingdom is not from this world. If my kingdom were from this world, my followers would be fighting to keep me from being handed over to the Jews. But as it is, my kingdom is not from here." Pilate asked him, "So you are a king?" Jesus answered, "You say that I am a king. For this I was born, and for this I came into the world, to testify to the truth. Everyone who belongs to the truth listens to my voice."

- We see two men standing side by side. One is obviously in authority and has control. The other man is in chains. Which of them is the King?
- Jesus says, "My kingdom is not from this world." What does he mean? How might his understanding of his kingdom affect what is important and unimportant for me?
- Can I stand and look at the King in chains? What do I want to say to him? What is he saying to me?

Monday 27th November   Luke 21:1–4

Jesus looked up and saw rich people putting their gifts into the treasury; he also saw a poor widow put in two small copper coins. He said, "Truly I tell you, this poor widow has put in more than all of them; for all of them have contributed out of their abundance, but she out of her poverty has put in all she had to live on."

- Jesus admires the poor widow because she gave her all.
- What does it mean to give my all? Could I do it? Is it wise or advisable? Have I seen others do it?
- What is this giving all that Jesus admires so much?

Tuesday 28th November   Luke 21:5–11

When some were speaking about the temple, how it was adorned with beautiful stones and gifts dedicated to God, Jesus said, "As for these things that you see, the days will come when not one stone will be left upon another; all will be thrown down." They asked him, "Teacher, when will this be, and what will be the sign that this is about to take place?" And he said, "Beware that you are not led astray; for many will come in my name and say, 'I am he!' and, 'The time is near!' Do not go after them. When you hear of wars and insurrections, do not be terrified; for these things must take place first, but the end will not follow immediately." Then he said to them, "Nation will rise against nation, and kingdom against kingdom; there will be great earthquakes, and in various places famines and plagues; and there will be dreadful portents and great signs from heaven."

- Again in these last days of the Church's year, we hear Jesus, in Jerusalem as he faces his own death, foretell crises and great upset facing his followers. Jesus does not minimize or water down the difficulties.
- Can Jesus' foreseeing this trouble for his disciples give me perspective regarding crises and upset in my own life or the life of the church and the world?
- Jesus himself went on to face the ultimate in crisis and upset. The crisis was not the last word.

Wednesday 29th November   Luke 21:12–19

Jesus said to his disciples, "But before all this occurs, they will arrest you and persecute you; they will hand you over to synagogues and prisons, and you will be brought before kings and governors because of my name. This will give you an opportunity to testify. So make up your minds not to prepare your defense in advance; for I will give you words and a wisdom that none of your opponents will be able to withstand or contradict.

You will be betrayed even by parents and brothers, by relatives and friends; and they will put some of you to death. You will be hated by all because of my name. But not a hair of your head will perish. By your endurance you will gain your souls."

- How do I respond to Jesus' talk of persecution and opposition for the sake of his name? Do I want to go and hide, stick my head in the sand? Does the prospect of righteous struggle excite me?
- Jesus says, "I will give you words and a wisdom . . ." when the time comes. What sort of words and wisdom does Jesus offer us for the time of crisis?
- How might I face crisis and opposition with Jesus' support?

Thursday 30th November, St. Andrew   Matthew 4:18–22

As Jesus walked by the Sea of Galilee, he saw two brothers, Simon, who is called Peter, and Andrew his brother, casting a net into the sea—for they were fishermen. And he said to them, "Follow me, and I will make you fish for people." Immediately they left their nets and followed him. As he went from there, he saw two other brothers, James son of Zebedee and his brother John, in the boat with their father Zebedee, mending their nets, and he called them. Immediately they left the boat and their father, and followed him.

- In this passage, Peter, Andrew, James, and John literally drop everything and respond to Jesus' invitation without any questions. It sounds almost too simple.
- Imagine Jesus walking into your home or your workplace and making the same invitation to you. How do you react?
- Perhaps your reaction is not quite so straightforward. Perhaps you have questions to bring into conversation with the Lord.

Friday 1st December   Luke 21:29–33

Then Jesus told them a parable: "Look at the fig tree and all the trees; as soon as they sprout leaves you can see for yourselves and know that summer is already near. So also, when you see these things taking place, you know that the kingdom of God is near. Truly I tell you, this generation will not pass away until all things have taken place. Heaven and earth will pass away, but my words will not pass away."

- "These things" that Jesus predicts are great trouble and strife. He doesn't flinch from that. But, in the same breath he affirms that the kingdom of God is near.
- How do I respond to the new developments in my life—in our world, particularly the fearful ones? What does Jesus' affirmation of the nearness of the kingdom of God say to this?

Saturday 2nd December   Luke 21:34–36

Jesus said to his disciples, "Be on guard so that your hearts are not weighed down with dissipation and drunkenness and the worries of this life, and that day catch you unexpectedly, like a trap. For it will come upon all who live on the face of the whole earth. Be alert at all times, praying that you may have the strength to escape all these things that will take place, and to stand before the Son of Man."

- Is there something that weighs down my heart? Dissipation, drunkenness, the worries of this life, or is there something else?
- How do I feel about the day of the Lord? Do I live with fear of being caught? Am I looking forward to meeting him?
- Is my praying today a preparation to meet the Son of Man with confidence?